Knowledge Management – A Blueprint for Delivery

Knowledge Management – A Blueprint for Delivery

A programme for mobilizing knowledge and building the learning organization

Tom Knight
Trevor Howes

Routledge
Taylor & Francis Group

LONDON AND NEW YORK

First published by Butterworth-Heinemann

First published 2003

This edition published 2011 by Routledge
2 Park Square, Milton Park, Abingdon, Oxon OX14 4RN
711 Third Avenue, New York, NY 10017, USA

Routledge is an imprint of the Taylor & Francis Group, an informa business

British Library Cataloguing in Publication Data
A catalogue record for this book is available from the British Library

ISBN 0 7506 4902 X

Composition by Genesis Typesetting, Rochester, Kent

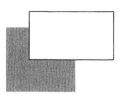

Contents

Computer Weekly Professional Series   vii

Foreword   ix

Acknowledgements   xi

1 Introduction – understanding knowledge management

1.1 Making sense of knowledge . . . and how you manage it   1

1.2 Why is it so important?   11

1.3 Understanding types of knowledge   20

1.4 To mobilize or manage?   24

1.5 So many influences   26

1.6 Introduction to the framework – where do we start?   28

1.7 Understanding the framework for action   35

2 New challenges, new vision   43

2.1 Stage 1: Understanding pressures to change   43

2.2 Stage 2: Define the organization's response – building a vision   59

3 From strategy to action   64

3.1 Stage 2 (continued): Define the organization's response – KM strategy and business case   64

3.2 Business case template   90

3.3 Moving into action   92

4 Designing the new reality   93

4.1 Stage 3, part 1: Leadership, people and process   93

4.2 Stage 3, part 2: Technology and information/content   144

5 Making it all happen   187

5.1 Stage 4: Implement the new reality   187

5.2 From pilot to programme   191

5.3 Programme design – additional considerations   198

6 Reaping the rewards   201
  6.1 Stage 5: Never rest – realize the benefits   201
  6.2 Managing risk   204
  6.3 Becoming a learning organization   211

7 Epilogue: Lessons from the journey   214
  7.1 The five-stage KM delivery network   215
  7.2 Five Golden Rules   219
  7.3 Looking to the future: mobilizing knowledge
      in a changing world   220

Appendix 1 Issue identification   230

Appendix 2 Knowledge role audit   233

Appendix 3 Knowledge process audit   235

Appendix 4 Resistance to change   237

References   242

Index   245

Computer Weekly Professional Series

There are few professions which require as much continuous updating as that of the IS executive. Not only does the hardware and software scene change relentlessly, but also ideas about the actual management of the IS function are being continuously modified, updated and changed. Thus keeping abreast of what is going on is really a major task.

The *Computer Weekly* Professional Series has been created to assist IS executives keep up to date with the management ideas and issues of which they need to be aware.

One of the key objectives of the series is to reduce the time it takes for leading edge management ideas to move from the academic and consulting environments into the hands of the IT practitioner. Thus this series employs appropriate technology to speed up the publishing process. Where appropriate some books are supported by CD-ROM or by additional information or templates located on the Web.

This series provides IT professionals with an opportunity to build up a bookcase of easily accessible, but detailed information on the important issues that they need to be aware of to successfully perform their jobs.

Aspiring or already established authors are invited to get in touch with me directly if they would like to be published in this series.

Dan Remenyi

Dr Dan Remenyi
Series Editor
Dan.remenyi@mcil.co.uk

Series Editor
Dan Remenyi, MCIL

Advisory Board
Frank Bannister, Trinity College Dublin
Egon Berghout, University of Groningen, The Netherlands
Ann Brown, City University Business School
Roger Clark, The Australian National University
Reet Cronk, Harding University, USA
Arthur Money, Henley Management College
Sue Nugus, MCIL
Terry White, Bentley West, Johannesburg
Ross Bentley, Management Editor, *Computer Weekly*

Other titles in the Series
Considering computer contracting?
Corporate politics for IT managers: how to get streetwise
David Taylor's Inside Track
Delivering IT and e-business value
E-business strategies for virtual organizations
The effective measurement and management of IT costs and benefits
A hacker's guide to project management
How to become a successful IT consultant
How to manage the IT helpdesk, 2nd edition
Implementing ERP
Information warfare: corporate attack and defence in a digital world
IT investment – making a business case
Make or break issues in IT management
Making IT count
Network security
Prince 2: a practical handbook
The project manager's toolkit
Reinventing the IT department
Stop IT project failures through risk management
Subnet design for efficient networks
Understanding the Internet

Foreword

I still remember the day in early 1996 that I stepped into a new role at IT services company ICL [since April 2002, merged with Fujitsu to become Fujitsu Services], as head of a new CEO-sponsored initiative known as the Mobilizing Knowledge programme. How I wish I could have referred to a book like this one! The challenge that I had been set was as follows: how could a company of twenty thousand people, spread across more than thirty countries, harness the knowledge it held so that its customers could benefit from its global breadth of experience, not just the knowledge base of the local office? The newly appointed CEO was determined to create a way of working that ensured that the company 'knew what it knew' and that its customers could benefit as a result.

I had been interested for some time in the practical challenges of creating so-called 'learning organizations', so I took on the role with great enthusiasm. What interested me was not academic theory but the nitty-gritty practicalities of what you do on Monday morning, to really make a difference. As I said, I didn't have the benefit of a book like this. I started with a largely blank sheet of paper and embarked on a journey that led in many fascinating directions.

The benefit of working in a new field is that you seek out fellow pioneers who share your interest and enthusiasm for the subject. In my time at ICL I discovered a number of fellow enthusiasts who believed in the huge potential of effective knowledge sharing and wanted to share ideas and experience with each other. We formed a cross-company community – nicknamed 'MobKnow' – which developed a pattern of meeting roughly every two months. We learned from each other, challenged each other and supported each other in times when it sometimes felt that we were speaking a different language to some of our colleagues. The authors of this book were two of the mainstays of that community and have kept its momentum going to this day, long after I (as community founder) had made the leap out of corporate life to mobilise my own knowledge in new settings.

Communities of people who want to share what they know – this of course is the foundation for the effective mobilization of knowledge. The 'MobKnow' network in ICL had its electronic space on the company's intranet but its vitality and usefulness came from the face-to-face discussions that took place. Community members came from many parts of the business, linked by their common interest in knowledge management. Every organization has these communities but they rarely appear on the organization charts. They cross business, functional and geographic boundaries and they are among the primary channels for knowledge flows. Technology acts as a supporting infrastructure but it is the connections between people that turn an individual's knowledge and experience into a real organizational asset.

Leaders in 21st century organizations are beginning to appreciate that the competitive advantage of their organizations depends on their ability to foster as many connections between people as possible, building the channels of trust and communication that ensure they will have not just intelligent people but intelligent companies. With luck they will have people like Tom and Trevor in their organizations, catalysts for change who will advise them on how best to tackle this challenge. And whatever happens, they now have this book to turn to for inspiration and practical advice.

Elizabeth Lank
Knowledge management and organizational learning consultant

Acknowledgements

Our gratitude goes to many people who provided help and support in the creation of this book.

First of all, our long-suffering partners: Tom's wife Kathleen, who put up with months of lonely weekends, entertaining Sophie and 'Wee Tom' while their dad was cloistered away at the keyboard, and providing emotional support when batteries started to drain; and Trevor's partner Sandie for her encouragement and support that flowed in abundance throughout the adventure, and also to Harvey, Rita, Thomas and Jessica for their sustaining love and understanding.

We also owe a debt to our colleagues in the Fujitsu Services Knowledge Management practice – the rich seam of expertise in this group, and the climate of lively debate, has provided both a rewarding environment in which to work, and the ideal foil for us to test some of our ideas. In particular, special thanks goes to Arif Azar for his help in crafting the technology section. Special thanks also to Jack Kenward and Tony Clack, who both freely gave their experience and skills to the knowledge types and knowledge workplace. Also the wider group of KM specialists across Fujitsu Services and Fujitsu Consulting that make up mobilizing knowledge community of practice, which Tom has had the privilege of leading for two years.

Finally, thanks for the help and inspiration received from other friends: Dave Norman of Dave Norman Associates, for his help in building self-motivation when the task seemed too big; Elizabeth Lank for providing insight and learning from the mobilizing knowledge regime she established in the pre-Fujitsu days at ICL; and Martin Green, whose commitment to help bring about positive change at the Department of Health, and more recently at the Department of Culture, Media and Sport, would challenge anyone's preconceptions about civil servants.

Introduction – understanding knowledge management

Learning is not compulsory . . . neither is survival.

W. Edward Deming

1.1 Making sense of knowledge . . . and how you manage it

What drives modern organizations to explore knowledge management (KM)? What exactly do we mean by the term? There have been some fairly unflattering answers to this question. It has been accused of being just a management fad, like the early 1990s enthusiasm for Quality Management or the hype around Business Process Re-engineering (BPR), which after their fairly brief moment in the spotlight, stood accused of being little more than the repackaging of a few genuine good ideas and practices, wrapped in a rich and largely unnecessary consultancy mystique (interestingly, both have since become part of the general business toolset, though the promises and project scope have become more moderate and realistic).

Others, meanwhile, have argued knowledge management is a new name for something else – information management, or document management. Still others see in knowledge management a revival of the 1980s enthusiasm for 'expert systems' created around a 'knowledge base' – a technology that at the time failed to achieve its potential, now reborn with the same promises of cost saving and easy access to expertise, but with the benefit of enhanced performance due to the rise of internet-related technologies.

There is some truth in all of the above, but the whole story is of a much richer picture. Clearly, we, the authors, wouldn't have written this book if we didn't believe that knowledge management as a discipline had significant potential to improve organizational performance. But as consultants working in some of the UK's largest organizations, we avoid imposing a strict definition of knowledge management.

This may sound like a cop-out, but we believe that one more definition of knowledge management doesn't really add anything to the debate, and certainly doesn't help us in a customer perspective. Depending on the individual you are speaking to, on the organization he or she works for, and the business sector involved, you can ask 100 people and get 100 different answers. Even where people agree on the basics, particular emphasis will vary according to experiences and priorities.

We believe there are two main reasons for this:

- First, knowledge management, which as a discrete discipline is certainly less than 10 years old, is not mature enough to have coalesced into a single, coherent world view (or even a smallish number of competing views) – a major difference from the patented, systematized Quality and BPR movements.
- Second, and consequent to this, practitioners themselves occupy a huge spectrum: from tightly drawn, technology focused purveyors of 'knowledge management systems', often with a mechanistic viewpoint, perhaps working for software vendors; through to practitioners with perspectives that are more focused on skills, behaviours and motivational issues – a 'learning organization' view.

    Theorists are also involved – in what is becoming a thriving academic knowledge management 'industry' – who more typically take a starting point in cognitive and behavioural science, or analysing the strategic choices organizations make. The non-academic literature available – much of it industry sponsored – tends to focus on the 'technical' perspective, and given that much of early interest in knowledge management came from those seeking to exploit new technologies such as the World Wide Web. Indeed this is the view that is most prevalent and we still often hear the phrase 'knowledge management system' in our daily work.

The authors' response is to acknowledge that there does indeed exist a plurality of viewpoints and approaches, skills and tools, and 'solutions', with a huge variety of reasons for taking action and many different desired and possible outcomes. All of these are valid in each specific context. If we insist on asking 'What drives modern organizations to look at knowledge management?' then we have to answer, 'lots of reasons'.

But this is not a reason for giving up on the struggle to make sense of this vast and growing area, for failing to seek patterns and connections, or finding a best way through the maze. As knowledge management consultants, organizations have looked to us to help them find an appropriate way forward, and their concerns can differ markedly from place to place: for example, one Fujitsu customer, the UK University for Industry, was conceived from day one to operate electronically (an e-business), with a unique 'centre and hub' configuration, essentially a franchised arrangement for course and tuition delivery, with very few staff at the centre and a heavy reliance on online systems for information distribution. Clearly, the knowledge management requirements of an organization like this will be radically different from those facing a very different customer, for example former gas utility company Centrica, which has made rapid strides to move away from its 'privatized utility past', but nevertheless controls its own extensive people and technology infrastructure, seeking to deliver value from its customer base and ability to handle mass consumer transactions across telecoms, motoring and financial services as well as energy supply. And Centrica's concerns are different again to those of a more asset-based organization combined manufacturing and services, like Nortel Networks, or a retail company like WH Smith where the overriding drivers are meshing together the demands of marketing, logistics, and stock control.

This book is our effort to capture and codify – make 'explicit', if you like – our own learning from the past seven years or so of knowledge management practice in the UK. It boils down to five Golden Rules that we will refer to repeatedly as we go along:

Golden Rule #1: Be crystal clear on the expected benefits – Always have a business case that details the agreed benefits that the knowledge management initiatives must deliver. Progress towards their realization must be properly managed and measured.

Golden Rule #2: People's behaviours must change for the long term – People's beliefs must be affected if long-term improvements in behaviour are to be achieved. You must do more than just 'build an IT system'.

Golden Rule #3: Nothing happens without leadership – Those responsible for running the organization must inspire and encourage all staff throughout the 'voyage of discovery' that is the change programme, continuing on after implementation to ensure lasting change.

Golden Rule #4: Process change leads to improved performance – Organizations need to build in new processes and routines through job redesign, to ensure knowledge capture and reuse, and to establish and reinforce desired behaviours and activity.

Golden Rule #5: Organizational learning leads to organizational success – Organizations can only survive and prosper by learning from the business environment, and putting that learning to practical use by responding to it in some way. The capability to do this learning well is what distinguishes successful companies from also-rans.

We believe that these principles underpin efforts to *mobilize knowledge in pursuit of business value* – ultimately, knowledge management must be about turning 'what people know' and what they know 'how to do' into outputs that create added value for an organization – the art of the knowledge management practitioner is to deploy appropriate approaches and techniques to achieve this end.

1.1.2 The roots of knowledge management

This is an essentially practical book based on experience of the process of helping organizations devise a knowledge management strategy and deliver the required changes that it requires. But we believe that it is vital to have some background in the context of modern approaches to mobilizing knowledge, so we will now step through a brief look at the discipline's history.

The ancient Greeks speculated a great deal about the nature of knowledge. From their deliberations, we have the modern science of epistemology. But alongside their academic speculations, the Greeks knew as well as anybody the importance of practical techniques for communicating knowledge. The practice of sitting alongside experts to learn their craft – from playwrights to carpenters – is as old as civilization itself. This notion of apprenticeship – a noble and ancient method of transmitting knowledge between individuals – was brought to something of a high point in the high medieval period, between 1200 and 1500. At this time, the keepers of knowledge were very separate and secretive.

- A very specialized kind of learning existed only in monasteries – the surviving knowledge of the Greek classics, along with knowledge of biblical and liturgical Latin. To a degree this kind of learning was communicated to the ruling classes – the aristocracy required familiarity with Latin as the language of diplomacy.
- A quite separate kind of learning existed among the merchant classes – knowledge of the rules of commerce, of interest payments and the rules of barter and exchange, again kept strictly within merchant families. From this period stems western use of the Arabic numerals for book-keeping (rather than the hard-to-use Roman character-based methods), along with sophisticated rules around ownership of property and conduct of trade.
- Another body of knowledge again existed among artisans and craftsmen (which at this time included certain trades we now think of as professions, such as medicine), who protected their knowledge through the creation of guilds, and transferred it through long apprenticeships where initiates were indentured to a particular master, and were bound to obey the rules of the guild and to give service to the master for many years in return for learning the trade. Such guilds are certainly the precursors to today's secret societies like the Freemasons, and even of trade unions (where the now defunct closed shop can be traced directly to medieval working practices). But in terms of their role in maintenance of standards and policing of behaviour, they are also the precursors to professional bodies such as the British Medical Association or the Law Society, who to this day police standards of teaching and practice in their respective professions.

To some extent, the walls in these divisions began to crack with the rise of the urban universities in the late medieval period, which opened up the world of book learning, previously the preserve of clerics and the aristocracy, to the sons (though not yet the daughters) of the merchant classes. The process was hastened at the end of the medieval period by the Reformation, and by the growth of mass literacy that accompanied the invention of printing. But a large-scale breakdown of the separate worlds of knowledge between different groups in society didn't seriously begin to happen in the mass population until the rise of industrialization, and moves to open up education to provide the baseline of skills and knowledge employers required of their urban workforce.

In today's world, the difficulties of coping with a skills shortage – attempting to leverage the skills of a small number of key staff, assisted by a combination of less-skilled individuals and the application of technology – is a common motivation for investment (call centres clustered around a highly developed knowledge base is a good example). To go back to the early part of the last century, the early industrialists faced similar problems, trying to manufacture goods on a large scale, while only having a small number of 'expert' staff. The first efforts at mass production really came along during the American Civil War, where the sheer demand for firearms led to the first use of sequential production lines. 'Armoury' methods, as they were known, took some time to work their way into general thinking about manufacturing, but by the early part of last century, advocates of large-scale mass production, such as Henry Ford, were trying to find ways to speed up and scale up the production process by breaking down the complex body of knowledge required by traditional craftsmen. This was done by reducing difficult tasks into groups of simpler ones which could be performed by less-skilled workers, many workers each having knowledge of just a tiny part of the whole.

Mass production techniques have moved on, of course, since the days of Ford. The industrial age was one of standardization (Ford's most famous saying is, after all, 'Any colour as long as it's black'). But as society has changed (post-war, and in particular post-1960s), expectations are considerably higher. Mass production is still with us, but increasingly we live in a world where individually held knowledge and specialization are the key requirements for individual wealth and productivity. By the 1960s and the dawn of the Information Age, it was already becoming clear that rather than semi-skilled production work, the complex web of knowledge held by groups of individual workers was becoming more and more important to organizational success. In 1969, the management guru Peter Drucker wrote:

> *Knowledge is the central capital, the cost centre and the crucial resource of the economy.*

This is quite a departure from Karl Marx's notion – which an industrialist like Ford would not have challenged – that 'Land, Labour and Capital' are the key economic resources. But while Drucker's statement may have been a quite radical notion in 1969, it appears common sense today.

Yet much of business thinking – and business decision-making – has still to catch up with this new world. For example, while accounting rules (some of which date back to the medieval period) are very firm on the management of capital assets, thanks to complex and long-defined bodies of custom, practice, law-making and professional regulation, the accounting profession is largely unable to properly value or manage knowledge assets (with the exception of a few intangible assets that might have a market value, such as brands or patents). This is a real management problem, having a real impact on the accuracy of things like company valuation, for which some creative solutions (incorporating concepts such as the Balanced Scorecard, which will be discussed in a later section) have been devised but are not yet in general use. Nevertheless, evolution of complex new sets of skills, and in particular (with the arrival of Internet technology) new tools for storing, aggregating and publishing information, have helped bring about a shift in the classical, market-driven view of the organization from one based on transactions to one based on knowledge.

The eighteenth century Scots 'inventor' of the modern science of economics, Adam Smith, held a fairly simple view of the firm: he believed that organizations come into being (growing from sole trader, partnership, small family concern) because the costs of doing business within a single organization – the transaction costs – are less than paying some outside body to perform the work. It was a simple cost equation to gauge whether managing work in-house, or buying in a particular product or service, was the correct course of action or not.

Of course, even back in Smith's time, organizations did not always behave that way. There are lots of reasons why firms might seek to keep in-house some activities that might be cheaper to buy in from outside – for example, 'national interest' might mean ensuring strategic access to raw materials or components, such as subsidizing shipbuilding in order to ensure supplies in time of war; unbusinesslike drivers such as sentiment or tradition might lead to owners keeping activities going against apparent logic. But as time goes by, new management theories have had to be developed to explain observed behaviour more accurately.

1.1.3 Knowledge and the organization

Current theories have a very different view of the world from those espoused by Smith. According to organizational strategy theorists like Gerry Johnson and Kevan Scholes, firms are nowadays better described as existing because they 'know' how to do things – defined in their 1987 publication *Exploring Corporate Strategy* as 'organizational capabilities'. In their knowledge-based view of the world, the success of an organization lies not just in its resources (money and buildings, people, tools and technologies), but in how it deploys these resources and builds them into capabilities to deliver goods and services to customers. Of course, although classical economics didn't recognize knowledge as an issue, firms back then were just as reliant on knowledge (for example, of weather conditions in the West Indies, and what that might mean for the state of the coffee harvest) as they are now.

Other writers on strategy, such as Robert M. Grant, and the Japanese academic Ikujiro Nonaka (whose work on innovation and knowledge we will discuss later), have helped foster the consensus that the ability to mobilize knowledge is increasingly one of the main drivers of organizational success. But, once again, it is obvious that in some sectors, management thinking has not kept pace with this reality. Mergers and acquisitions are one area where senior managers consistently fail to consider the knowledge implications of their actions. From the financial pages, we regularly read that mergers and acquisitions undertaken with great optimism after detailed negotiations consistently fail to deliver the value promised to shareholders at the time of the grand announcement – in fact, a significant number end up destroying value.

In the writers' view, it is precisely because too much attention in merger and acquisition deliberations is paid to capital assets, and not enough to the knowledge base of the organizations concerned – the intangible, 'soft' ways that organizations build their capability through people working together in certain ways, or using particular tools – that causes this failure to thrive. It takes a clear understanding of the dynamics of knowledge and the melding of company cultures to make a success of a large merger. It could be argued that a strategy for maximizing the potential of knowledge assets is more important in such a scenario than one aimed at accounting assets – but how many times is this even addressed? Even at a mechanistic level, the difficulties of merging information systems are a substantial blocker to progress in grasping the benefits of mergers – it can take years even to achieve relatively simple things such as common desktop tools and access to common information sources – while the challenge of building a culture where information is freely shared and its value maximized is often not even on the agenda. The authors have experience of at least one UK financial institution where, five years after a large merger, staff are often still identified (by each other) by the 'colour' of the logo of the pre-merger company they came from!

Downsizing presents a related problem. When companies get faced with short-term problems, they often cut staff to improve the profit and loss figures. But when the upturn comes, these same companies can be very slow to get going again – in the recession of the early 1990s, companies that shed large numbers of staff (particularly in the US, where there is a culture of mass layoffs in such a situation, made easier by the general lack of social responsibility legislation) were slow to get going again when the upturn came, while companies that retained staff and deployed numbers of them to do, for example, new product development or quality management work were able to mobilize again very quickly once things improved.

The fashion for removing layers of middle management in the early 1990s, and the loss of thousands of middle ranking employees often did far more to harm than strengthen organizations, and certainly hampered efforts to cope with a revival in economic fortunes. This was the fundamental flaw in the doctrine of 'de-layering' proposed in the 1980s by the management gurus like Tom Peters, and his followers in some of the large management consultancies – and the main reason why so many restructuring projects failed. Middle managers are much more than 'messengers' as Peters and cohorts claimed at the time – as the sometimes-derided 'knowledge brokers' in organizations, this group provide context, translate head office jargon into terms that are real at the level of the workgroup, and retain in their heads much of what might be described as organizational memory. An organization disposes of this at its peril. Peters has since recanted – but the damage was, by then, done, at a serious cost in competitiveness, responsiveness and organizational ability to learn lessons and 'remember' how to succeed.

Unfortunately, while many HR professionals and other senior managers are aware of these issues to some extent, it can be hard for companies, when the crunch comes, to act on this knowledge and look for alternatives, when there may be extreme shareholder pressure to stem losses or at least be seen to be taking action – and sometimes, of course, there is genuinely no choice but to scale back activity or make a strategic exit from a market sector.

Nevertheless, organizations do need to learn lessons about the true costs of retrenchment. In his book *The Living Organization*, former Shell senior manager Arie de Geus described the distinctive differences between companies which had been around a long time (the book was based on a Shell study of organizations more than 100 years old – a very exclusive club), compared with more 'normal' organizations (average age at the end of their independent existence just 8–12 years). De Geus found a number of common characteristics, but a key one was a distinctive 'family' feeling among employees and senior managers, partly engendered by a culture of mutual long service (workers and company). These companies were slow to expand core staff in the 'good' times (using contractors and outsourcing to cope with additional work) but also slow to get rid of people in a downturn. This had many positive benefits – not least engendering a culture of loyalty. But perhaps the most significant benefit of long service is the capability it gives organizations to recall the past and apply its lessons, and often (due to rotation of jobs and localities) to hear and act on the intuition of individuals so steeped in the culture that they are able to 'feel' for how the changing world might impact the organization as a whole.

The notion of organizational capabilities includes all this, but extends out even more broadly. In project management, for instance, the capability to learn lessons and apply that learning is crucial as a risk management tool. One example is an engineering-focused company the authors worked with which was faced with repeating a similar project task in different countries throughout Europe. We began with a requirement to find ways to 'reuse' project-planning material. But the logic of 'lessons learned' was continued into other areas – and the result was a range of new processes geared at using outputs from the project review stages as inputs to up and coming projects. This was a far more powerful way of learning from experience than the traditional method of writing a report and filing it on a system for people to find and digest if they knew it existed at all.

Armed forces are another example of crucial capability being derived directly from shared knowledge. One of the authors recalls a conversation with a senior manager in defence procurement. He pointed out that he had 3000 staff in a building, whose job it was to make sure that the right number of tanks, bullets, blankets, screwdrivers and a million other things were purchased at a sensible price and made available to the right people, at the right place, at the right time. 'But we don't make tanks, or bullets, or screwdrivers. What we have is the knowledge of where we can buy them, how many we need, where we want them to go, and how we get them there. What we trade in here, the only thing we work with, is knowledge.'

Armed forces also depend on another kind of knowledge, a kind that is deeply embedded in organizational routines. Armies all over the world have access to similar tools and equipment these days – so what makes, say, the British Army so relatively successful? There is a strong argument that the British Army's 'competitive advantage' derives in strong measure from 400 years (more in some cases) of the regimental system. The strong culture of regiments, their discipline, history, and the symbolism shared between a group of people, the trust and dedication engendered by 'belonging' to something greater than themselves, is a very powerful tool for building effectiveness. Knowledge embedded in culture, practice and symbolism is the hardest knowledge of all for a competitor to copy.

Without a hard definition of knowledge management, we have come quite far in assessing the importance of knowledge to modern organizations. In the next section, we will examine the phenomenon of knowledge in some more depth, and look at some practical examples of how it can be managed or mobilized in pursuit of organizational goals.

1.2 Why is it so important?

1.2.1 The rise of the knowledge worker

The previous section raised the idea that soldiers are knowledge workers, just as much as software engineers or call centre staff. Some may see this as a little far-fetched, but there is a story from the late 1990s that illustrates it fairly dramatically. This was a period when a growing economy and the increasing availability of well-paid jobs for school leavers was hurting recruitment to the armed forces, which were significantly understaffed. To counter this, there was a proposal from politicians to urge the

Services to consider recruiting from society's hard cases – particularly young offenders (previously barred from applying), but also from unqualified school leavers, the adult long-term unemployed. An outcry followed as brigadiers and generals popped up all over the media to dispel the notion that today's professional army could get away with anything less than switched-on, intelligent young people. Army recruits were now required to use (and if need be, repair and rebuild) sophisticated information and communications technology, as well as all sorts of high-tech weaponry. The politicians backed down.

We are all 'knowledge workers' now. Rather than being paid for what we do (as in the old days of industrial production), we are increasingly being paid for what we know.

Some in business remain uneasy with this shift, unsure whether the term 'knowledge worker' is just another instance of management-speak. But the knowledge economy is here to stay. Increasingly, according to the media, business journals, and countless academic papers, the Information Age has come and gone, replaced (at least in the developed world) by a new business environment based on knowledge. But what exactly is 'knowledge', what is this 'knowledge economy'? Is it related to the 'new economy' that we heard so much about in the 1990s internet boom (and which proved to be illusory), and what are the implications for the world of work, for those of us (managers, IT professionals, consultants) whose role it is to make sense of the present, and take action in order to ensure that our companies (and, of course, ourselves in our personal lives) are ready to embrace the future?

Part of the key to all this lies in the various meanings of the term 'knowledge'. There are many kinds of knowledge, and many routes to formalizing a definition, each in their own way contributing to a rounded understanding of the richness that embodies the concept. This section aims to explore several of these routes.

1.2.2 Data, information and knowledge

In many business situations, the terms data and information – and sometimes knowledge too – are used interchangeably (knowledge management software companies are the worst culprits here, and some IT managers have adopted this habit). Yet to do this is to obscure the relationships between them, which can tell us a lot about how we think about knowledge,

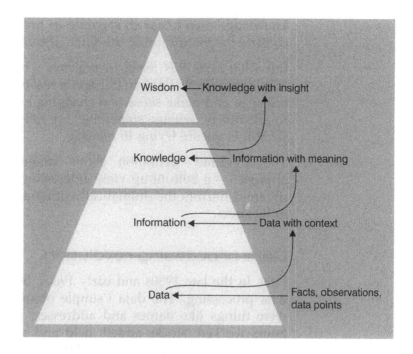

Figure 1.1
The knowledge hierarchy (reproduced and adapted from *Creating the Knowledge-Based Business*, Skyrme and Amidon 1997)

and in turn about some of the things we need to start taking more seriously in the knowledge economy.

In their 1997 work *Creating the Knowledge-Based Business*, Skyrme and Amidon make clear distinctions between data and information, and between information and knowledge. They also looked at the role of wisdom in this context – not normally a topic for management research (though perhaps it ought to be!), but important as a reminder that the acquisition of knowledge has a higher purpose – that full integration and realization of individual knowledge can lead to mastery, something that remains important even in today's high-speed business environment.

The authors of the influential knowledge management study *Working Knowledge*, Thomas Davenport and Larry Prusak (2000), concur with the thrust of this approach. They also came up with some detailed definitions. For them:

Data is:	*'simple observations of states of the world'*;
Information is:	*'data endowed with relevance and purpose'*;
Knowledge is:	*'valuable information from the human mind'*.

This comes with a health warning that, in practice, such categorizations may be impractical. 'Data, information and knowledge aren't easy to separate in practice; at best you can construct a continuum of the three' (Davenport and Prusak).

But what does this mean in practice? The reality is that such considerations do have an impact on real organizations trying to organize and make sense of a changing environment. If we are to attempt to manage something, we need to be able to know what it is we are trying to manage.

The 'pyramid' definition above suggests an evolutionary approach – a bottom-up view. Interestingly, the content of the pyramid mirrors the dramatically different 'eras' of computing in business.

Data processing revolution

First, in the late 1950s and early 1960s, began the great age of data processing. The data ('simple observations') in question were things like names and addresses, payroll numbers and hours worked, stocks added, held and sold, and transactions recorded and billed. The power of being able to process this data – by which was meant capture, order, collate, totalize and compare the masses of individual transactions – was a huge step (in terms of efficiency, speed and availability of access) over manual book-keeping systems that had existed in the past. The technology gave firms that invested in it such significant competitive advantage – initially, with a focus on reducing costs – that very soon the technology was widespread. Data processing is still very much with us – it is hard to imagine a firm of any size at all doing without data processing at its core. This era left us with an organizational legacy too. Historically, data processing departments came under the control of the finance director – the former owner of company book-keeping. MIS and IT departments even today often maintain this connection.

The Information Age

A change in emphasis in the 1970s and 1980s – stemming directly from increasingly powerful computer systems, along with a greater awareness of their potential – changed the nature of thinking about what might be asked of technology. Data processing is essentially about recording and processing transactions. But, in the process of handling these transactions, new information is generated – information 'about' information (so-called 'metadata') about the types, volumes and speed of transactions, allowing greater control over management of the overall process. Without necessarily forcing a clear break from the data processing approach, these faster systems and more sophisticated software (including the radical new desktop technology – the personal computer and personal productivity software, which widened computer access enormously) enabled a new generation of management, who had grown up with the technology and understood its potential, to make demands that had not been made before.

At this point, the Information Age – the age of management information systems, of database queries, and spreadsheet summaries – can be said to have arrived. The power of these new tools propelled information systems to the heart of business, providing detailed information on customers and their preferences, stock movements, and, of course, information on performance (especially cash flow and profitability, but also other performance measures related to production or customer transactions) with a speed and often to a level of detail that had never been available before. The data collected, organized 'with relevance and purpose', transformed managers' ability to forecast, predict and generally control their organization. In this period, the IT director or Chief Information Officer (CIO) acquired a crucial role in guiding business strategy and exploring new ways to exploit improvements in infrastructure and productivity tools. The majority of companies (and senior managers) are still, on the whole, most comfortable viewing the world in these comfortable, late-1980s terms.

Information overload and the knowledge economy

But the new technology – especially the growth of desktop tools in the hands of non-technical staff – led to their own problems, and combined with more widespread social, economic and political change, began to alter the business environment. Increasing amounts of important information – reports, spread-sheets, memos, presentations – became marooned on individual desktops and laptops. Not backed up or centrally stored, or easily available to the wider organization, frequently not even printed out for distribution but marooned on email systems, the consequent vulnerability of companies to unpredictable events like hard disk failure and laptop theft meant the situation was increasingly unsatisfactory. Management of all this became a nightmare, complicated by the introduction of technologies based on the World Wide Web, which allowed people to carry out wide-ranging research without leaving their desks, and download documents and software (and, of course, viruses) from anywhere in the world (and potentially, export company secrets just as easily).

The evolution and impact of intranet and related tools will be explored in a later section. However, what is clear is that, particularly since the mid-1990s, the confluence of a number of important trends has led to a new phenomenon: *information overload* from overwhelming amounts of company-generated paperwork, printed sources, and electronically held material accessed via databases and search engines. At the same time, management trends away from central control and hierarchy towards a flat 'networked' organization has contributed to a rethink about the nature of work, and the risks to the business from potential loss of the many knowledge workers. These workers go home every night with significant amounts of the knowledge assets of companies in their heads, in their briefcases and on their laptops.

The impact from this scenario – increased working hours, decreased job satisfaction, faster job turnover, which in turn have led to wider debates about work-life balance – has made companies begin to look much harder at the 'human' costs of doing business in today's marketplace, and the vulnerability they suffer from changes in things like greater employee mobility. Increasingly, this vulnerability – as much as any drive to improve productivity, innovation or knowledge reuse – is a key driver for companies looking seriously at managing these softer issues.

By the mid-1990s, knowledge management – as an active discipline for addressing these concerns – began to be defined and described. Dorothy Leonard-Barton, writing in 1995:

> *Companies, like individuals, compete on the basis of their ability to create and utilize knowledge . . . expertise collects in employees' heads and is embodied in machines, software, and routine organizational processes. Some of this knowledge and know-how is essential simply to survive or to achieve parity with the competition.*

This growing importance is not just acknowledged by management writers, for in business this realization is now making its way into the boardroom. A survey by Breu, Grimshaw and Myers in 2000 had 576 responses from senior UK business decision-makers, with 50.4% stating that exploiting knowledge was on their board agenda. In the same survey 28.5% of companies had responded as having an organization-wide knowledge exploitation strategy. This in turn followed a survey in 1997 by Murray and Myers which found that more than 89% of 100 European business leaders said that knowledge was the key to business power.

The dynamic of attempting to manage knowledge leads us further into definitions of what knowledge actually is. One possible view (again from Davenport and Prusak) is that knowledge is

> *created by human interaction with information: each individual's interaction with information can bring about different inter-pretations depending on their previous experience and current abilities.*

Another pair of academics, Ikujiro Nonaka and Hirotaka Takeuchi, writing in 1995 in an attempt to compare Japanese and western approaches to innovation, investigated this notion of interaction and interpretation, concluding that to define knowledge from a single cultural perspective is to miss out on a richness of understanding. To elucidate this distinction, they called on the different traditions of eastern and western philosophy for their analysis.

I'm a believer: the western perspective

Nonaka and Takeuchi noted that western philosophers have generally followed Greek tradition, and agreed that knowledge is essentially 'justified true belief'. The word 'justified' implies that anything an individual believes to be true can be termed knowledge (provided that belief can be satisfactorily defended). This definition of knowledge goes right back to the teaching methods of Plato and Socrates, and can be seen in our own society in, for instance, the impulse to assemble a 'panel of experts' – the Great and the Good – to enquire into and attempt to resolve complex questions in the legal, technical or ethical fields. For Nonaka and Takeuchi, this defence of belief is a mental activity (an attempt to impose rationality and structure on what is 'known').

The Japanese approach: whole person

By contrast, the Japanese view is less focused on the workings of mind and thought, and more on a holistic approach that includes the mind, body and soul of a person. For example, from the western view, the knowledge a salesman possesses about winning new business essentially equates to what that salesman has in his mind – the steps involved, the processes followed, the procedures typically undertaken. The Japanese view goes beyond this, emphasizing, for example, issues of whether the salesman is physically comfortable with the tasks, and is also morally and spiritually comfortable too.

This might be seen simply as from the perspective of cultural difference, but there are important questions raised about the meaning of work, and the possession and development of what people 'know' and how they come to know it.

East meets West: the consensus view

It is possible to come to a more commonly accepted definition, such as the one presented below, which includes elements of both western and Japanese viewpoints:

Knowledge is the whole body of cognitions and skills which individuals use to solve problems. It includes both theories and practical everyday rules and instructions for action. Knowledge is based on data and information, but unlike these, it is always bound to persons. It is constructed by individuals, and represents their beliefs about causal relationships. (Probst, Raub and Romhardt 2000, p. 24)

This definition, which includes within 'knowledge' an awareness that much of the time, people make decisions on the basis of rules of thumb (heuristics), and is held individually by people (rather than owned by corporations or somehow organized in computer systems), matches rather well with Nonaka and Takeuchi's research, and forms the basis of the approach to knowledge that informs this book. It can also be put more simply. In www.dictionary.com (2002), knowledge is:

- *Familiarity, awareness, or understanding gained through experience or study.*
- *The sum or range of what has been perceived, discovered, or learned.*

(www.dictionary.com 2002)

According to these definitions, we conclude that knowledge is built by individuals who make sense of information and causal relationships, not just with their mind, but also with their entire personality. Once this has happened we say that new knowledge has been internalized. Individuals will have a new, or updated, set of cognitions and skills that they can apply to many tasks.

So there we have our definition of knowledge: something bound to and belonging to people, able to be applied in multiple situations. In a business context, where we need to use knowledge to give advantage and add value, this definition raises more questions than it answers. How do we liberate knowledge? Improve the effectiveness with which it is put to use? Grow and capture it, refine and build on it? In effect, manage it?

What the authors have found is that before an attempt can be made to 'manage' knowledge, we need some more granularity as to what we mean by knowledge in specific situations. We need an understanding of the various 'types' of knowledge, in order to build approaches to deliver business value and advantage.

Many studies of knowledge in organizations have made a distinction between knowledge that exists in people's heads – 'tacit' or hidden knowledge – and that which is somehow made more concrete or 'explicit'. Polanyi (1967) was one of the first writers to use the word 'tacit' in this context and he described it as 'practical knowledge that is hard to express'. According to Nonaka and Takeuchi (1995, p.59) *explicit* knowledge, by this definition, is transmittable in formal, systemic language while *tacit* knowledge is personal, context-specific and therefore hard to formalize and communicate.

As we shall see later, part of the challenge of mobilizing knowledge is to make tacit knowledge more readily accessible and available – a goal at the heart of every technology-based knowledge management approach and tool, with a number of areas of emphasis:

- To reduce vulnerability from staff leaving the organization with key knowledge which only they hold.
- To add to the stock of measurable 'intellectual property' or knowledge assets within the organization.
- To make it easier to diffuse knowledge among staff – without ignoring the importance of context, and the need for pre-existing knowledge to understand and make sense of it.

The interaction of 'tacit' and 'explicit' elements is a key component of any mobilizing knowledge programme, and is a key theme of this book. According to our experience, however, there are real dangers in organizations pursuing strategies for knowledge management that overemphasize the 'explicit' at the expense of strategies for mobilizing individually held 'tacit' knowledge.

Ultimately, while organizations can collect so-called 'explicit knowledge' in repositories, and filter, organize and deliver back this material in one form or another, this material only becomes truly useful when combined with or interpreted in the light of individually held knowledge. In this context the more appropriate term, the authors believe, is information collection. Systems don't know things – only people do. While the potential for using electronic systems to assist in, for example, report or proposal production, or as the basis for decision-making, is substantial, ultimately any technology is essentially there primarily to enable better human performance. Therefore, the authors believe that the terms tacit and explicit knowledge should be used with great care: in fact if only people (not systems) can 'know' things, then we would argue that there really is no such thing as 'explicit' knowledge at all – only various types of information that can be gathered from people and understood by others within the appropriate context.

1.3 Understanding types of knowledge

The science of epistemology has evolved over the past two millennia, generating categorizations and generalizations about the sorts of things that can be defined as knowledge. However, in a situation such as a workshop, where people are being invited to examine their own knowledge and the people round about them, a more simple method of analysis is required. Even when conducting a full-scale knowledge audit – where quite detailed input may need to be gathered on what information organizations possess, and on the overall climate for fostering, sharing and capturing information (and by extension, how people act on this information and turn it into personally held knowledge) – a simple framework still has some validity, though it may need to be supplemented by other approaches. In fact, any practical frameworks that assist a project by clarifying, simplifying, standardizing, and enhancing knowledge understanding will deliver benefits.

We will come to leveraging the outputs of attempts to classify knowledge later, but in the meantime want to introduce a method of classification – the six investigators. This goes beyond a simple classification of knowledge into 'explicit' and 'tacit' categories and allows us to dig a little deeper into how knowledge is created, used and shared. In IT and business-related projects this greater understanding can be invaluable.

1.3.1 The six investigators

Skyrme and Amidon (1997) have produced a framework of six different types of knowledge, building on the five investigator questions (Know-how, Know-who, Know-when, Know-where, Know-why) plus a sixth, 'Know-that'. Of these 'Know-that' is the closest to 'wisdom' as shown in the previous 'pyramid' figure, p. 13. When using the following questions they can help identify certain areas that are essential to performance, yet are weak within the organization.

An approach based on these questions has been widely used by the authors to structure workshop or interview sessions geared at building a picture of knowledge within organizations. These concepts are easy to grasp, yet when pursued in depth can provide a great deal of material which can be captured or used to illustrate a new way of thinking about people's roles within organizations.

In workshops, the six investigators can be presented as the following (this is the order typically used in workshops):

Know-how

How well do people know how to get things done? This may be explicitly stated in written organizational procedures but, in practice, much of it will be found only in people's heads (i.e. in 'tacit' form). Everyone knows much more than they can easily describe: for example, almost any common task (running a meeting, writing an email) requires people to perform a number of sequential steps – but this process is seldom if ever written down, as we assume most people 'know how' to do it. We may think we hire people on the basis of their formal qualifications – but the real measure of suitability is experience, 'know-how' – of having done something comparable in the past. In terms of competitive advantage, company know-how may be hard to define but is precisely that factor that can't be easily written down or easily taken away from its context and replicated elsewhere.

Know-who

How well do people know who to ask? Assuming that significant know-how exists only in people's heads, access to people (the right people) becomes crucial. For example, how do workers know whom to ask when faced with a specific problem? How did they first find out whom to ask? This knowledge of people is 'know-who'.

Depending on the culture and size of the organization, access to know-who knowledge may be easy (a directory look-up, a simple phone call to one person) or extremely difficult (no systems, or a 'silo' approach to management where there is little access to expertise outside the immediate group of co-workers). Knowing 'who' can help with a specific task can enhance organizational performance enormously (just as 'not knowing' can be a significant blocker to progress or in worst cases lead to reinventing the wheel or otherwise repeating a significant chunk of work).

Like other categories, successful 'know-who' knowledge relies on interpretation skills – reading the runes of the organization, being able to understand which skills or strengths to seek out, understanding the various contexts in which knowledge can exist within the organization. This can be primarily through individuals' personal networks, or through contact databases, or directories of expertise. Since the overwhelming majority of organizational knowledge lives in people's heads, addressing 'know-who' knowledge should be a priority of any knowledge management programme.

There can be substantial and immediate benefits to this. An example was a consultancy group – not a large group, only about 50 people – who implemented a directory of expertise. The group had recently sent a team to Russia to do some work there for the Russian government. Once they had the directory of expertise up and running they found out that they had a fluent Russian speaker among the group who had not been sent on the trip – a big opportunity wasted to get behind the scenes and engage better with their hosts, to say nothing of the additional language translation costs.

Know-why

How well do people know why they are doing something? The wider context and the vision, the value system and sense of purpose that exists within organizations. This 'context' knowledge allows individuals to go about unstructured tasks in the most appropriate ways. An example is doing what is right by a customer rather than slavishly following a procedure. In a wider context, this might also involve being in tune with the wider philosophy – the mission and vision – of an organization.

Most individuals join or elect to stay with organizations that on some level match their personal beliefs and goals. It is becoming more and more important for organizations to be able to communicate what they stand for, what their principles are, to employees, customers and their wider stakeholders. In addition, clear business goals must be expressed and communicated to staff. If employees are working in alignment with the goals, objectives and overall ethos of the company, this is an important component of organizational success.

This is a context where techniques such as storytelling can be quite powerful. The stories, myths and legends told and retold within an organization tell staff and newcomers a great deal about how the company views itself, what it will take to 'fit in' and which behaviours are acceptable, and which are not.

Know-that

How well do people instinctively know that a course of action is the right one? The basic sense of knowing. It represents accepted 'facts' (perhaps acquired through formal channels such as training courses and formal education) but also experience. A skilled repair person, for example, instinctively knows that the cause of a problem is likely to be found in a particular component. 'Know-that' knowledge is often best expressed or understood in peer communities – for example, groups of scientists, engineers or doctors possess their own vocabulary or ethical code which might not be in wide currency in the organization in which they belong, but is very important in their own professional community.

Know-when

How well do people know when to do something, and when not to? A sense of timing. For example, skilled stock market operators seem to have the knack of buying when everyone else is selling. Their ability to know-when to do something can differentiate them above their work colleagues. Some companies have made a virtue of their timing of takeovers and market entry strategies.

Know-where

How well do people know where to find what they need? A mixture of basic information management skills and knowledge of how to navigate information (on systems and on paper) specific to the workplace or wider organization. Knowing where to go to find key information in a bid situation or when problems occur can make an enormous difference to performance and customer satisfaction.

1.4 To mobilize or manage?

We, the authors, generally prefer the term 'mobilizing knowledge' to the more usual phrase 'knowledge management'. We believe this is a more 'active' term – indicating a hands-on approach which suggests a company-wide mobilization of individually held knowledge in pursuit of organizational goals, rather than a defined task to be carried out by appointed specialists in an organization. Simply understanding what knowledge an organization possesses, where it sits in the organization, and how it can be categorized, is not enough to generate any benefit. The whole point about undertaking any kind of programme to mobilize knowledge is to see what can then be done to improve performance. We will now briefly look at some of the levers by which knowledge can better be put to use, in order that its value to the organization can be better realized.

There are essentially three approaches to mobilizing and delivering benefit from knowledge. These are not by any means mutually exclusive, but nevertheless somewhat contrasting in emphasis.

Approach 1: From the ground up

This involves analysing local needs and developing changes to processes, technologies, and overall working culture and contexts. This approach focuses on knowledge sharing in workgroups and teams, on developing an enthusiasm for organizational learning (largely fostered through leadership by individuals), and on motivation of staff towards participating in knowledge sharing activity: in short, on finding ways to change the behaviour of individual people (supported and encouraged, as appropriate, by technological infrastructure, changes to process and working practices, and leadership activity).

Approach 2: from the top down

This approach involves activity by senior management, usually with the aim of maximizing value from intellectual capital, in line with the achievement of medium- to long-term business strategy. The focus is on recognizing company-wide the importance of knowledge as a prime differentiator, source of competitive advantage, and basis of present and future earnings for the organization, proscribing downwards through the organization changes for all major business units and staff.

Approach 3: middle-in, then up-down

This approach is when small projects that deliver significant benefit from knowledge management techniques are then taken up by the organization as being a 'good idea'.

For example, a new discussion area may be developed on an intranet for a project team. The success of this may spark a request from other new projects for similar tools. Soon senior managers see this happening and start applying the lessons of small-scale successes to company-wide initiatives.

Internal case studies are some of the most powerful tools available for winning converts to the cause of knowledge management. Many of the more noted knowledge management practitioners – Steven Downing at the World Bank, for example – began as departmental champions who have 'walked the walk'. Nothing succeeds like success.

In the authors' experience, Approach 3 is the most common. Visionary, 'intrapreneurial' staff – often (but certainly not exclusively) in IT or information management disciplines, kick off projects which then gain visibility. KM consultants seldom find a 'green field' situation when they visit a company – generally they have been called in to move things forward – or join things up – that have already been started by internal visionaries.

There are many examples in the literature of each of these sorts of approaches to mobilizing knowledge, essentially dependent on the level at which knowledge management was initially championed within the organization. For example, when former chief executive Keith Todd took over the helm at the former ICL, his first appointment was of a chief knowledge officer, Elizabeth Lank, who was a key player in his efforts to transform the company from a product-focused company (selling hardware, mainframes, and a variety of software-related products) to one focused on selling IT services. These services – for example, the know-how surrounding years of experience of very large infrastructure installations – had been little valued in an IT market focused on hardware sales, but which in a changing environment, a shift from selling product to selling know-how became crucial as margins on hardware evaporated as the 1990s progressed.

However, for every ICL, which used a top-down approach, there are a dozen companies where the focus has instead been 'bottom up' and 'middle-in, then up-down'. Organizational visionaries (sometimes within business units, sometimes in a central IT or information function) have worked to create the necessary conditions for small-scale leaps forward.

As we shall see, to be truly successful in reaping the benefits from mobilizing knowledge, all the approaches are vital.

1.5 So many influences

As we shall see in later chapters, many of the activities undertaken as part of knowledge management programmes are not new, but they do provide a fresh focus for an organization to improve the way it views, measures and values knowledge. Such an approach is re-enforced in the reference below.

Generation, codification and transfer all occur constantly, so management does not create these actions. The power of knowledge management is in allowing organisations to explicitly enable and enhance the productivity of these activities and to leverage their value for the group as well as for the individual. (Ruggles 1997, p. 2)

But if many activities that now come under the banner of knowledge management have been around for some time why has this discipline recently emerged to be a significant movement in business? We would suggest it is largely a matter of timing, with a number of factors emerging as issues and opportunities together. These factors include:

- A focus on wealth generated from knowledge, with a shifting importance on the value of people as holding the key to this wealth.
- Environmental conditions such as globalization and the increasing service nature of products, which are encouraging

the sharing of knowledge across networks. Virtual organizations are emerging with blurred boundaries, alliances, and changing staff relationships.

- Learning and innovation are increasingly being viewed as a means to long-term competitive advantage.
- A view of technology as an enabler in organizational success has also grown in importance through the advent of Business Process Re-engineering and the impact on business and society of the use of internet technologies.

These and other drivers have found a common theme in knowledge management expressed in Figure 1.2. This applicability across many crucial areas has led to knowledge management being described as a set of 'core underlying business principles' (the KM consultancy, TFPL).

An understanding of the related disciplines influencing knowledge management allows KM proponents to appreciate the different perceptions that people may have about knowledge management. For example, a human resources specialist may stress learning and reward factors, while an intellectual property lawyer may focus on the explicit capture and registration of knowledge. They each will rightly believe that they are focusing on knowledge management, yet there will also be value gained by considering viewpoints from the other perspectives.

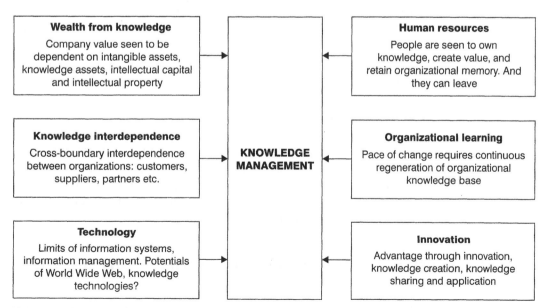

Figure 1.2 Drivers of knowledge management (from course materials, B823 'Managing Knowledge', Open University)

For IT and other projects, understanding these different points of view allows the KM champion to deliver projects that have a greater chance of adding real business benefit, enabling the different stakeholders to see the wider value and opportunities that you can and will deliver.

Given the broad nature of influences on knowledge management, claims on how it can provide business benefits across the areas have become frequent. Murray (1999) makes the following observation:

> *Knowledge has been around since the beginning of time, since people began codifying their knowledge in cave drawings or other primitive means, but now the business interest is clear. Stories began to appear in the business and academic press showing how knowledge management can generate competitive advantage, increase profits, bring about the creation of new products or services, identify new markets, improve business practice so lifting efficiency and organisational effectiveness* (Murray 1999)

What organizations require is a breakdown of the specific business benefits gained from exploiting knowledge that can be used in investment appraisal, project monitoring, and in internal communication. As part of a Cranfield research project Breu, Grimshaw and Myers (2000) identified a set of business benefits that can be expected from exploiting knowledge in an organization – grouped under the following headings:

- Innovation and growth
- Organizational responsiveness
- Customer focus
- Supply network
- Internal quality.

We will return to these areas in more depth later in the book, when we will also be setting out a range of techniques for defining a business case for knowledge management initiatives. For now, it is sufficient to note that the potential impact of KM techniques is substantial.

1.6 Introduction to the framework – where do we start?

So what are the typical starting points for addressing knowledge issues in organizations?

The main two we encounter are:

- The point solution: 'Things would be better if only we had access to XYZ . . .'
  Frequently following our 'middle-in, up-down' approach to introducing knowledge management defined earlier, someone tends to spot a gap in how well the organization does things, and looks to undertake or commission some work to address this. It could be a database, intranet, discussion board, or some kind of specialist software deployment. Such initiatives are often labelled as 'knowledge management', but in reality they are usually focused on new ways to structure information.

The other main starting point is:

- The big infrastructure initiative: 'If we build it, then people will use it.'
  Almost all large companies have an intranet now. Some of them are truly remarkable structures, full of features and large amounts of carefully selected and published content. But ask staff how useful they are, and most will have misgivings. Where intranets are concerned, unless they are firmly embedded into the culture and processes of organizations, and appropriate motivation and reward systems are in place, they will fail to deliver what the architects promised of them.
  A great deal of the work we do as KM consultants arises from conversations with customers who are trying to revive 'failed' intranet projects. The issues are seldom technical – usually the sites work fine, it's just that they are not fulfilling their potential. The same applies to desktop infrastructure. No medium to large business these days could function without a reliable desktop infrastructure, with internal and external email, file storage, backup, and all the things that go along with this. But again, few companies feel that they are getting a proper return on this investment. Infrastructure exploitation is an extremely fertile area for knowledge management consultancy.
  This is not to say that 'big infrastructure' initiatives or 'point solutions' don't have their merits – sometimes very specific benefits can be achieved from well-run projects. But there are two major drawbacks with these approaches:
  - First of all is the fact that they only address elements of the problem, usually focused on provision of 'tools'.
  - Also, organizations which go for multiple point solutions can end up with staff experiencing 'initiative fatigue', the result of change piled on top of change in no predictable pattern.

Typical 'point solution' approaches might be technology initiatives such as intranets or database projects. Another typical area is marketing and customer relationships. For example, the authors are aware of a major insurance company whose whole knowledge management approach is focused on customer relationship management (CRM) – a reasonable place to start, but the big challenge is not just to capture customer information, but to link this better to the overall capabilities of the organization in ways that will improve end-to-end service. Simply knowing the customer is not enough. Another typical project area is human resources – for example, grafting on 'self-service' HR tools to an intranet. Sometimes, the business benefit is clear and relatively easy to achieve, but often these initiatives are carried out in isolation from real business need. CRM is a typical case in point, often badly thought through and consequently seldom delivering benefits promised by the consultants or software vendors (estimates of 'failed' first-generation CRM projects – meaning ones that didn't achieve what those who bought them intended – now typically hover around the 60% mark).

An alternative, and more comprehensive route into dealing with knowledge issues is to use a 'knowledge needs' approach. The 'needs' chosen by an organization depend to a large extent on the particular culture, business activity, its industry sector, and the particular management focus. Here are some generic categories that will be refined and expanded on later:

- **Product and service knowledge** – effectively the core of any organization, the 'business content', and always a mix of structured, formally held, and personal, informally held knowledge.
- **Process knowledge** – how to get things done, again a mixture of explicit and tacit knowledge.
- **Customer and/or supplier knowledge** – the focus of many customer relationship management systems and also of procurement and enterprise resource planning systems, the emphasis can vary enormously depending on the nature of the organization, its customers and transaction volumes.
- **Project knowledge** – in delivery organizations, organizational memory from projects may be the crucial knowledge resource, but this resource is often poorly managed. Learning opportunities exist in all categories, but project knowledge may offer perhaps the best opportunity to leverage this in terms of

lower risk, and also cost savings from reusing materials and applying lessons learned.

- **Technical or expert knowledge** – often the focus of knowledge management projects and certainly of many of the software tools. Such projects often miss the point that most technical experts share only a tiny fraction of their knowledge, and then only with colleagues with sufficient context and pre-existing knowledge to gain benefit from the sharing. Therefore, the focus in this area is clearly on tacit knowledge, and the various techniques (such as communities of practice or directories of expertise) which might prove effective in support of an expert or professional group.

A 'knowledge needs' approach begins to address some of the wider issues – such as skills gaps, content lifecycle management, and communication outside organizational boundaries – that are often not properly addressed in 'infrastructure' or 'point solution' approaches. When added to awareness of the 'tacit vs explicit' dimension of knowledge, and the 'six investigators' approach, we have the beginnings of a useful toolset to structure thinking, as well as the start of a holistic approach to mobilizing knowledge.

1.6.1 Being pragmatic

But there are still significant limits to what can be achieved using these approaches. Neither really begins to answer the question: where do we start? The problem is, at its core, a change management one. Every time you change something (in mergers, acquisitions, downsizing, or just a reorganization) – it has a knowledge implication – you are dealing with holistic systems that evolve over time.

The answer as to where to start is that you need to take a step back from the operational side and develop a KM strategy. But it can be hard to persuade senior management that it is the correct approach, when the specific benefits of doing so may still be unclear.

Senior management tend to be busy focusing on what they view as the 'big problems' – profitability, efficiency, effectiveness in the marketplace, perceptions of key stakeholders, and therefore can't see the need to get involved in things like knowledge management. Their first instinct is to delegate – but this risks missing both the strategic importance of knowledge to the business, and also the need for leadership as a key success factor in any mobilizing knowledge initiative (more on leadership later). Consequently, those driving the knowledge agenda tend to be stuck with a classic infrastructure or point solution approach.

The typical consequences of this are:

- lots of local initiatives
- potential for in-fighting over areas of influence
- tight budget constraints
- a narrowly scoped business case with little opportunity to present the wider benefits
- little chance of truly leveraging knowledge to achieve solid cross-organizational benefit.

The danger of this is that knowledge management as an approach can quickly come to be regarded as ineffective, or become too associated with a particular stakeholder group (for example, it is seen within the organization as a technology thing, a marketing thing, or an HR thing). In short, knowledge management gets the reputation of not delivering and becomes discredited. We have seen this in particular where the emphasis is on technology, when the term knowledge management typically has the word 'systems' appended, and where the focus is all on capture and classification of information.

This view is based, quite simply, on an illusion that knowledge is somehow 'out there' in an organization, and that it can be actively captured and managed in isolation from the people who possess it. This illusion maintains that 'knowledge management' is primarily about tools, infrastructure, software, or point solutions. Of course, there *are* some important infrastructures, particularly technology, prerequisites for any successful mobilizing knowledge initiative. But the ultimate goal of a successful programme is to change what people actually *do* – how people interact with each other, with suppliers, with customers, and with the systems and tools they have at their disposal. Impacting on what processes they follow, and what skills they have and how they put them to use. Rather than focusing on systems, a successful knowledge management initiative will focus on building awareness of the importance of knowledge flows at every level of the organization:

- for improving efficiency – with the goal of cost savings (from reuse rather than reinvention)
- for improving effectiveness – with the goal of better quality of delivery and improved ability to perceive and meet the needs of customers, and development of a 'corporate memory'

- for increasing the level of innovation – with the goal of developing the ability to recognize, nurture and develop new ideas and approaches, and to respond and react to the ever-changing business environment.

The degree to which knowledge is shared, accessed, captured and reused is all dependent on how people structure their time, and the behaviours they choose to adopt. Behaviour will change only if ways of thinking begin to change – hence the importance of leadership, to build a new consensus:

- where mobilizing knowledge is seen as central to the business
- where it is recognized as a fundamental capability that needs to be developed and nurtured to help organizations reach their potential to compete in a crowded marketplace.

So how do we (as consultants, or as managers) go about working to build this consensus? Well, as with any attempt to change people's thinking, you can't necessarily do it by rational argument. Scope is limited for confronting the issue head-on. But we can use the power of story – of case studies, particularly internal ones – to demonstrate the potential of changed processes, behaviour, development of skills and deployment of systems to make a difference within the organization. To generate the right sorts of stories, it is essential that pilots or local initiatives are undertaken with strategic potential in mind – not point solutions, but beacons of potential that can be shown to have universal, or at least widespread, appeal, benefit, and be replicable across other parts of the organization. It is also essential that those responsible for the programme are prepared to capture and use these stories to demonstrate the potential of knowledge initiatives.

'Storytelling' as a knowledge management technique has a long pedigree and, indeed, some literature of its own. But there are other effective techniques that can be used. For example, for both internal and customer projects, companies sometimes use freelance journalists to come in and capture case studies. Journalists are able to read project documentation, interview staff, quickly come to the core of the issue, and then present the story in a concise and readable way, from a very different perspective than a consultant or project manager's approach. Rather than a technical description or a formal report of what was done, the goal is to capture a story that people at many levels in the organization can relate to on a personal level. We have found the approach very valuable – in fact, internal case studies are without doubt one of the most powerful change tools at our disposal.

1.6.2 Being strategic

But there comes a point where individual initiatives are not enough: when the role of knowledge in the organization needs to be fundamentally addressed, and a clear strategy set forward for how it can be mobilized in support of business goals. Over time, we have evolved a five-stage process for defining and implementing knowledge management strategy:

- We begin with defining the pressures on the organization, and investigating the potential for leveraging knowledge in delivering corporate objectives.
- We then move on to develop the knowledge management strategy itself: assessing the current state, defining a vision for the role of knowledge in the 'future' organization, and defining the benefits which any programme will be required to deliver.

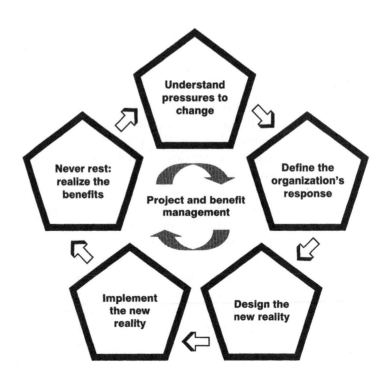

Figure 1.3
The five-stage knowledge management delivery framework

- Next comes design of the 'new' order using the 'levers' for change – the appropriate mechanisms or enablers for achieving the desired new reality (we have defined these as leadership, people, process, technology and information).
- Next follows implementation – planning the change, apportioning responsibility for delivery and for management of the initiative, and determining budgets, priorities and the overall shape of the programme.
- Finally, the benefits management stage – ensuring that the expected benefits are being realized, and continued energy and resources are spent identifying further opportunities for improvement. In addition, focus is placed on ensuring that the benefits delivered are maintained and not lost as circumstances change.

Consideration of this framework – which has been used successfully with a number of our customers – will be the focus of the remainder of the book. The overall theme is one of change management – how to identify what changes we want to see, and how to ensure that the desired change is delivered.

1.7 Understanding the framework for action

The five-stage strategic framework for devising and implementing a programme for mobilizing knowledge has now been briefly introduced. Further chapters will build on this framework and demonstrate how we can start to use it to deliver real benefits to organizations as they attempt to deliver on their mission to shareholders and stakeholders.

In the long term, all organizations must continuously improve what they do to survive and prosper. To do this, they must come up with a winning formula – something that enables them to compete effectively in the marketplace, or (in the case of charities or public sector organizations) to meet the expectations of staff, volunteers, clients/recipients, and fund holders by providing appropriate and efficient levels of service. But while finding such a formula is hard enough, maintaining effectiveness while the world changes all about is even harder. A strategy that works in one decade (or, in some fast moving industries, one year or even one quarter) might be the wrong one in a future one. Corporate history has many high-profile examples of this – market leaders who, by not rising effectively to meet the challenges of a changing world and sticking to a proven recipe, fall rapidly from grace.

The difficulties continue even after a strategic course is set. To compete effectively, as we have stated, organizations need to be in a state of continual improvement and adjustment. The difficult questions are: precisely what should be improved, what innovations should be introduced, and what practices, products, even markets should be left behind? In a knowledge management context, the questions take on a different form:

- How can organizations get greater value (greater return) from what they know and know what to do?
- How can information and knowledge resources be better put to more profitable or more efficient use?
- How can organizations unlock the potential ideas and innovations of their staff?
- How can intelligence about the changing macro business climate, industry focus, or customer base, be gathered, made sense of, and acted upon?

The answers to these questions, and specifically issues of appraisal of projects and investment, form the backdrop to the business case that must be created in order to gain resources and win approval to proceed with activity in any of these areas.

The overall framework is a suitable model for knowledge management programmes, a roadmap to guide organizations on the journey.

Knowledge underpins all significant activity in all organizations, so, as we have seen, the opportunities for change may stretch far and wide. The framework is intended to assist those responsible for delivering change to focus in and prioritize their efforts and resources to gain the maximum benefit. The framework should be used as a prism through which all analysis of knowledge and information use and requirements can be viewed. It is focused on the interrelationships between knowledge, information and productivity. The object of using such a framework – which can be applied at many different levels in the organization, from workgroup level to overall strategic management – is to ensure a consistency in approach, and also to reinforce the link between strategy, implementation and measurement. Although presented as a loop, it should not be regarded as a sequential journey or a simple set of prescriptive stages – knowledge management is an iterative process and it is also 'messy'.

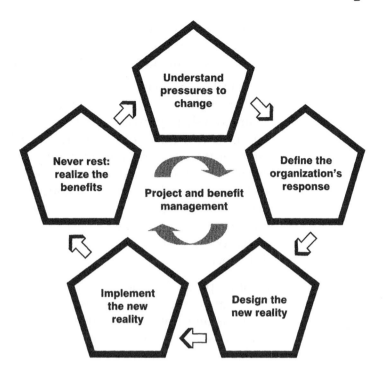

Figure 1.4
The five-stage
knowledge management
delivery framework

In a consulting context, the authors have evolved the framework through practical experience in developing strategies for knowledge, including such diverse customers as the UK Department of Health and the Nortel Networks European professional services group. However, we have also used it repeatedly to develop knowledge management programmes at lower levels in organizations, right down to individual workgroups.

One conclusion we have repeatedly arrived at, to the point where we now regard it as a fundamental principle, is the view that at the core of any change must be a crystal clear identification of the business benefits that are expected. Without a clear and compelling business case, where the expected benefits, costs, risks, and assumptions are stated, then the changes will have a high risk of failure. These benefits must describe the case for action and clearly state priorities of projects.

The world does not stand still: projects must be constantly monitored and checked to ensure it is still realistic to expect the benefits anticipated at the outset. Therefore, at various stages in a project benefit checks should be carried out and changes to the project made as necessary. This is why benefit and project management are at the 'hub' of the framework.

A typical example is the classic approach to corporate intranets. Whatever has been subsequently said about the limits of technology-led approaches to knowledge management, what is certain is that much of the interest in KM has been as a direct result of the excitement generated by the potential of corporate intranets, in the wake of early development of the World Wide Web. As web technologies developed – better publishing tools, better search and classification, automated indexing and topic linking, as well as messaging and collaboration tools – there appeared to be increasing potential for intranets to make a real difference.

Most corporate intranets began life as 'skunk works': groups of technical people, keen to do two things – first, get their hands on the tools and learn how to use them, and second, to 'show the way' to some extent to the business. Sadly, most have later evolved into not much better than a noticeboard – 'one to many' publishing – as internal communications or marketing departments took over content provision. In the vast majority of cases, efforts to use intranet tools to enable or encourage information sharing have not been successful – we believe largely due to the 'let's build an intranet' philosophy that engendered the majority of early (and subsequent) intranet efforts.

As consultants, a great deal of our work starts off either as a discussion with senior managers about the potential of these technologies, or with us being called in to resolve problems or 'make work' a failed intranet project. The reason for this is that the untold story of web and KM technology implementation has been to retrofit business needs to the potential of new tools – almost never the other way around.

At the risk of getting ahead of ourselves the moral of all this is straightforward:

> **Golden Rule #1: Be crystal clear on the expected benefits** – Always have a business case that details the agreed benefits that the knowledge management initiatives must deliver. Progress towards their realization must be properly managed and measured.

We will return to this – and our other 'Golden Rules' – repeatedly throughout the book.

1.7.1 About each stage

We are now ready to outline the various stages of the framework before the subsequent chapters go into further detail.

Stage 1 is all about developing an approach to gain a clear view of the challenges and issues facing the organization, and relate these to the various ways knowledge management principles can be applied in pursuit of larger goals. Using this understanding we are able to move on to strategy definition.

Stage 2 is where the current situation regarding knowledge and information access and use within the organization is assessed, and a knowledge management vision created which directly addresses the main strategic concerns facing the organization. How radical the thinking and analysis that goes on in these early stages will depend on the amount of control, choice, and resources that managers involved in a KM programme have. For example, in public service organizations a significant amount of direction and resources are defined by central government, restricting the amount of control and choice of managers. Within large, independent and successful companies the degree of control and choice may well be far wider as there may be fewer constraints imposed centrally.

In *Stage 3*, using the vision as a guide, detailed analysis and definition of required changes will be carried out – enabling the new reality to be 'designed'. It is important that we understand all the key structures and attributes of an organization before we go about reinventing and changing things. This is one of the essential principles of any change project: to build on existing strengths, and move away from areas that hold little value. The degree of experimentation – how radical ideas can be – will determine the scope of this stage. Encouraging experimentation is the cornerstone of innovation for many companies – and KM can play a key role in turning this experimentation into organizational success. Organizations must be clear from the outset of the level of discretion and scope for change that may challenge the existing culture, beliefs, and procedures.

An example of a company that has, for many years, actively encouraged experimentation is 3M, where staff, for 15% of their time, are free to carry out 'pet' projects, drawing on company resources to do 'blue skies' research or to mix and match across organizational areas. Some of 3M's more high-profile innovations – such as BluTac and Post-It notes – could not have come about without this toleration of activity at the margins.

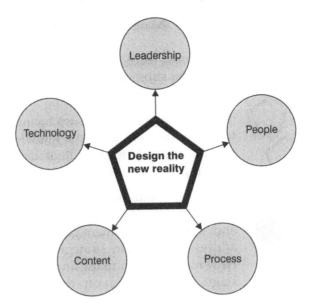

Figure 1.5
The five levers and enablers of change to shape the new reality

Stage 3 focuses on how to work with five broad 'levers and enablers' of change, pulling them together into a detailed strategy with a plan of action. These are represented in Figure 1.5.

Leadership: Analysis leading to development of vision and strategy for the role of knowledge and information in the organization. Apportionment of responsibility for delivery of a knowledge management programme and interpretation of the meaning of the vision for knowledge within the organization at large, and for providing direction, boundaries, inspiration, and role models. KM strategy development activity should begin the process of helping leaders and managers define and demonstrate the sorts of knowledge sharing behaviours that need to be developed in order to build value.

People: Analysis of the role of people in the knowledge management programme – looking at behaviours around communication and knowledge sharing, and the skills to carry these out using the various tools at their disposal. This all occurs within an environment and culture that may encourage or hinder effective knowledge management – motivation and reward are key areas for analysis and action.

Process: Business processes exist to add and deliver value to the end customers of the organization. The strategy should examine the potential for new processes to improve knowledge identification, use, creation, sharing, and recording. Processes in an organization can be likened to clothes in a wardrobe – it is very easy to add new clothes but sorting and clearing out those not required any more is a challenging task. In a similar way, processes tend to build up and need clearing out every so often. With knowledge processes, there will likely be significant opportunities to improve the value they can add, and to link them together to improve end-to-end performance.

Technology: Addressing the technology component as it is often confused with the disciple of knowledge management itself. Technology offers significant potential in terms of tools that are important enablers of business processes, and as catalysts for changing the culture and behaviours of people in the organization. Any knowledge management strategy needs to look at the issues and potential offered by technology infrastructure, collaboration tools and specialist KM software, while recognizing the very real change management problems that go along with technology implementation.

Information: Finally, any strategy must consider the basic ingredient that underlies the personally held knowledge of the organization's employees and partners. The relevance, availability, context, and quality of available information in and across organizations will determine in large measure the success of any knowledge initiatives. Included within the definition of information is what has become known as 'content', information that resides within web-based solutions such as the internet, extranets, and intranets, plus information contained in structured repositories such as databases and data warehouses, and in document management systems and online text or image libraries.

Stage 4 is concerned with implementation of the knowledge management strategy, and delivering planned improvements in the way the organization operates. It is rare that a corporate-wide knowledge management programme will be initiated solely from the top of the organization and stretch across and down in one single wave. Due to the very people-focused nature of knowledge management it is more likely that a number of smaller projects will build from the bottom or middle of the organization, creating interest and involvement as they grow, bubbling up and organically growing through the rest of the organization. Introducing knowledge-based change will need to follow similar patterns – activities must be encouraged at all levels of the organization to evolve and develop. Projects will then either build on successes and thrive, or have difficulty in delivering the benefits required and be stopped.

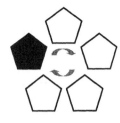

Finally, *Stage 5* is concerned with improving the results of the changes and on delivering measurable benefits. The pressures and circumstances of an organization are constantly changing and there must be a permanent monitoring and improvement process.

1.7.2 Golden rules for mobilizing knowledge

To conclude this section, we will again set out our five 'Golden Rules'. These come out of our experience in creating and running KM projects in organizations of all kinds – and represent our thinking on the biggest influences on project success, from benefits management to leadership. We will continue to make reference to each of these in various places in the book as we go along.

> **Golden Rule 1: Be crystal clear on the expected benefits** – Always have a business case that details the agreed benefits that the knowledge management initiatives must deliver. Progress towards their realization must be properly managed and measured.

> **Golden Rule 2: People's behaviours must change for the long term** – People's beliefs must be affected if long-term improvements in behaviour are to be achieved. You must do more than just 'build an IT system'.

> **Golden Rule 3: Nothing happens without leadership** – Those responsible for running the organization must inspire and encourage all staff throughout the 'voyage of discovery' that is the change programme, continuing on after implementation to ensure lasting change.

> **Golden Rule 4: Process change leads to improved performance** – Organizations need to build in new processes and routines through job redesign, to ensure knowledge capture and reuse, and to establish and reinforce desired behaviours and activity.

> **Golden Rule 5: Organizational learning leads to organizational success** – Organizations can only survive and prosper by learning from the business environment, and putting that learning to practical use by responding to it in some way. The capability to do this learning well is what distinguishes successful companies from also-rans.

New challenges, new vision

2.1 Stage 1: Understand pressures to change

2.1.1 A vision for knowledge

Every organization has a corporate strategy or plan that defines the business, sets out medium- to long-term direction, and provides a series of goals on which managers can focus to drive the business forward. By understanding this strategy, those leading knowledge management projects can gain insight into how the position of the organization can be improved to give it some advantage. This strategy may not be published for public scrutiny – though in most cases, a flavour of it can be picked up from the 'mission' and 'vision' statements commonly set out in annual reports – but the essence of strategy will certainly be in the minds of those in leadership and influencing positions. All organizations need clear statements of purpose and intent to reduce 'drift' from the intended direction and as a basis for setting performance targets.

What we need to understand now is how does knowledge management strategy fit into this? The accepted meaning of the term 'strategy' relates to both

- the interaction of intent – of the mission, long-term goals and sense of purpose of an organization, and
- efforts to deploy resources in pursuit of these goals.

The authors view the role of a knowledge management strategy as complementary to corporate strategy: setting out a

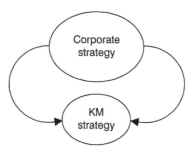

Figure 2.1
Knowledge
management strategy
must support the
corporate strategy

vision and plan for knowledge and information within the business, in pursuit of the organization's larger aims. The corporate strategy must be our starting point, and we should understand and use it to craft our knowledge management strategy.

We can see from this that knowledge management strategy makes sense only if it derives directly from the vision, mission, goals and objectives of the organization. This linkage must be maintained at every stage – from development of the strategy, through to its implementation and measurement – if demonstrable success is to be achieved. One common failure of the first wave of knowledge management projects – especially ones focused on technology exploitation, typically intranets – was that the goal was often to 'do' something related to knowledge management ('go and check out the potential for XYZ') rather than to deliver on specific business objectives. As a consequence, many projects were successful in delivering working intranet sites or software installations, but generated a very large 'So what?' response from employees and managers alike. Such failures were so common in the field of corporate intranets that a famous phrase from the great days of American showmen, turned on its head, became common currency: 'If we build it, they won't come!'

Ensuring proper linkage between a KM programme and corporate strategy involves work defining precisely what the particular burning problems or major challenges are within an organization, and matching these to the known potential for KM (using case studies, experience, and from understanding the activities of competitors and partners in this area – both at a corporate level, and at the level of individual business units and departments).

2.1.2 Pressures to change

If a corporate strategy is about deployment of resources in pursuit of particular goals, then strategy development is about setting these goals, investigating resources, and coming up with feasible and acceptable options for achieving them. We can therefore say that a knowledge management strategy is about deployment of resources in pursuit of particular knowledge related goals that support the corporate strategy. Developing this knowledge management strategy is about setting these knowledge-related goals, investigating resources, and coming up with feasible and acceptable options.

In the development of a knowledge management strategy we use questions that any would-be strategist needs to ask:

- Where do we want to be?
- Where are we now?
- How do we get there from here?

When answering the first of these questions – the focus of this section – we need to gain an understanding of the pressures on the organization, and the challenges it faces. These will typically include macro-pressures such as industry changes, demographic trends, and the position of the local, regional and sometimes global economy. Closer to home, stakeholder pressures – from customers, suppliers, shareholders, banks and funding bodies – also have an impact, as do issues of availability of raw materials or expertise, and the activities of existing and potential competitors.

'Where do we want to be?' is not a licence for asking the impossible. Journeys (and organizations) always start from somewhere and with the opportunities there will be various constraints (financial, cultural, operational). In particular, existing culture, or 'the ways things are done around here', may be a significant block to better sharing and reuse of knowledge. People tend to be comfortable behaving in certain routine ways, so persuading them to change is often hard: the reasons for change must be clear and compelling to each individual, and they need to have appropriate tools, training and time to make the transition. It is not until these are in place that the required behavioural changes will be possible.

In addition, KM advocates may have to battle upstream against other potentially 'unknowledge friendly' changes such as structural reorganization (for example, through a merger or following downsizing). The organization's structure and management processes may constrain – rather than encourage – the flow of knowledge and information by adding complicated communication channels and distance between people. Job uncertainties in difficult times tend to hinder free communication – with people falling back on an attitude of 'knowledge is power', keeping information to themselves. If, in difficult times, an organization sheds staff, then there is a risk that valued knowledge about products, operational strengths and weaknesses, or core capabilities, will leave the company and either be lost altogether or – perhaps worse – will end up being put to use by a competitor.

Because of the various constraints and the complexities in the changing environment, the questions 'Where do we want to be?' and 'Where are we now?' are never entirely separate. It is always important when trying to visualize the future to comprehend and take account of various influences and factors affecting an organization (and we will look at tools in the next section to conduct this exercise in a structured way). An initial simple and effective approach is to examine your organization's annual report. Take a highlighter and mark the areas where knowledge-related issues crop up: the sections where 'people and skills', 'experience', 'goodwill', 'relationships', 'intellectual property' and so on are mentioned. With most of today's organizations, you will soon end up with a mass of yellow ink.

Information on the pressures to change will come from many sources, for example consider what knowledge and information-related activity is going on with industry partners and competitors? This can be done by keeping an eye on key publications, websites, and identifying case study material by attending conferences and calling on the help of consultancy organizations. Those close by in the same industry sector are likely to be facing the same sorts of macro issues (in the economy or industry sector) as your own organization – for example, pressures for more focused or personalized service with customers and suppliers, the need to speed up innovation and to move quickly into action when new ideas emerge. These pressures provide strong clues as to what sort of knowledge management projects will help the most to deliver maximum strategic impact to the organization.

Most importantly the senior leaders, managers, and those with a 'stake' in the organization's success should be asked what they feel the organization should be like, or at least be moving towards. With these people identified the task turns to generating ideas for knowledge management strategy. For this learning from others is an ideal starting point.

In the previous section, we discussed the headings identified in a research project at Cranfield University where a set of generic business benefits that can be expected from exploiting knowledge in an organization were set out. Here we reproduce the table (Table 2.1) in full as a useful prompt to help uncover possible options for improvement. In a consultancy environment, we have found this table ideal for use with groups of stakeholders to facilitate discussion on knowledge-related issues.

In your organization, will improvements in any of these areas make a difference?

Opportunities have been identified using this method at all levels in the organization: at the macro, organization-wide level; at business unit level; and at the level of the individual workgroup.

There are a number of ways this table can be used, depending on size, seniority of the group chosen to be involved in the strategy creation process, and the amount of time allowed, for example:

- **Sample method 1:** Break into subgroups and consider the issues arising for the organization for each of the main headings, and come back with a list/description of issues and what it would mean for the organization if these issues were resolved. Check back towards the end of deliberations to see how many of the subheadings (in the left column) were raised in the discussion.
- **Sample method 2:** Go through each point on the list in detail and consider the relative importance of each heading and subheading. Map this to the vision, mission and corporate goals laid out for the organization/group concerned (e.g. from the annual report, in the business unit report, or in the objectives of the workgroup concerned).

See Appendix 1 for an initial template and example to assist you with such an exercise.

Table 2.1 Knowledge-based business benefits (Breu, Grimshaw and Myers 2000)

• New products/services • Research and development • New business opportunities • Developing new markets • Innovative capability.	**Innovation and growth**
• Reducing geographical barriers • Organizational integration • Organizational flexibility • Sharing ideas • Organizational learning • Speed of decision-making.	**Organizational responsiveness**
• Customer retention • Customer service • Meeting customer needs • Product/services quality.	**Customer focus**
• Supply chain efficiency • Integration of logistics • Supplier relationships • Sustaining existing markets • Time-to-market.	**Supply network**
• Process innovation • Capability for change • Operational efficiency • Project management • Product/services management • Staff morale • Quality of decision-making.	**Internal quality**

Regardless of the method used, don't be constrained in the first pass through. Be prepared to be open to criticism of existing delivery methods and work processes, and be receptive to ideas about possible new ways of doing this. The important question that follows at this stage is not the difficulties or otherwise in achieving results. Rather it is whether improvements in any of the areas identified will prove compelling for senior management because they link to existing strategy and goals, or whether they are instead just things that might be 'nice to happen'. And it should never be too far from participants' thinking that the ideas generated must at some point be firmly linked to clearly defined business benefits – a business case that lacks rigour, agreement, or proof is unlikely to lead to strong commitment and a successful implementation.

Once the pressures to change and the knowledge opportunities have been teased out from the stakeholders and linked to the overall goals and objectives, we find we have obtained the tools to gain a better high-level understanding of where we want to be and where we are now. It is now time for a more detailed understanding of where we are.

2.1.3 Inside the organization – a workplace audit

We now come to the next of our strategic questions – 'Where are we now?' – in which we come to an understanding of the size of the task ahead – essential if priorities are to be decided – and come to a view of where the main deficiencies are in terms of capability: what does the organization do well, less well, badly, or is unable to undertake at the moment as a result of lack of availability of information or knowledge; what resources and skills are missing before this capability can be built.

'People are our most important asset' has been repeated like a mantra in recent decades, to the point of meaninglessness. But no matter how often it gets used, or the degree of conviction with which it is expressed, the fact remains that people have a special and essential role in knowledge management – indeed it could be argued that in some organizations (as diverse as consultancy groups and government departments) – the principal function of their people is to process information by applying their knowledge. One of the authors recalls a conversation with a senior individual in UK defence procurement and logistics, who insisted that the only thing that his people did was gather and apply knowledge.

The way people work, the skills they have and apply, and how people interact, all offer potential areas for improvement. The workplace audit allows us to make an assessment of how a given organization, business unit, or workplace performs in these areas.

It is worth empathizing that the purpose of the audit is not just to uncover issues, shortfalls, and problems. It is equally important to identify and give recognition to areas of strength that can be learned from and the lessons applied in other areas. The audit, therefore, is not a 'witch-hunt', but more of a discovery exercise.

The main audit areas are as follows:

- Knowledge intensive roles
- Knowledge intensive processes
- Main community/workplace groups, where people work together and exchange information and knowledge
- Technology used to support the activities of individuals and workgroups
- Information and content – 'explicit' sources
- The culture of the organization – an assessment as to what degree it helps or hinders knowledge sharing and organizational learning.

Figure 2.2 shows in summary how all of these elements interact before we expand on them in more detail. We term this the 'knowledge workplace'.

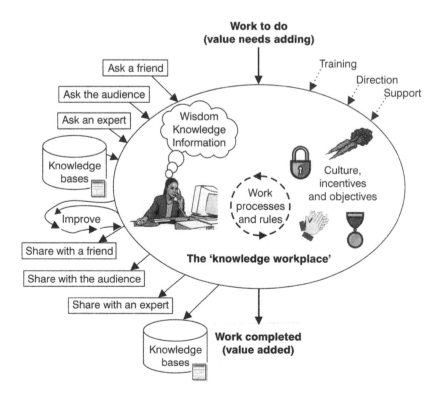

Figure 2.2
The knowledge workplace, developed by Trevor Howes and Tony Clack

In the workplace people will already know certain information and have an amount of knowledge and wisdom. They are employed to perform a range of activities, or work processes, and are often supported in this by technology. In addition, they will have specific objectives, and be influenced by the incentives on offer and surrounding culture. They will also receive varying degrees of training, direction, and support to guide their actions for the corporate and their personal good.

Work will then flow to them, whereupon they may ask 'friends', a wider audience, or specific experts for advice. They may also use paper and electronic systems to find what they need. In doing their work they may also improve the information and knowledge. For example, by adding what they have learnt from their own experiences. So as well as completing the work, they may also share this knowledge with friends, a wider audience, specific experts, or record it within paper and electronic systems.

The knowledge workplace is where a cycle of work constantly flows, where the individual adds value and contributes to the wider community of knowledge.

Knowledge-intensive roles

People get hired for a job partly because of formal qualifications, but among a group of similarly qualified individuals, the person with experience will always come out on top. In the workplace, experience and personal expertise count for almost everything. For example, a Channel 4 television series, *Faking it*, revolved around the efforts of specially chosen experts in a particular field in teaching a skill to an individual with no background in that field – examples included teaching a vicar to sell used cars, and a classical cellist to be a dance DJ. It achieved this by giving them special coaching to get them up to a standard where they could be judged alongside 'real' professionals. From a knowledge management perspective, these shows demonstrate the importance of things like professional jargon and 'tricks of the trade' or rules of thumb in establishing credibility and enabling people to function confidently. These are no less important for 'real' professionals than for bogus ones!

In this context, it is clear that the way a role is defined and the make-up of the workplace (which adds context as well as specific processes that people follow) are very important in influencing performance. These in turn are also impacted upon by managerial actions, including direction given from a management viewpoint, as well as decisions taken regarding training, skills, and workplace support. For example, an individual may know a great deal about a certain computing language from an intellectual perspective, but his or her skills in actually using it may be a little rusty, and he/she may be encouraged to go on a training course that emphasizes gaining practice. The individual may also be given access to software that will help debug and test programs, and perhaps also a set of best practice information containing details of previous experiences of people who use the language. Here the *training* is the course, the *direction* was the instruction to attend the course, and the *support* is in terms of the software tools provided.

A knowledge-intensive roles audit will go through the organization, workgroup by workgroup, identifying the key roles – sales managers, for example, or second-level customer support – that place the most demands on individual and organizational knowledge and information. Each business unit might identify the 'top 5' roles (with a number of people in each role noted) for example, with descriptions and perhaps a list of key information sources associated with each role. Commonalities and patterns can then be mapped – for example, there may be insights to be gained in whether roles tended to be clustered in customer facing positions, mostly internal facing, or more support oriented.

See Appendix 2 for an initial template and example to assist you with such an exercise.

Knowledge-intensive processes

Each of the roles identified will be associated with a set of formal and informal processes – anything from completing timesheets, to running a bid, and dealing with complaints. In order to perform these an individual must use several kinds of knowledge, first of all personal knowledge to understand the context of the request or requirement to do something, then knowledge of the (formal or informal) process associated with carrying it out, then knowledge of how to use any systems or technical components (such as forms or communications devices) required by the process.

A process audit is useful in setting out what the top five knowledge-intensive processes are, associated with each of the 'knowledge-intensive roles' previously identified. The rationale for this is that optimum functioning of knowledge processes are essential to the organization, for through them value is directly added which is then passed onto the customer. This is the cornerstone of organizational advantage and success.

At this point, it is not required to redesign processes (though ideas arising about efficiencies that might be made should be collected) as more detailed process analysis will take place in the next stage. All that is required here is an understanding of which processes add the most value to the organization.

See Appendix 3 for an initial template and example to assist you with such an exercise.

Functional groups

Here we look at the main communities/groups where people work together to exchange information and share knowledge.

The organization chart is a good place to start – but most organizations now have teams or other working methods that cut across formal boundaries. An important element of knowledge management strategy is finding appropriate ways to foster communication and knowledge sharing across these boundaries, as well as finding ways to capture 'shared' knowledge within groups and subgroups, and make it available to other group members, business units, or indeed the whole organization.

Formal and informal groups are recognized as the main conduit for sharing of experiences, and for giving and receiving of feedback and advice. To analyse these, we need to move beyond the organization chart, and start to map out the linkages between formal workgroups; charting the strengths and weaknesses of these links and their effectiveness helps form a picture of the relationships that exist to support one another. Do these groups help the individual? Do they provide enough support and quality of information? Also can you easily find an expert to gain advice from in specific circumstances?

If working on a knowledge management strategy for the whole organization, it may not be possible to do much work on groups other than to identify some of the key issues facing workgroup performance – thinking of the needs of a few 'sample' groups will help keep the work at a pragmatic level.

Technology audit

Technology infrastructure plays a crucial role in today's workplace: joining people together to enable communication through many different media and channels, and providing access to content creation, access and manipulation tools.

An information and knowledge technologies audit examines the status of an organization's technology estate, looking at the infrastructure (desktop, server and networks) and the software available to users. Questions need to include aspects such as:

- Does the technology support knowledge sharing (do tools exist)?
- How useful do people find existing tools?
- Is performance adequate (network speed, compatibility issues)?
- What are the most useful elements of technology for the key roles and processes?
- Do communities and workgroups use technology appropriately?
- What is the potential for new technologies or upgrade of existing ones?
- What standards are in place and are these appropriate for the future?

These questions should uncover potential problems, such as the suitability of the underlying networks, platforms, infrastructure, and applications services. The responsiveness of the IT team to business needs and operational change may arise as an issue – also effectiveness and appropriateness of security – for example, even where security measures such as virus protection or firewalls are in place, the way they are implemented may be preventing people from being able (or feeling able) to share sensitive information.

Many organizations will already regularly conduct such an audit under efforts to manage IT strategy. However, while material assembled for this purpose may be extremely valuable in a KM strategy context, it should be recognized that there is a particular knowledge focus that requires a fresh and holistic look at IT provision.

Information, content and skills audit

The information and content audit seeks to identify if the quantity and level of information is available to support the key roles and processes. This is a sizeable task – a recent audit conducted for a government customer, for example, turned up more than 10 000 Lotus Notes database files in an organization of around 4000 people. Many of these databases were things like group diaries, but more than half of the total were thought to be no longer in use. Most organizations use a very complex patchwork of internal and external information sources, some of them shared between many owners in the business and some even shared with or wholly provided by external partners.

Information sources can be databases, news feeds, intranet sites, memos, books, and 'expert' opinion. 'Content' is a term more specifically used to mean information which is delivered via the web, a category covering quite a large subgroup of information, from tiny snippets of information in intranet pages, to very large aggregated files containing Microsoft Word, Excel or Power-Point documents, or PDF files.

Methods of assessing workgroup-level information and content management needs are discussed in depth in Stage 3 (together with a much more detailed information and technology audit, aimed at assisting with development of a detailed implementation plan), but for the initial audit, the essential questions are ones of fundamental and business-wide relevance:

- Is the information architecture adequate in terms of scope, classification, and access? Can staff access the information and documents they need – are they captured and stored, and if so, are they available, quickly, at the point of need?
- Is there clarity on what information and documents are business critical?
- What are the main frustrations regarding access to information?

Once again, the goal at the level of knowledge management strategy is to get to a top-level view of the issues and challenges. Detail analysis and input to project design comes in Stage 3.

Culture and knowledge climate

The interplay between the culture of an organization (the unwritten 'rules' and customs, which in turn reflect the overall tone and value system) is frequently the dynamic that most clearly distinguishes one organization from another. The degree to which firms are risk-taking or risk-averse, homogeneous or diverse in terms of people mix or behaviour across geographies, or resistant or embracing of change, all dramatically affect what it is like to work for these firms; the sorts of people attracted to work there (or repelled by the culture) can also have a major impact on its performance and success.

From a knowledge perspective the cultural imperatives or constraints matter enormously. Questions such as 'What behaviours are supported and rewarded by management?' (which in turn influence what distinctive competences are developed over time) are important. Culture is essentially driven by the expectations and actions of senior management over a long period, relating to what results are expected and most importantly how those results are achieved. If management try to change things too quickly, differences can rapidly develop between the 'official' corporate culture espoused and the unofficial culture that may hang over from an earlier era, or have developed by itself over time.

This is particularly prevalent with professional cultures – groups of academics, lawyers or doctors, for example, have a strong professional culture that in many cases is more potent than local organizational cultures where they physically work.

Assessment of culture, and local or organizational impact on knowledge issues, can be a tricky exercise but is most commonly attempted by questionnaire. Fujitsu's Knowledge Assessment toolkit is based around a series of questions (several hundred in the fullest version) that assesses attitudes in organizations to such things as information strategy, people and skills, knowledge sharing, incentives, use of technology, collaboration, partners, and customers.

Such an assessment process can be used at various different junctures – at the earliest stages, when a knowledge management programme is being evaluated; in fuller form, in development of KM strategy; and in bespoke form, working with individual workgroups as part of a change management or KM implementation process. With the questionnaire, elements of information, content and skills are also rolled into the tool, enabling a fairly comprehensive picture of the status of an organization to be quickly established.

The following represents the sort of questions typically asked. In Fujitsu's case, the tool is customized to suit the particular company and industry sector in which it is being applied. Respondents – who will vary in role, seniority and number according to the circumstances in which the questionnaire is used – are asked to grade the following using a scale 1 to 5 where 1 = strongly agree, 5 = strongly disagree. The results should be brought together and averaged out across the group.

Please grade the following:

- *Your organization is open to constant change*
- *Your organization uses a recognized business model*
- *The leader is committed to knowledge sharing*
- *Your organization understands why better use of what people know is required*
- *Your organization has a long-term vision for the role of knowledge*
- *Your organization has the information to meet its critical business needs*
- *Management focus wider than financial performance indicators*
- *Information flows regardless of hierarchical structures*
- *Staff are encouraged to share information*
- *Mistakes are tolerated*
- *There is a 'no blame' culture*
- *Staff are rewarded for information sharing*
- *Staff are trained in the use of information access and retrieval tools*
- *Staff are aware of their performance relative to customer delivery*
- *Non-standard and constructive challenge are encouraged*
- *Exit interviews are conducted when staff leave the business or move to another unit*
- *Staff are encouraged to work in teams*
- *Information is shared between business/departmental units*
- *Staff are free to share and work with other parts of the organization*
- *There is a community spirit*
- *People feel they can define their own working practices*
- *Companies create their own business opportunities and are not totally led by the market*
- *Knowledge sharing is part of the company culture*
- *Staff feel they can contribute towards business strategy*
- *Business performance is evaluated using more than financial indicators.*

There have been instances where organizations have chosen to re-run this sort of evaluation at fixed intervals, to assess whether the culture supporting knowledge and information sharing is improving.

2.1.4 The external environment

The final piece of the audit puzzle relates to the external environment – the issues and challenges posed by the wider macro-economic climate, conditions in the specific industry sector, experience in meeting the demands of external stake-holders such as funding bodies and major shareholders.

The standard discovery tool for this is a STEP analysis, typically used in a workshop to capture and assess the importance of various factors, as they impact on issues relating to knowledge and information. The focus is on teasing out and agreeing significant drivers of change.

This can be a very powerful approach as it forces people to take a step back and look at the issues in a wider context, something people tend not to do as they become engrossed in the day-to-day pressures.

External factors may also influence the various knowledge-intensive roles and processes previously assessed for internal purposes. As part of the analysis, it may be worth reviewing the various topic areas previously discussed, this time from the external (STEP) perspective, attempting some kind of bench-marking or comparison with industry norms and best practice:

- Key knowledge-intensive roles
- Key knowledge-intensive processes
- Groups and communities (including professional groups)
- Technology used to support roles, processes and groups
- Information and content innovation
- The culture and motivation of external competitors.

For example, process innovation adopted by a competitor may be putting pressures on innovation within your organization, or highlight some weaknesses in current processes or responsibility gaps across existing roles.

With knowledge roles, for example, the market for skilled and knowledgeable staff constantly changes. The cost of losing staff, obtaining new staff, retraining them and the time to get up to proficiency can be significant. Reducing the attrition rate of staff can, therefore, have a positive impact on costs and on the retention of knowledge within the organization. In such circumstances it may be worth considering what is being done to help retain staff and encourage knowledge sharing and creation.

In terms of process and the development of new communities of expertise – are there new areas developing in your industry? If you had more knowledgeable staff, might this make a difference to customer satisfaction? A need to boost skills is often apparent in changing environments, when learning and innovation are key to adapting and remaining competitive.

Table 2.2 An example STEP analysis

Sociological – e.g.:
- Increasing trend towards teamworking
- Increasing trend towards partnership working and alliances
- Demographics – major loss of staff in certain industries likely due to many reaching retirement age at same time.

Technological – e.g.:
- Competitors leveraging KM and other technologies (mobile, extranet)
- Roll-out becoming cheaper through economies of scale
- New tools coming on stream.

Economic – e.g.:
- Increasingly competitive climate in industry sector – highly skilled staff turnover
- Need to demonstrate better return on intellectual capital
- Threat or aftermath of merger/acquisition.

Political – e.g.:
- For private bodies – issues of regulation, deregulation, integration with EU, data protection
- For government funded bodies – political agendas, 'joined up' government, Public Records Office requirements, Freedom of Information Act.

By the end of this audit stage, we now have a high level, yet comprehensive, understanding of the organization's resources, circumstances and priorities.

2.2 Stage 2: Define the organization's response – building a vision

As we have seen from our five-stage approach, the second element is the creation of a vision for the organization – a look into the future at how the organization can be, or should be in the context of knowledge. In an ideal world, how would knowledge and information best be created, captured, used and shared?

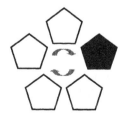

- What sort of resources would we see deployed? For example, technology or role changes.
- What capabilities should the organization and its people have in this future state? For example, skills and experiences.

Out of this, a vision for knowledge can be distilled, hopefully a succinct one where the benefits are obvious to all.

Depending on the genesis of the push for mobilizing knowledge within the organization, there are two main types of strategy – those that 'fit' the needs of the organization (focused around incremental improvement and efficiencies), and those that 'stretch' the organization to do things differently, leveraging resources and capabilities in new ways. How the vision is drawn up will to some extent determine the balance of 'fit' and 'stretch' which the strategy will likely adopt.

The vision might be the product of much discussion, but it should be succinct enough for non-specialists to understand. An example of a good vision for knowledge is this one, adopted by the UK Department of Health (2001):

- **Create the knowledge base**, both tangible (books, articles, databases etc.) and intangible (expertise, skills, social networks).
- **Make it available in user-friendly ways** (exploit infrastructure, improve process, join up information assets).
- **Encourage and skill people** to seek out, use and share knowledge and information.
- **Build a culture** that fully rewards, encourages, values and supports knowledge and information sharing.

The important thing about this vision statement is that it derives directly from the pressures for change on the Department of Health, and wider pressures on the UK Civil Service for 'joined-up government'. Although the language of knowledge management is used, the picture it paints is substantially driven by targets and goals set out by ministers and senior managers. If this vision were suddenly to come about tomorrow, it would represent in some sense the 'ideal' department it is striving to become.

It is important at this stage to remember that a vision is not the same as a strategy, which is concerned with the actual deployment of resources in order to achieve the vision. The vision – by definition – lies in the future. Whatever is contained in the knowledge management strategy, the stages must be pragmatic enough to be followed in practice. Too often there are cases where strategy is made in an intellectual ivory tower, without being challenged and validated by a wider circle.

Due to the far-reaching impact of knowledge management strategies, people in key roles are likely to be impacted, and a successful implementation is dependent upon their cooperation. It is therefore essential that the strategy is not owned solely by those at the top of the organization but also that key people throughout feel like they own it too, and see the benefit in implementing it and bringing others on board.

So how can those charged with getting KM off the ground in organizations make this happen? This is normally achieved through a combination of interviews, workshops, and a communication plan that involves listening as well as telling, focusing on what is important to people across all parts of the organization and grades. Both 'carrot and stick' approaches must be used – building understanding the 'carrot' element is often the hardest, but once key areas of personal motivation are understood then the chance of success is more certain.

Widening involvement across the organization and grades has another advantage, that of bringing together other similar initiatives under a common focus. By coordinating knowledge-related projects, the resources, experience, and knowledge of those involved can be joined together and a greater variety of requirements consolidated. As we have previously emphasized, there is no such thing as a green field site for knowledge management these days – lots of initiatives are under way in any organization, whether with a KM label or not.

When formulating a vision, it is important to consider widely the implications for the whole organization. Peter Senge has written extensively on the 'learning organization' – about how organizations (as a whole) can come to learn from their environment, and from their own successes and failures. We previously mentioned the work of Arie de Geus, a former senior manager at Shell, who wrote a seminal book on how organizational learning works in practice. Entitled *The Living Company*, it emerged from work conducted at Shell into company longevity. Its premise – that long-lived companies have management philosophies that in some sense treat the organization as a living being – has interesting implications for the management of knowledge. A living being requires an ability to respond appropriately to environmental stimulus. Indeed, de Geus puts this ability to respond at the top of his list of key characteristics of a living company:

- **Sensitivity to the environment** (which, he says, represents a company's ability to *learn* and adapt).

- **Cohesion and identity** (aspects of a company's ability to build a community and a *persona* for itself – related to some extent to the 'know-why' knowledge discussed in the previous chapter).
- **Tolerance and decentralization** (symptoms that a company is aware of the importance of *ecology*, of constructive relationships inside and outside the organization).
- And finally, **conservative financing,** which helps the organization control its own *evolution*.

(Arie de Geus 1997, p. 16)

It is unlikely that many knowledge managers will get – at least immediately – the opportunity to remodel an organization (though sensible organizations might include them, along with the IT director, in the strategic discussion!). However, there are significant lessons here about the underlying rationale for knowledge management. These may not be apparent at present to senior managers, but with appropriate promotion and tie-in to the overall organizational direction, can be brought forward in a very powerful way to begin to shift the viewpoint of those setting organizational or business unit direction.

Of course, it can be great fun discussing ideas for the future, and creating a long shopping list of ideas. It is important to avoid 'paralysis by analysis' by analysing only what is needed and no more. Bringing groups of ideas together into theme areas and questioning how they link to the corporate strategy are both excellent ways of weeding out unnecessary ideas.

However, as we have mentioned before, every journey begins at a starting point . . . and in knowledge management, that starting point is crucial in determining the appropriate course of action. The following section looks at how this can be achieved.

2.2.1 Moving forward – strategy

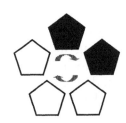

Precisely how the stages in this chapter are used in practice depends on the circumstances faced. For very large organizations, it will not be possible to go into great levels of detail at this stage – the intention must be to create a reasonably complete picture to a comfortable degree of resolution. For a business unit, the process as outlined above is still valuable, but a great deal more detail can be sensibly assimilated.

We began this chapter with the idea that strategy development was about seeking answers to the following questions:

- Where do we want to be?
- Where are we now?
- How do we get there from here?

So far, we have looked at the formulation of a vision, and the conduct of various kinds of audit and assessment. The final step – formulation of a strategy – involves considerably more work than this, as we have yet to properly formulate options and assess whether they are suitable for purpose, feasible to implement, and acceptable to all parties. However, by this stage ideas should be forming as to the sort of shape a knowledge management programme might take, the business issues it might address, the difficulties the organization might encounter in implementing it, and the degree of change that might be required to achieve measurable results.

At this point, it is appropriate to begin to build the business case – the essential step in ensuring that a programme properly meets the business needs and issues identified.

3

From strategy to action

3.1 Stage 2 (continued): Define the organization's response – KM strategy and business case

3.1.1 Shaping the strategy

Earlier, we defined the process of strategy creation into three parts, and the previous chapter focused on the first two:

- Where do we want to be?
- Where are we now?

The challenge from here on is to answer the question:

- How do we get there from here?

Some organizations proceed without a formal strategy – working on an ad-hoc basis, project by project, or with some broad principles, typically grown from a set of IT and data standards. But it is the authors' view that once a certain maturity is reached, ownership and coordination of knowledge and information activity in the business becomes essential: in particular, a strategic approach to infrastructure and technology choices is vital, otherwise individual business units and divisions can run off and build incompatible systems with differing underlying architectures; but beyond this lies real value in a dedicated individual or group being responsible for reflecting on the end-to-end processes involved in knowledge flows throughout the business. This 'ownership' approach also offers real potential for building true organizational learning through the creation of case studies and collation of lessons learned, evangelizing the results, and helping others use and integrate that learning within new projects.

The lower level details of the knowledge management strategy will evolve as we progress through the stages, as greater clarity comes from more informed analysis. But what does a knowledge management strategy look like? Organizations differ in their interpretation of the word 'strategy' but the authors have tended to use roughly the following report format.

Management summary

- Summarizes the findings: the drivers, audit results (what was 'found' in the organization, the status quo), the 'vision', top-level results from the analysis, and conclusions and recommendations. It is vital to keep this tight, and free of KM 'jargon' – it must be accessible to decision-makers who have not been party to the background thinking and work, but who nevertheless have budget authority. Recommendations must deliver on clear problems the organization knows it is facing – while the management summary is not the place for a full business case, a benefits-based approach to specifying recommendations is useful in putting the top-level programme in a business context. Unless organizational custom dictates more, we would keep this to one to three pages.

Method outline

- When using a methodology such as the five-stage KM strategy framework, we have found it useful to describe the approach taken. It is also useful to briefly log the work done – workshops and interviews conducted, background research undertaken – and any assumptions or exclusions.

Analysis and conclusions

- The 'meat' of the strategy. Precisely how this is structured depends on the shape of the organization – it can be done in a variety of ways to reflect the degree to which the organization is chopped up into business units (for example, by market sector or technical specialism), or integrated (such as organizations structured around brands with key shared 'group' functions run at 'group' level).

Typical structures might be based on:

Knowledge types – Using categories from the introductory chapter such as the 'six investigators' (p. 21) or generic grouping such as product, process and customer knowledge (p. 30). Alternatively, there are some more advanced category analysis tools in Chapter 4.

Business issues – Analysis based on the key challenges facing the business (for example, 'coping with regulation', 'implementing e-business', 'improving production efficiency', 'improving market penetration', and so on. This can be a powerful way to show the possible impact on specific areas of the business, but risks becoming repetitious if different areas (as they are likely to) call on the same proposed central initiatives in areas such as IT infrastructure, training, and process re-engineering.

Levers and enablers – Using the knowledge management levers and enablers (*Leadership, People, Process, Technology and Information*) as the units of analysis. The difficulty with this is that while it makes sense from a KM point of view, this view of the business may not be familiar to key stakeholders. Consequently, it may be better to mix this approach with one of the two others in order to arrive at an analysis intelligible to the wider organization.

Whatever the structure, this section focuses on looking behind the picture uncovered so far, examining how they move the organization towards vision, and understanding the future potential, and coming to some conclusion as to a suitable way forward.

A programme of action

Individual recommendations or proposals may accompany the various areas for analysis – but if we return to our original idea of strategy as some kind of purposeful allocation of resources in pursuit of specific goals, then the strategy must conclude with a specific plan of action – divided for our purposes into proposals for action (accompanied by an outline benefits case) – and a prioritized programme plan.

The recommendations must describe three principal elements:

- **Business area** – usually based on the categories from the analysis sections.
- **Business priority** – which projects (or pilot initiatives) need to be done first.
- **Ownership** – where responsibility for change lies within the organization.

Business area

Mirroring how the organization is structured, or some similar sensible groupings of the actions..

Business priority

The time dimension is an important one, affected by many different factors, for example there may be dependency on something being in place – such as the roll-out of an intranet portal. Alternatively, there may be an immovable business target (such as a merger or product launch) which needs to be supported by the particular initiative concerned.

Typical project categorizations are:

- Quick win – a project that is perceived as quick (but not necessarily cheap) to implement but has potential to deliver visible benefits quickly – great for case studies.
- Prerequisite – a dependency for later projects – for example, if a later project aims at developing communities of practice, the technical infrastructure needs to be in place first.
- Pilot – various kinds of pilot exist, from proof of concept (where the final solution may look very different to what was piloted) through to a 'test' roll-out of a process or software product that it is already scheduled for large-scale deployment. The ability of an organization to learn from pilots is a key knowledge management capability.
- Main project – a mainstream programme element that contains a significant piece of work – may follow on from a pilot as a roll-out phase, for example.

- Potential/optional – a project for which the business case, budget or stakeholder support is not assured, but which is shown on the programme as a recommended option.

Certain timeframe designations are also useful:

- Milestone – an assumed decision point or anticipated project completion.
- Short term (e.g. 1–6 months) – may fall into the same category as quick win.
- Medium term (e.g. 6–18 months) – typically dependent on other factors (such as delivery of earlier projects or on future budget approval).
- Long term (18 months +) – not necessarily well defined in terms of benefits case and certainly liable to change in detail.

Once the strategy has been formulated to an acceptable level then it is time to understand in greater detail the benefits that individual projects, or a programme, will bring: indeed, only once this is done will most organizations free up sufficient budget for the programme to commence.

3.1.2 The business case – clear benefits

Before a project or programme can be put forward for approval, a business case must be produced which makes clear what the resulting benefits are expected to be. Different organizations require different degrees of rigour in business case creation – some companies are fairly loose about this process, requiring only that a clear improvement be promised, and that costs are proportionate to the anticipated benefit. Other organizations apply much more scrutiny, applying all sorts of investment appraisal methods, including discounted cash flow techniques that require a project to demonstrate that they can produce a significant financial return over and above the effects of interest rates and inflation on the money invested.

Historically, it has been difficult to make the business case for knowledge management projects, but some organizations have gone ahead regardless, without formal efforts at working out return on investment, on the assumption that, for example, the building of an intranet may have intrinsic benefits that do not require precise measurement (with an awareness that any benefits delivered may be extremely hard to measure anyway).

Unfortunately, the other side of this coin is that, in other organizations, the case for knowledge management has been unclear and unconvincing. The benefits – which relate to things like 'intellectual capital', 'knowledge sharing' and 'innovation' – are seldom clearly calculable, or proven to result in dramatic productivity gains – and in cultures where the doctrine of 'if it can't be measured, it can't be managed' is pursued in a fundamentalist way, this has led to KM projects never getting off the ground (or never being pursued in the first place).

The third way is perhaps the most familiar one (though perhaps becoming less prevalent as time goes on): a business case is cobbled together that jumps company hurdles for investment approval, but which is set aside almost immediately once approval for a project is gained.

Figure 3.1 presents a story all too common in IT projects – where a 'chasm' of faith separates the activities proposed and the benefits aimed for. Such a gap requires a gamble by those authorizing the project – a gamble managers are less and less inclined to take, as IT management matures as a discipline, thanks in no small part to experience of many technology projects which have failed to deliver significant benefits to the business.

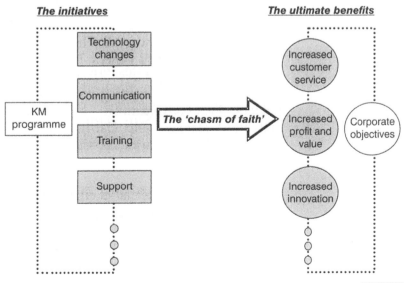

Figure 3.1
The 'chasm of faith' often seen in business cases

Consequently, when using funds from IT budgets, those signing off knowledge management projects have increasingly required a watertight business case, due in no small part to confusion as to what KM actually is, and the wide range of expectations and perceptions that follow from this.

We have dedicated so much of this book to the question of a KM business case to help those developing KM programmes create a robust and compelling case for change, based on the benefits of mobilizing knowledge.

Figure 3.1 shows, on the left, some proposed initiatives – these can be projects, activities, or tasks. (Only a small sample of typical initiatives is shown in the diagram – any real programme is likely to differ substantially.) The items in this column make up the majority of cost and resources required for the investment.

On the right are the ultimate end benefits that the decision-makers are really interested in. Here we are talking about such end goals as lower costs, higher revenues, improved profits, higher market share, return on investment, and increased shareholder value.

In an ideal business case – one which comes across powerfully to justify significant investment – the initiatives must be clearly linked to outcomes: for example, if we do X then this delivers benefit Y. Sadly, all too often, initiatives and ultimate benefits are both spelled out, but the direct linkages are unclear or ill defined. We call this the 'chasm of faith'.

It follows that what is needed is something else to fill this chasm and prove cause and effect – some intermediate benefits, which form a bridge to the end goals. The following section looks at how we might use a set of generic business benefits which can be deployed to construct this 'bridge', and which are also useful in structuring early benefits-focused conversations with stake-holders. Such conversations – carried out alongside the vision and audit steps – help clarify priorities and uncover risks associated with the various possible courses of action.

Balanced Scorecard approach

One of the most useful tools to link up initiatives with ultimate strategic benefit objectives is the Balanced Scorecard, as defined by Kaplan and Norton (1996). There is substantial literature associated with the development of scorecard-based approaches such as the Kaplan and Norton method, or the Navigator method developed by the Scandinavian insurance giant, Skandia. These developed out of a coming together of a number of influences:

- The growing concern at the failure of traditional accounting measures to provide an accurate company valuation – difficult when balance sheets are built around cash and the book value of assets, while stock market valuations are based essentially on sentiment surrounding potential future performance.
- Related frustration with the backward-looking nature of traditional company measures.
- The apparent inability of traditional accounting to adequately value intellectual capital, leaving a sizeable gap in tools for performance management.

Measurement systems within organizations have long been focused on financial measures – most accounting rules are property-based, going back to the Middle Ages – ignoring the core non-financial competencies that are needed in today's environment. With the increasing focus on measurement that has been the legacy of the 'Quality' movement, this has proved a serious gap. From a KM perspective it is largely through non-financial indicators that knowledge management gives its most immediate impact. The four perspectives proposed by Kaplan and Norton allow a robust and balanced view of measurement, essential if knowledge management initiatives are to success-fully fight for funding alongside other pressing matters. For our benefit framework, specifically focused on knowledge manage-ment, we use the Balanced Scorecard concepts as our basis. It is therefore essential that a basic understanding of it is gained before we progress.

Scorecard – four into one

Within the main body of the Balanced Scorecard are four perspectives:

- **Financial**
- **Customer**
- **Internal business process, and**
- **Learning and growth.**

These four perspectives are shown in Figure 3.2. The aim is to represent a balanced view of business, to improve managers'

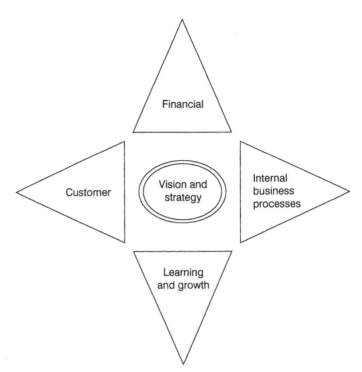

Figure 3.2
The four perspectives
of the Balanced
Scorecard
(Kaplan and Norton
1996)

ability to make sense of a range of measures, and so improve how the organization is managed.

The following are extracts from Kaplan and Norton (1996) are reproduced, with additional comments, in order to further explain the concept:

> The **financial perspective:** 'serves as the focus for all of the other perspectives ... The financial themes of increasing revenues, improving cost, and productivity, enhancing asset utilization, and reducing risk can provide the necessary linkages across all four scorecard perspectives.' (p. 47)

The financial perspective is the area where the most compelling business cases are strong. Demonstrating how the knowledge management initiatives can make a difference to the financial perspective is powerful message from. Perhaps the best opportunity for knowledge management techniques in this area is in knowledge reuse – demonstrating that cost savings can be made from reusing or repurposing existing content or collateral.

> The **customer perspective:** 'represent[s] the sources that will deliver the revenue component of the companies' financial objectives

... [It] enables companies to align their core customer outcome measures – satisfaction, loyalty, retention, acquisition, and profit- ability – to targeted customers and market segments.' (p. 63).

Being customer 'obsessed' is the key objective for many organizations. By meeting customer objectives (and by demon- strating this to stakeholders), the organization is more likely to have a stronger performance financially, for example with improved customer satisfaction leading to reduced medium- /long-term costs of doing business through happier and more closely tied customers, more repeat business, and lower cost of sales. In addition, better knowledge about customers' prefer- ences and behaviours helps individuals and groups better meet their needs. If you don't understand what customers want and need, then the chances of increasing their satisfaction are slim.

*The **internal-business-process perspective**: '[is where] managers identify the processes that are most critical for achieving customer and shareholder objectives ... We recommend that managers define a complete internal-process value chain.'* (p. 92)

The business processes that organizations follow, and the day- to-day activities performed, should be adding maximum value. Like clothes in a wardrobe, processes can build up and turn into clutter if not cleared out regularly. Are there processes still performed even though they no longer add value? Are there processes which are too complex, slow, or not delivering the right level of quality? By getting the business processes right, and focusing on those that make a difference, then organizations can directly contribute more to customer satisfaction, and help meet financial objectives.

Knowledge and information are used in and produced by business processes. As proposed during the previous audits, knowledge-intensive processes that actually make the most difference to an organization are where initial energies should be focused. If knowledge creation, sharing, and reuse is poor within an organization then the potential for business processes to add value is probably not being realized.

*The **learning and growth perspective**: 'provide[s] the infra- structure to enable ambitious objectives in the other three per- spectives to be achieved ... [it] stresses the importance of investing for the future ... [there are] three principal categories [of objectives]*

- *Employee capabilities*
- *Information system capabilities*
- *Motivation, empowerment, and alignment'* (pp. 126–127).

This perspective is the very essence of knowledge management – it deals with how people obtain information, and whether they have the means and motivation to add meaning to it, act on it, and build value from it.

Efforts to improve employees' ability to learn and innovate, and to develop and share knowledge they hold, directly impacts their performance and of those around them. This has many positive side-effects. People become more flexible as they understand more choices and the 'bigger picture'. They can better uncover and deal with business process inefficiencies – leading to continuous improvement. Consequently, they are better able to add value to the organization and its customers, as well as increasing their own value in the employee marketplace.

The first thing required when creating a business case is to understand the organization's objectives using the Balanced Scorecard perspectives and how they interrelate. For example, the objectives from the learning and growth perspective are likely to support objectives in the other three perspectives. Figure 3.3 shows typical cause-and-effect links between perspectives.

Here the financial perspective is at the highest level, with objectives from the lower perspectives contributing to its objectives. Second the customer perspective objectives are

Figure 3.3
The cause-and-effect nature of objectives in each of the perspectives (adapted from Kaplan and Norton 1996)

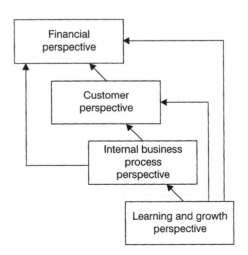

contributed to by the objectives of both the internal business processes and learning and growth.

The learning and growth perspective, therefore, underpins all the other perspectives, and this is where knowledge management efforts should focus. For example, by learning and growing, the organization will be able to better improve its business processes, these will better be able to meet customer needs, and therefore financial results should be improved.

Bridging the chasm

With the occasional exception, it is unlikely that chief executives or other senior managers will ever be interested in knowledge management for its own sake. Strategic considerations aside, the business of day-to-day management, focused on quarterly trading figures or performance targets, tends to be about generating short-term profit, whether by going for sales growth or by cutting 'slack' or spare capacity from the operation. Short-term thinking is very much at the heart of management culture in most organizations – and this is unlikely to change any time soon. Preparing and presenting a compelling case for action where the financial payback from the investment may be more long term is a challenging task – but there are ways to improve the chances of a business case being successful in winning support.

This is where understanding the key corporate drivers' is important – knowing what the hot buttons are, and the areas of pain in the business, will allow you to identify appropriate strategic action, and articulate beneficial outcomes in the form of tangible benefits.

In order to create a compelling case, there is an important challenge for those creating it: to leave behind our tendency to be subjective. We can illustrate the possible confusion of being too subjective by taking the survival and growth of a tree as an example. Can one objectively say which of sunlight, water, soil quality, wind strength, and temperature variations is the most important variable for a tree? They all contribute to the tree's well-being, but can we monitor and measure and create the ideal mix?

As we cannot understand all the relevant influences, or really have any control over them, then all we can do is single out those which we are most certain about. What to select will depend on a number of factors, including the specialisms and enthusiasms of the people involved, and the qualities most desired from the tree – for example, quality of seeds, flowers, leaves, or long-term growth? We could also question if we should just be talking about trees. What about all the different kinds of shrubs? A health warning should be applied to this type of thinking – too much detailed analysis can be counterproductive!

With knowledge management there are many influences as well, and the emphasis chosen will depend hugely on specific organizational needs, culture and values. The moral of the tree example is to focus only on those elements that will make a real difference. Widen the scope too much and the questions become impossible to answer, and the case for knowledge management will become too confusing.

The suggestions for business case creation in the following pages can provide only a generic framework with some rules of thumb that the authors have found valuable in working with customers. It is then down to readers to apply these ideas in their own organizations in the most appropriate manner. We also recommend the text *The Information Paradox* (Thorp and DMR Consulting, 1999) for further reading on realizing business benefits from IT.

When preparing a business case, it is useful to work with adapted Balanced Scorecard categories:

- Knowledge and information availability (learning and growth) and personal competence (learning and growth)
- Internal business process
- Customer and stakeholder
- Corporate.

We begin by using these benefit categories to start to bridge the 'chasm of faith' as shown in Figure 3.4. Note that our methodology assumes that the majority of the links across the 'chasm' will likely be sequential, with the personal competence improvements contributing to internal business process improvement, and so on. However, in practice, there will also be many examples where the links skip the sequential flow. One such example is where efficiency savings arising from research and development activity are not visible to the customer, but go straight through as corporate cost saving.

Going through these benefit categories enables us to choose which, if any, are likely candidates for inclusion in the benefit map associated with our KM projects.

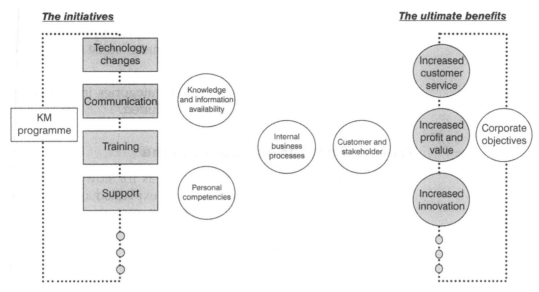

Figure 3.4 Using interim benefits to fill the 'chasm of faith'

Clarity is essential when identifying benefits, the temptation is to express potential improvements in language such as 'better quality information', 'improved processes', or 'happier customers'. But this is highly subjective language: what is precisely meant by 'better', 'improved', or 'happier'? This leaves the exercise open to misunderstanding.

The way round this is to formalize the language of 'benefit'. We use only five verbs, with the useful mnemonic acronym CRIME:

- **Created**, e.g. created pricing structure
- **Reduced**, e.g. reduced number of complaints
- **Increased**, e.g. increased satisfaction
- **Maintained**, e.g. maintained market share
- **Eliminated**, e.g. eliminated costs.

Clarifying what is meant by 'better' is made much easier when you can use this list.

With precise language should go precise measurement – only with this can the ability to manage the benefits be demonstrated. It is essential that for each benefit appropriate measures are stated. These can be very difficult to define for certain knowledge management benefits, although it is an essential step along the way to a compelling business case. We will now go through each benefit category, and explain its possible use in a

KM context. Alongside each benefit entry is a proposed measure. This is not meant as definitive or prescriptive, but as a useful guide and reminder that all benefits must have some quantifiable measure associated.

In the list below, only the key benefit categories important in knowledge management, have been included.

3.1.3 The benefit categories

The following benefit categories are ideas for how mobilizing knowledge may help in projects. Each is explained and, because measures are required for a business case, examples are provided to help with this challenging process. For each benefit that is applicable to a project then the CRIME test must be made – ensuring the benefits are clearer than simply 'to make things better'.

These are common mobilizing knowledge benefits and are by no means meant to be comprehensive or complete. Each situation will bring new opportunities and so these are intended to 'jump-start' the benefit discovery process.

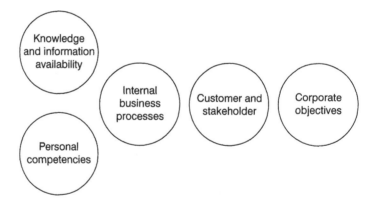

Figure 3.5
The benefit categories

These five benefit categories are now examined, starting from the left where the direct link to the strategic objectives is likely to be weakest, moving onto where the strategic relationship will be the most clear.

Knowledge and information availability

The information and content audit previously carried out should have begun to tease out the problem areas and potential opportunities. The availability of corporate information, the ability to access it, reuse it, is of vital operational importance, while the issues surrounding record-keeping and corporate memory are also of great significance.

The opportunities around knowledge and information availability focus on providing increased access to:

1 Experienced/expert people
2 Skills and training
3 Formal business processes, structures and standards
4 Reference material for professional roles
5 Drivers for customers, suppliers, and markets
6 Organizational information
7 Individual support
8 Workgroup support
9 Social, human resource and personal information.

1 Experienced/expert people

This benefit area is about allowing people to understand **'who knows what'** in the organization (the 'know-who' knowledge defined earlier). Benefits include access to expertise and advice from experts, as well as improved overall efficiency in internal communications. There is a lot of anecdotal evidence about the importance of repositories of expertise – one manager in a government department, running a small internal consultancy team, said that getting such a database was like getting 10% more staff – suddenly he found out his people had skills and capabilities he didn't know about before.

A measure of the usefulness of improvement in this area often includes the percentage of 'new' contacts made by individuals, or a measure of the usefulness of the system using a 1–10 scale, gathered from interviews or questionnaire.

2 Skills and training

Improving the information technology skills, as well as the information management skills, of key staff can have a significant impact on performance and is, of course, absolutely essential when rolling out new technology tools. In addition, learning of new skills can increase the confidence and competence of individuals, encouraging wider thinking and generating feelings of increased self-worth, as well as increasing their ability to deliver better quality and goods and services in a consistent fashion.

Measures can include the percentage completion rate of formal training courses, or time spent on self-development. Data might be gathered from time recording systems.

3 Formal business processes, structures and standards

Achieving among employees an increased understanding of preferred and mandatory ways of working (an aspect of **'know-how'**) can bring many benefits, from the basic saving of time and effort through following the right process first time, to reducing business risk as staff become less likely to get things 'wrong' in sensitive situations.

The percentage of formally documented processes, organizational structures, and standards of expected performance available and accessible to all is a key measure here.

4 Reference material for professional roles

Examples of 'good and best practice' material for key documents will aid the individual in his or her role, as will current information about the latest news and developments in their area. Good practice material may be document templates or previous presentations to customers. These materials may be the 'bread and butter' knowledge and information that are used at work – the main inputs used and outputs produced every day.

Measures might include the number of items available per role – for example, sales or production – and an independent judgement as to the quality of material available. Ideally measures would also be available on usage and 'usefulness'.

5 Drivers for customers, suppliers, and markets

Information on specific customers or groups of customers can help people understand more about the circumstances and pressures on them. Appropriate information would also increase awareness of customers' likely priorities, while information about previous dealings the organization has had with them is also useful in building relationships and generating/supporting repeat business. As well as records of past transactions, information may be provided about any major technology breakthroughs relevant to the customer, and the financial health of the market sector.

From an IT perspective customer relationship management (CRM) systems have been aimed, at least in part, at capturing and sharing customer information. Just putting in a CRM system is a failure to recognize the wider implications of knowledge management that are covered within this book. In many ways CRM and other relationship projects are in fact KM projects, as they are centred around using information and knowledge about customers to improve the strategic performance of the organization.

Measurement of the value of this information should be based around usage volumes, as well as usefulness ratings gathered from those accessing it.

6 Organizational information

For example – when joining an organization it can be many months before a new starter pieces together a comprehensive picture about the products and services sold, the management structure, the meaning and priority of communications, and what is 'important' in terms of the overall value system. (Quality of induction, which might be assisted by access to appropriate online information, is a regular focus area for KM projects.)

Measures typically include number of items available and accessible, usage, and also quality ratings and feedback from users.

7 Individual support

Good performance by individuals may require access to information and other people's personal knowledge that is often taken for granted. This might include unofficial telephone lists, maps and directions to other company buildings, and informal information about how to escalate problems about organizational issues or how to book meeting rooms. Often this can be addressed only at individual workgroup level.

Informal information is very difficult to measure but subjective ratings from new employees might be taken on how long it took them to become productive. More formal measures might also be gathered as before on published information.

8 Workgroup support

Working in groups is becoming increasingly common, and specific information and access to expertise outside the group can support and enhance their performance. For example, statements of what the group should achieve in terms of objectives and key measures might be made available, with details of team composition, appropriate documents and information issued, and specific rules or constraints placed on the group. (When we say workgroup you can also take this to mean groups with various names including projects, programmes, and community of practice groupings, divisions, functions, and even business units, where appropriate.)

Again, usage statistics and usefulness ratings gathered from users might be appropriate measures.

9 Social, human resource and personal information

In some workplaces it may be appropriate (and performance enhancing) to publish and make available social and personal details including information about social activities, details of personal objectives or career development plans, as well as employee-related information such as entitlements to holiday and pension details.

Again, usage statistics and usefulness ratings gathered from users might be appropriate measures.

Moving on, from 'knowledge and information availability', the next benefit category is that of personal competence.

Personal competence

As we have repeatedly stated knowledge in organizations is, for the most part, individually and personally held – anything else is really just information, which people need to access, understand and contextualize before it is of any real value. In this context, the role of individual skills (especially IT literacy and information management and processing skills) is vital. Beyond this, we have already mentioned the importance of induction – people are hired for their 'know-what' or 'know-that' ability – their formal qualifications and their body of personally held knowledge – but until they are up to speed with the formal and informal processes of the new organization, and know where and how to access people and information, they will fail to be productive. The following categories link knowledge management with personal competence:

1 Reduced time to competence
2 Increased competence profile
3 Increased personal value

1 Reduced time to competence

Speeding up the induction process, particularly by having appropriate information (especially contact information) to hand is an important way to reduce time to competence. This logic applies, however, in any change situation – by making the main tasks better supported with information tools then 'new' staff should benefit by being productive quicker.

A possible measure of this is the number of working days that someone requires to reach a competency level. In Fujitsu, a scale of 1–5 is used to judge the competency level of someone with, for example, presentation skills. An appropriate measure might be the number of days taken to go from level 1 to 2, with the aim of reducing this downwards through improved access to information and expertise.

2 Increased competence profile

All organizations need a certain number of people with specific core competences, and this measure is about increasing the numbers of people with the required profile – getting the mix right.

For example, a large IT department supported 140 new and legacy systems, while also developing new solutions. The challenge for this organization was to balance the knowledge of COBOL and other third generation languages with the desire of staff to gain knowledge of newer web-related skills. The organization recognized that a certain mix was essential if it was to maintain the old systems, while also being an attractive place to work for skills hungry IT professionals.

The measure is sometimes based around a target number of people assessed or possessing a certain competence.

3 Increased personal value

This is about satisfying the inner needs of people through such things as recognition and an increased sense of purpose. Improving the quality of life for staff through career development activity – from courses to placements – may help with job turnover, and boost self-esteem and contentment within the organization.

Having more information and advice available will allow people to make more sense of situations, and when combined with opportunities to debate and challenge they can add real value from a personal and organizational perspective.

Measured mainly through employee surveys.

Moving closer to benefits that are more clearly strategic, we now look at the benefit category of internal business process.

Internal business process

According to our Golden Rules:

Golden Rule #2: People's behaviours must change for the long term – People's beliefs must be affected if long-term improvements in behaviour are to be achieved. You must do more than just 'build an IT system'.

The implications for this are quite profound. If the goal of a knowledge management programme is to deliver better value from knowledge and expertise, then some effort needs to be focused on formal knowledge capture, but the hardest job (and also the most beneficial) is to change the way people behave, in how they think about their expertise, the documents they write, and how they learn from their colleagues and the wider environment. It is also likely that it will be necessary to change some formal processes, to help embed good behaviours and build in 'knowledge capture' steps, ensuring that insights not previously gathered or stored are now captured in some form, for sharing with others.

The main behavioural and process focus is increased providing access to:

1 Sharing of best practice knowledge
2 Quality of knowledge resources
3 Management of knowledge resources
4 Individual and workgroup effectiveness
5 Individual and workgroup efficiency
6 Capacity
7 Capability to innovate
8 Capability to change
9 Understanding of customers

1 Best practice knowledge

Organizations need to examine how they identify, appraise, learn from and share insights and best practice. This can range from formal methods – such as formal 'after action' reviews or debriefing – to less formal 'suggestion box' approaches. Internal briefing or conference events are also useful.

There are a wide range of potential measures in this area, from 'costs saved' by spreading best practice process or procedure, to impact on such things as appraisal schemes (asking people to demonstrate that they have shared their knowledge in some way in order to meet performance targets, for example). It may also be possible to measure things like reductions in bid costs or project start-up times.

2 Quality of knowledge resources

This is about having information that is current, relevant to workplace needs, consistent, timely, and covering the topic comprehensively.

As before under knowledge and information, usage statistics and usefulness ratings gathered from users might be appropriate measures.

3 Management of knowledge resources

Content that is not useful or current is more of a hindrance than a help. The publication process must be transparent, easy to use, and if possible, capable of alerting people when new content they are looking for arrives. If not actively managed, information can build up into an unstructured jungle, where valuable information and knowledge may be lost, or only found after frustrating and significant searching.

As before under knowledge and information, usage statistics and usefulness ratings gathered from users are appropriate measures.

4 Individual and workgroup effectiveness

Improving effectiveness, or doing the right things, means delivering greater strategic value. This can be achieved by having appropriate information available when needed, staff with the right competencies ready for action when called upon, and help and expertise accessible to all. These will all support people in doing the 'right things' when faced with decisions or while under pressure.

Example measures of effectiveness can include review and quality control checkpoints during the processes, and monitoring the number and type of rejections in a manufacturing or service process.

5 Individual and workgroup efficiency

This specifically applies to achievement of a reduction in time it takes to do something because of the increased information and expertise available. It also covers reduced costs through less wastage or better ways of working. With activities being simplified, there may be additional savings, including allowing lower skilled staff to perform them due to additional support that is available.

Traditional efficiency measures include elapsed time (from start to finish); work time (time of effort required); costs (fixed and variable); and the number and level (including costs) of skilled people required.

6 Capacity

Increasing capacity in this context is about the organization being able to take on increased workloads without the need for extra people. This is possible through the effectiveness and efficiency gains raised previously. There are many knock-on effects of this, from not needing additional office space due to increasing people's workloads, to performing the same work with fewer staff when appropriate.

In can also mean being able to employ innovative ways of using existing resources and technologies. For example, one international company redesigned its restaurants to encourage people to sit and chat (share knowledge) over coffee; and it took the opportunity to install 'work points' so that visitors could set up their laptops and work. This not only reduced the need for 'visitor desks' in each department, but also allowed people to work more flexibly.

Measures of this are the same as for efficiency and effectiveness.

7 Capability to innovate

Organizations can use increased capacity to drive cost savings, or it can be used to increase the firm's capability to innovate, largely through allowing staff to spend time on experimentation and generating ideas for improvement, as well as different approaches to familiar problems. With increased information and expertise available, there should be an increase in the variety of ideas, while improved communications should also stimulate additional challenge and encouragement. An example of these practices was quoted earlier, with 3M encouraging staff to innovate.

Measures include the additional revenue from new ideas and approaches, also measurable differences in the customer's perception of the organization as an innovator.

8 Capability to change

Through improved communication, knowledge sharing, and a constant striving to improve, the organization as a whole should begin to place a higher value on the need to constantly change and improve. In time, the organization should be ever more used to change, and be better prepared for it. By having a wider variety of information and expertise on tap, there will be less constraints placed on the organization by narrowly focused systems, structures, and people.

Measures include employee surveys on attitudes to change; audits of organizational culture; and changes in elapsed time required to develop or amend products and services to meet changing needs.

9 Understanding of customers

A culture of sharing information and knowledge internally in the organization should also extend to the relationships with customers. This is about enabling staff to better understanding the drivers, pressures and motives of customers, to reduce unnecessary barriers and improve the value delivered.

This goes beyond simply having the benefits of having increased customer and market knowledge. It actually means building and tailoring how work is performed to work better with, and for, customers.

Measures include customer surveys, the number of cross-organizational knowledge sharing meetings that take place, and their effectiveness as viewed by all parties.

The next benefit category is an essential focal point for all KM projects – that of customer and stakeholder needs.

It is worth remembering at this point that the previous benefits will also contribute to these customer and stakeholder benefits – benefits frequently combine on our model as we build up towards the end strategic objectives.

Customer and stakeholder

In the private sector, measures of customer satisfaction are hugely important to organizational success. In the public and not-for-profit sectors such as charities, 'customers' may be just one of many stakeholders whose views and experience of service are part of a complex picture which may include fund holders, government, and lobby groups. Improving customer service is a core knowledge management goal. Here we have two initial areas for improvement:

1 Increase customer value delivered
2 Maintain the 'right' customer prices.

1 Increase customer value delivered

Factors such as understanding the customer better, having efficient and effective processes, and an increased ability to change, will help increase the value delivered to customers. Such value may be in terms of delivering the 'right' solutions to meet customer needs, consistency and accuracy of services and interactions, reduced response times, and an increasingly personalized service.

The value added will be very personal to the customer and measures will include customer survey rating your products and services; repeat requests for individuals for additional work; and the meeting of agreed service level objectives.

2 Maintain 'the right' customer prices

Through efficient processes and operation, and understanding better the needs of customers, it should be possible to achieve better flexibility and accuracy in pricing decisions. This will help with corporate measures such as profitability, but also with customer retention. With greater trust and communication, only valued products and services should be offered, with a knock-on effect on prices.

Measures will continue to be customer surveys and questioning on price, but also win/lose ratios for new business with existing customers and profit margin on the business taken.

The last benefit category is that which we have labelled 'corporate' – a selection of high-level strategic aims.

Corporate

Ultimately, improvements in financial indicators must be the goal of any knowledge management programme. Significant financial impact might arise from the following factors:

1 Increased customer base
2 Reduced risk/lower cost business

88

3 Increased exploitation of intellectual assets
4 Managed headcount
5 Controlled costs
6 Improved profit, increase in shareholder value.

1 Increased customer base

A key goal might be to improve the position of the organization in its chosen markets, supported by increased value added, and better flexibility to meet any change. Closer relationships with customers should help with retention, while better willingness to communicate and innovate should be attractive to potential customers. Appropriate pricing will, of course, also be an important factor.

Here standard measures include market share in target sectors, and the overall meeting of strategic objectives.

2 Reduced risks/lower cost business

Lack of key information about areas of the market, customers, or operations can pose a significant risk. Improving knowledge sharing and communication throughout the organization can help people understand what is important, and help them act accordingly.

Measures might include the number of contract disputes, the severity of complaints, the percentage of contingency normally allowed for risk, and the number of lawsuits won or lost.

3 Increased exploitation of intellectual assets

Adding knowledge assets to the financial balance sheet is a move made by an increasing number of organizations. Areas include patents, knowledge bases, and copyright materials.

Measures include 'rent' from exploitation of innovations and copyrights. Also, the increased estimated cost of replacement of key databases and information.

4 Managed headcount

Retaining the right people and expertise in the organization means adopting a managed approach to employee turnover, to support the organization's strategy and corporate goals. Improved knowledge of 'who knows what' in the organization, along with skill levels and individual performance data, should make this task easier.

Measures might include employee turnover in favourable and unfavourable areas.

5 Controlled costs

Cost control is essential in any business, and this can mean both cost avoidance and cost reduction. By retaining the right staff and customers, improving efficiency of recruitment, and lowering the cost of winning new business – all typical goals of KM projects – many significant costs to the business can be controlled. This is in addition to process efficiencies, capacity savings, and added organizational flexibility gained from other KM initiatives.

Performance against budgets is a key measure.

6 Improved profit, increase in shareholder value

Depending on the type of organization, these benefits are often the core driver. Areas that might benefit from KM include finding ways of sustaining or increasing profitability, margin, and revenue (approaches outlined in some detail earlier in this section).

Financial measurement and management systems should already be in place to provide appropriate indicators.

These benefit categories have been provided to help readers to get a business case together. They are not meant to be comprehensive or complete, but are intended to 'jump start' the benefit discovery process to enable a strong case to be developed.

3.2 Business case template

A business case must show justification for the investment required, describing the estimated costs and anticipated benefits from the project. These benefits must be linked to the corporate strategy in a clear enough way to allow a 'what to do next' decision to be easily reached.

As a result of presenting this case the project(s) will either be given the go-ahead, they may ask for changes to be made before approval, or they will be stopped. This is the most crucial time for projects, and the way the business case is presented must be in line with the expectations of the decision-makers.

So far in this process, we have gathered a great deal of information that will allow a business case to be developed.

Areas for change have been identified through the involvement of stakeholders, and from a number of audits. The vision for mobilizing knowledge and a strategy to achieve it have also been defined. Lastly, benefits have been identified, forming a benefit chain from the initial initiatives through to the strategic objectives – reducing the 'chasm of faith' that is so often a risk to projects. These benefits will have measures associated, and any risks to their realization explained.

Each organization may have a different structure for a business case, but that introduced here has been found valuable for knowledge management.

1 Management summary
2 Overview of issues identified
3 Vision of a KM future
4 Possible options
5 Benefits
6 Impact
7 Risk
8 Financials
9 High-level plan.

The case for knowledge management can never be a purely financial one; there are always subjective arguments for and against. This is why an 'overview of issues identified' and 'vision of a KM future' are invaluable. They must describe the current and future states and the strategic importance of mobilizing knowledge.

Always keep in mind that those reading and deciding on the business case may not have a clear understanding of the language and practice of knowledge management. The best advice the authors can give is to explain your points objectively, pragmatically, and with stories where available, rather than using academic reference or extensive explanation.

The management summary will briefly outline why the business case has been produced, the main options considered, the recommended way forward, and the decision(s) required. The size of a management summary section is often cause for debate, but as a rule of thumb this should be no more than a single page. Busy executives should be able to read the management summary during the walk to the meeting room from their desks.

There may be a number of different ways that the project could progress, each having its own benefit; they will impact the organization in different ways, have specific risks associated, and require different investments. These must be explained, and the key milestones of the plans shown to give an idea of time scales and priorities.

Also remember that 'doing nothing' is always an option, especially when the case for investment is too weak: there may be occasions where this should be recommended.

3.3 Moving into action

With the business case submitted, the project has now defined its response to mobilizing knowledge. We have worked sequentially through Stage 1, which is about understanding the drivers for change; Stage 2, which focuses on the process of defining the organization's response: creating a vision for knowledge in the organization (looking ahead to a knowledge-friendly future), auditing the current status of information and knowledge, formalizing the strategy, and building a business case for knowledge management activity around measurable improvements. But, although each of these activities is generally conducted individually, they interact at a fairly fundamental level.

In the next chapter, we look at the five levers for change – leadership, people, process, technology, and information/content. This will enable us to fully assemble a plan of action, and to start designing the new reality in detail, so we can understand specifically what changes are required and how they can be implemented, and how we can begin to realize the benefits expected from mobilizing organizational knowledge.

4.1 Stage 3, part 1: Leadership, people and process

Once a business case for change has been assembled and approved then the challenge turns to some detailed analysis and design to shape what will be implemented.

This part of the process is about designing the new reality – laying down a path through uncharted territory. We can now see the goal ahead of us, we know the reasons why change is necessary, and the sorts of benefits we are aiming to achieve along the way. Now comes the detail part – deciding what, specifically, should change, and what implementation activities are required to move things along.

To do this, we need to go into considerable detail – beginning with considerations of what can go wrong, followed by detailed analysis of possible options using our chosen 'levers' for change. Lastly we will look at the change programme itself in its entirety – how all the areas of change can be knitted together to deliver the business benefits and changes in behaviour necessary.

Throughout Stage 3 there will need to be 'proof of concept' development activity, alongside more extended pilot projects, to prove the design ideas and check how suitable, acceptable, and feasible they may be. Designing the new reality is, therefore, about getting the right ideas and technologies together into a 'mobilizing knowledge architecture' that will allow low risk, high benefit, and practical changes to be agreed and implemented.

4.1.1 Blockers and levers of change

We have already spent some time considering the dynamics of change in organizations, and the implications of moving away from a 'command and control' model, to one where managing change is viewed as a process of influencing, leading and motivating people (we will develop these themes further later in the book).

But the biggest implication of a people-centred view of management is this: if people are essential in helping deliver change (by changing what they do and how they do it), then they also have the power to block change, too. In this context, the biggest blockers can be expressed as people-centred questions, the sorts of questions that come up every time we discuss knowledge management with groups of workers:

- **What's in it for me?** – 'Why should I share what I know if someone else gets the benefit/credit?'
- **Time is money** – 'I'm measured on financial results, not what I give away to other staff.'
- **Not invented here** – 'That solution was invented by another workgroup/division/company and doesn't do the job as well as the one we are developing . . . we know best.'
- **Information overload** – 'There isn't time to check through all this information' or alternatively 'We're drowning in paper, we can't meet the deadline.'
- **Knowledge is power** – 'If I share what I know, that'll reduce my control/influence/make me redundant.'

These are familiar to anyone who has ever spent a day in an office. There are methods (as we will discuss) that can be adopted to deal with each of these and other blockers – but there are some guiding principles for managing change worth introducing at this stage, not least:

- **People need to be made aware of the reasons for change**
  Why is change really required? – is it in response to pressures from competition or changing customer demands? Is it a change of focus, or a complete change organizational direction? It is not enough for an organization just to create a strategy – people must be helped to understand the vision and objectives and what is required to deliver on it.
- It may be the case that the whole story cannot be told – in order to throw competitors off the scent, for example – but the story told to staff must nevertheless be convincing if people

are to buy into it. People respond to change in different ways, bringing their own emotions into play. These reasons for change must be felt as real and compelling, otherwise the risk of failure will be significantly increased.

- If at all possible, **people need to be able to influence the outcome of change**

  Senior management do not always know best – often it is the workforce on the ground who really know most about trading conditions or best practice. Consultation is crucial if change is to be successfully integrated and implemented.

Any forewarning of things that may block the changes will allow sensible methods to work through them to be developed. We have identified five key areas for change when designing the new reality. These are shown in Figure 4.1 and descriptions of each follow.

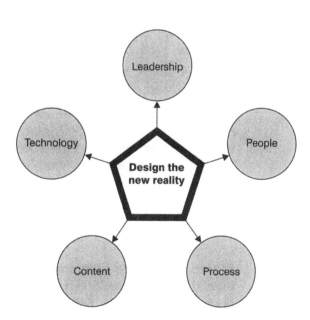

Figure 4.1
Five levers and
enablers of KM change

4.1.2 Leadership

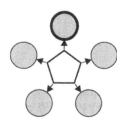

First, what is a knowledge worker? Here's a definition that is loosely based on the thoughts of Peter Drucker, who is credited with inventing the term back in the 1960s:

- A knowledge worker is a worker who knows more than his/her boss about how to do their job, *or alternatively*...
- A knowledge worker is a worker who can do his/her job better than the boss could.

The authors have tested this definition out in many situations and there are some that it doesn't fit – for example, in work situations where the 'boss' is a craftsman surrounded by apprentices or semi-skilled support staff. But the principle remains, as these are the exceptions that prove the rule: workers now know more than their bosses, indeed they are expected to do so – the notion of 'team working' or workgroups assembled from a range of people with different skills relies extensively on the concept of deploying specialists with relevant knowledge to tackle specific situations, managed by someone who does not have the in-depth knowledge of the individual team members.

Leadership and change

But where does this leave the 'boss'? In the days of Henry Ford (and of the division between white collar and blue collar workers, and trade unions who saw the world in very clear terms of 'us' and 'them') the division was clear cut. Managers managed, workers worked, and leadership primarily existed at the level of the foreman (rather like the army model of non-commissioned officers).

To help us understand more on leadership and change we will briefly look at some descriptions from some of the leading writers on the subject. Philip Kotter, in a Harvard business review article examining 'What Leaders Really Do' (2001) noted that

Management is about coping with complexity, whilst leadership is . . . about coping with change.

Within any change programme (such as a knowledge management initiative), leadership is an essential component. In his book *Leading Change*, Kotter defines a leader's responsibilities as

- establishing the direction of the change
- aligning people to that direction, and
- motivating and inspiring people to overcome major political, bureaucratic and resource barriers.

Kotter held the view that successful change programmes are '70 to 90 per cent leadership' (as defined above) and '10 to 30 per cent management'. In Kotter's view, it is really wrong to talk of *change management*: more accurately it should be about *change leadership.* If we accept this definition, then it has substantial implications for how we think about projects – instead of the traditional emphasis on budgets, planning, discounted cashflow and so on (important though they are), project management (*project leadership*) becomes much more focused on motivating, inspiring, informing and enabling people to do what they do best – using their skills and experience to good effect.

This is reinforced by the work of Robert Goffee and Garath Jones in the same issue of the *Harvard Business Review* (December 2001). The role of the change leader is to ensure that people involved with and affected by the changes must be led willingly, and to do this three key responses must be felt:

- First, workers need to feel valued, to *feel significant*, to feel as if they really matter – enough effort must be invested to ensure this comes through.
- Workers also want to *feel like they belong in a community.* Communities of practice have been a key component of many knowledge management initiatives, and the work in taking them forward is strongly in the hands of the change leader. People need to feel a unity of purpose around work and be willing to relate to one another as human beings. This is best achieved when the leader is successful in fostering a feeling of community and trust.
- Lastly, the people involved need to *feel some kind of buzz, excitement, and challenge* from the programme. Creating this feeling tends to come easiest from leaders who are more extroverted, energetic, and committed to the change.

So if this is the role of a leader of a change programme, what sort of specific implications are there for leadership of knowledge management projects? The first element is obvious enough: there has to *be* leadership of an organization's knowledge management efforts. This may seem obvious – but in our experience, lack of leadership (or the wrong kind of leadership) is one of the main causes of failure in knowledge management efforts.

KM leadership roles

So what kind of leadership roles are appropriate? These depend largely on the kind of organization, its culture, the scale of the project, its importance and relevance to the organization's future, and the degree of top-level buy-in and visibility that it has.

There are a whole variety of possible roles in a KM initiative, each of which exert some kind of leadership at different levels in the organization and require different skills.

Chief knowledge officer (CKO)

More often seen across the Atlantic than in the UK and continental Europe, this role is generally at senior level – most often a direct report to an executive board member. There are many interpretations of the role, but the most common one is one of formal responsibility for tailoring KM strategy to organizational strategy, for developing and designing the overall KM programme, and for the allocation of resources. Resources for mobilizing knowledge are seldom clustered under the command of the CKO. They generally are a mix of a 'seed' budget (for central infrastructure and support initiatives), and resources required to deliver specific benefits identified in business cases.

It follows that the CKO role needs to enthuse and engage business units and help them develop their own initiatives with their own budgets. The CKO needs to be far more than a thinker – he or she must also be an evangelist or salesperson for the benefits of mobilizing knowledge, making the case, explaining compelling examples from other organizations, and providing the passion that drives the effort forward.

Knowledge programme director

This is not quite the same thing as the CKO, and though the roles are often combined in a single individual, the skill sets are subtly different. While a CKO's role is to enthuse and lead, a knowledge programme director's role may have a greater emphasis on hands-on management, with more focus on delivering specific projects and having more of a responsibility in managing staff and budgets. Few organizations have the luxury of both roles, yet few individuals are expert at carrying both out, so support may be required depending on the individual and on the organization's particular characteristics.

In any case, the titles are often confused, or substituted to make a particular symbolic point: for example, when Elizabeth Lank was appointed Director of the Knowledge Programme by ICL in 1996 she was the incoming chief executive's first appointment. Her role was, however, very much like that of a chief knowledge officer (not that the title was a common one at the time). The idea of a programme in this case was to some extent symbolic, in the sense that it conveyed the intention to deliver change – an important leadership message.

Information professional/knowledge officer

Organizations have a variety of information professionals – from librarians and file and records management specialists to database administrators – who bring a variety of literacy, numeracy and technical skills to bear on the enterprise-wide management of information. This has been the case for a long time – but increased use of technology, as well as better skills in searching, sifting and using information tools, is changing these roles, bringing people out of the back office into a much more prominent role within the business.

Indeed, many people driving knowledge management programmes in organizations have been information professionals – highly appropriate given the depth of understanding required about how the many information sources needed by today's large companies interact and are managed.

As an example of this changing role: one of the authors worked in a newspaper office which simultaneously introduced both a web-based 'cuttings' library (a fully searchable text archive to replace a large room full of manila folders stuffed with newspaper clippings and bound volumes going back 200 years), and a digital photo system that was used to manage current/recent pictures. The library staff had once spent their time finding files, putting them away, adding new items into files, and generally organizing information. The new system took away the need for much of this – and with conventional management thinking, its introduction would have led to some redundancies. But all the staff were kept on – and suddenly emerged, blinking, into the light of day to become a fantastic resource for journalists who could suddenly interact far more with these information professionals, getting far better value from the encyclopedic knowledge of the archive they had at their disposal.

As digital information technologies proliferate across an organization, if the temptation of cost saving is resisted and instead the changing role of information professionals is exploited, then there is huge potential to mine vast, currently unexploited reservoirs of corporate knowledge. The professionals themselves will have plenty of ideas on this score!

Knowledge broker

Of course, information professionals are not the only workers who concern themselves with the gathering, making sense of, and sharing of knowledge and information: this is the very stuff of knowledge work. But in every workplace, every team, there is an individual who excels at this: who knows precisely who is doing what, or what article appeared in what publication, or who knows their way best around the forest of paper or the myriad folders on the shared drive. At one time their role might have been the source of some amusement, and depending on the environment, might have earned them the name of office gossip . . . but smart organizations are beginning to see the benefits of developing these people into an entirely new breed: the knowledge broker.

It makes sense to develop and build these skills and talents, and to recognize in them essential things that every workplace needs. Within Fujitsu Services, for example, such individuals are identified and given project coordination roles, or roles as intranet 'community' administrators (we'll come to the role of communities of practice later). In the Department of Health, plans are afoot to identify and use these natural knowledge sharers to help deliver the programme – it makes a great deal of sense to build knowledge projects around the very people who would bring massive commitment. In time, such individuals may be given a formal role or developed as information professionals – but we have found in Fujitsu that it is more likely that, due to their talents in 'networking' at the centre of activities, they will be promoted and move on to other things in the organization, leaving a gap for new blood.

Technology and process specialists

A major theme of this book is that knowledge management is about changing people's behaviour – and that the use of technology is very much subordinate. However – as we established in Chapter 1 – the principal reason for the interest in knowledge management over the past 10 years or so has been (and to some extent remains) a wish to exploit the potential of the revolution in information capture, search and retrieval that has accompanied the bursting forth of a raft of digital technologies, from HTML and global email, to collaborative applications and powerful new data mining tools.

To manage technology selection, system design, implementation and roll-out, or ongoing support and user training, requires input from technology specialists. Likewise business analysts are required to make these systems function and to achieve other benefits that may not be so heavily technology dependent. Experts in analysis and review of business processes must form part of any implementation team.

Leading from the top

Beyond the KM-specific roles, of course, leadership in knowledge management can be at any level, and indeed must be present at more or less every level of the organization in some form or other. One big mistake that senior management can make is to appoint a chief knowledge officer – even one at senior level in the organization – dedicate a few helpers and some budget, and think that that individual can deliver knowledge management. No – things will change only if the leadership in the organization demonstrates, though the various communications channels at their disposal, that knowledge management is important. This brings us to another of our Golden Rules:

> **Golden Rule #3: Nothing happens without leadership** – Those responsible for running the organization must inspire and encourage all staff throughout the 'voyage of discovery' that is the change programme, continuing on after implementation to ensure lasting change.

Although senior management can delegate the burden on matching the vision for knowledge to the wider needs of the organization, developing the change programme, and even managing the fine detail of implementation, what they cannot do is opt out of their responsibilities to lead. The appointment of Elizabeth Lank at ICL was backed with a clear statement that mobilizing knowledge was vital in transforming the business from a product-focused company (selling mainframes and computer hardware) into a services delivery organization where all it had to sell was the knowledge, expertise and experience of its people. This was a classic case of a knowledge management initiative being put at the heart of corporate change.

In addition to this kind of large-scale, 'on-message', rather symbolic kind of support, the wider management circle are also responsible for more practical steps – such as aligning targets and measurements – which we'll discuss shortly.

Building a KM delivery team

So what sort of team do you need to deliver KM? We've looked at the typical roles above, but what of the wider balance of the team? Any change effort is not just about leadership, but also about supporting roles. In 1995, the writers Michael Hammer and Steven Stanton came up with a list of change roles which focus the responsibility for success and help drive through change in a balanced manner. Table 4.1 paired these up with possible roles in a typical KM delivery programme.

Table 4.1 Comparison of roles for a knowledge management team

Hammer and Stanton's five Roles	Possible management or KM team roles
Leader of change	Board sponsor; chief knowledge officer or knowledge programme director
Process owners who have end-to-end responsibility for change within specific process areas	End users (from business units working with the KM team); knowledge officers
Insiders who bring knowledge, experience and credibility	Information professionals/knowledge brokers
Outsiders who bring creativity that flows from a fresh, objective perspective	External consultants; external KM, technology or process specialists
Czar who provides advice to the process owners and helps coordinate the teams within the programme	Chief knowledge officer

These five roles are essential as part of the change team, and it can be seen from this that they do not necessarily form part of the core KM team – in fact, participation from people on the ground in business units is critical, as is appropriate top management support. The usefulness of the table is that through anticipating the need for specific roles, it becomes easier for you to plan the resources required.

In the authors' experience the time commitment requirement by those people taking part in the change, to think through, unpick and reconstruct the way business is conducted, is almost always underestimated. Not least people must understand the need for, and the detail of, the changes required. The worst thing that can happen is that those running the programme come to believe that involving staff on the ground is an unnecessary burden and do not invest the required time and effort – this can only be a recipe for failure.

Building the team, appointing leaders, and making individuals accountable for the carrying out of various elements of delivery is a key part of any KM initiative – indeed, in a consultancy situation we typically specify this as the first step in launching any knowledge management programme. Without leadership, accountability, and some kind of goal, any initiative is doomed.

4.1.3 People, motivation and skills

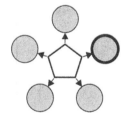

Human beings, who are almost unique in having the ability to learn from the experience of others, are also remarkable for their apparent disinclination to do so. (Douglas Adams)

A discussion of leadership inevitably leads on to a discussion of the wider role of people. As we stress throughout this book, there is no such thing as knowledge independent from the people who 'know' things, anything else is just information, which (if it is to have any value) has to be understood and acted upon by people.

It follows then that the people element of mobilizing knowledge is both the most important and the most complex area to work with. It is also the hardest in which to deliver lasting change. There is a dictum – almost a piece of folk wisdom – in the discipline of Neuro-Linguistic Programming (NLP) which states: 'If you do what you've always done, you'll get what you've always got'.

If we are attempting to change things for the better, people need to change what they do, or how they do it: this is another one of our golden rules:

Golden Rule #2: People's behaviours must change for the long term – People's beliefs must be affected if long-term improvements in behaviour are to be achieved. You must do more than just 'build an IT system'.

But just what are the 'people' elements of mobilizing knowledge? We have grouped this complex topic into four main areas:

- Beliefs, values and motivation
- Culture, custom and environment
- Skills and competencies
- Collaboration, sharing and community.

The following examines each of these in some detail: the link between each is that in combination they allow us to come to understand better why people behave in certain ways – essential if we are to identify what people-related barriers exist, or if we want to map out the type of behaviours aimed for.

Beliefs, values and motivation

People hold, develop, share, and use knowledge. To do this well they must have the appropriate skills and be motivated to use them. We have stated our belief that change is not successful until behaviour is affected, i.e. until people:

- do something they have never done before,
  or
- do existing things differently.

People's behaviour is principally driven by their belief system – what they believe to be true, and how this interacts with the value system they have created for themselves in the course of living their lives. Professors Icek Ajzen and Martin Fishbein have produced a useful model which attempts to show how people's belief systems interact with their behaviour in the working environment.

They propose that what we believe at work is influenced by three key elements:

- our immediate work environment
- our past experiences
- the external environment.

They suggest that people's belief systems are fluid, and that past experiences cannot be altered, but beliefs about them can be when processed alongside new information – a function of learning. Some of the areas affecting beliefs (shown in the list above) can be altered by management action, for example, by improving the working environment or tools available, also by communications that stress certain things about the external environment that are relevant to the firm, workplace or individuals concerned.

We have already stated that our behaviour is influenced by what we 'believe' to be true; it is also the case that what we believe in-turn influences our values and attitudes. Values lead us into or away from certain situations – people's belief systems and values tend to chime in some way with the work they end up doing. For example, those with a caring bent may become nurses or teachers; those driven by monetary concerns are drawn towards sales or a job in the City. Values and beliefs also drive attitudes – enthusiasm, compliance or hostility to a project, depending on how it is perceived, and consequently all of them drive behaviour.

How does this help us when mobilizing knowledge? One way would be to recognize that to change behaviour we need to look at the role of beliefs, and work out what kind of workplace or environmental changes might help bring about the changes required. By influencing what people believe, this should lead to changes in attitudes, values, and ultimately behaviour.

Some examples of how changes to desired behaviours may be encouraged are shown in Table 4.2.

It is useful to consider this type of cause-and-effect approach when planning any favourable changes in behaviour. This brings us to the wider question of motivation. This is not the place for a full-scale discussion of motivational theory, and the role (or otherwise) of money or other incentives. However, anecdotal evidence from knowledge management projects where monetary incentives are specifically aimed at enticing people to publish documents on repository systems have generally failed. Far greater success has been seen where incentives exist to encourage people both to reuse or incorporate previously published material and to credit the original publisher. These have the multiple effects of motivating people to make original contributions, to research and reuse those contributions, and to give credit and recognition to colleagues in the first place (very important in those many workplaces where recognition and approval of peers is a stronger motivation than a small addition to pay which gets instantly eaten up by income tax).

Table 4.2 Examples of how desired behaviours may be encouraged

Workplace stimulus → →	Impact on beliefs → →	Desired behaviour
Changes in appraisal system to measure information publishing	'It's becoming more valued that I publish things on the system'	More people publish information
Mobile working introduced, some desks removed, more sofas and coffee machines	'It's OK to sit on a sofa and talk about a work problem – I don't need to be sitting at a desk all the time'	An increase in casual knowledge sharing
Praise/awards/other incentives for reuse of solutions or other previously published material	'Designing my own way of doing things is a challenge I enjoy, but it's more valued by the firm if I check first whether someone has already worked this out'	More people check to see if there is anything published that might help them in an assignment or with a problem they are trying to solve

Creative approaches to motivation do exist. One of the major reasons for failures in the first wave of customer relationship management implementations was the reluctance of salespeople to hand over information about customers. This was for a variety of reasons ranging from defensiveness about their position (fearing that by passing on what they know, they become much more replaceable), to more creditable reasons of wishing to protect the relationships they have built up with customers from demands from numbers-driven superiors they fear might compromise those relationships. To tackle this, one organization had a quarterly award for a top salesperson who then 'won' an assistant for that period – a win–win scenario (if carefully managed) where the young assistant was able to learn techniques from a skilled professional, as well as gaining useful insights into that salesperson's customer base.

Indeed 'sitting by Nellie', the apprenticeship route, has long been recognized as a rich (if not always efficient) method of knowledge transfer – more modern versions include internships (or graduate job placements), secondments, and job exchange programmes. If knowledge exchange is the goal, there are indeed better ways to achieve it than by publishing documents or reading up on available literature.

Other common 'people'-focused knowledge management issues and techniques include the following.

Staff induction

At knowledge management workshops, when personal or workgroup efficiency is examined, one topic that almost always arises is the quality of staff induction. Addressing this in a more structured fashion (or one more personally relevant to the new worker, rather than focused on fire escapes and HR department form-filling) can pay big dividends in helping staff to become productive quickly. One high-turnover workgroup which the authors took through an analysis exercise introduced handover folders. These contained details of the main processes, contact details and background information which where needed to do the job.

Exit interviews/knowledge harvesting

Many organizations have introduced the practice of exit interviews – usually run by trained HR professionals and aimed at getting to the bottom of why people leave (better salary, personal problems, or a difficult boss?). Because of the confidential nature of these interviews, specific information about the content of jobs or insights about how things might be done better is seldom made available to the business at large. However, some organizations are beginning to go further by exploiting structured interviews with departing staff, aimed at extracting key contacts, processes, insights, and advance warning of up and coming issues. Videotape experiments have proved useful for this purpose – though the burden of transcription and the sheer effort of making sense of this sort of information makes management of knowledge harvesting projects a rather difficult exercise. The value to organizations can be immense, however, compared to what is common practice of no debrief at all, or a cursory effort to ask individuals to 'write down what they know' in the few days before departure.

Nevertheless, the loss to organizations of individually held knowledge simply walking out of the door can be immense: it takes six weeks, for example, to train an operative to do telesales or telephone support, at great cost to the organization; this individual may take another six months before they are up to speed and as competent as the general run of experienced staff.

If staff turnover is high (say nine months or a year) then the cost of training, plus the cost of learning on the job, represents a huge cost to the organization. And if this applies at the level of a single telephone support operator, think of the cost of losing a salesman with 10 years of contacts and established relationships, or a project manager with 15 years' experience of managing people and controlling budgets. Companies need to get creative about what they do when staff leave, but they also need to be very clear on the true costs of them leaving and take appropriate steps to recognize and retain important knowledge and skills within the organization.

After action reviews

First established by the US Army, and adopted as part of knowledge management initiatives by large corporates such as Shell, these are based around a very simple format, posing three questions in a no-blame environment:

- What was supposed to happen?
- What actually happened?
- Why was there a difference?

To speed up learning, this process is built on the idea of 'no blame' – removing judgement from the equation in order to ensure that nothing gets covered up that could instead be learnt from. The result has been to increase trust within the fighting units concerned, and by replacing long 'after the fact' written briefings with quick, to the point verbal ones, has enabled local commanders to get a far quicker picture of conditions on the ground. This technique also works exceptionally well in a project management environment – as we'll discuss in Section 4.1.4, 'Business process'.

As an example, there is pressure within the UK National Health Service to institute a similar 'no-blame' environment surrounding the handling of babies who are brain damaged at birth. At the moment, the rather regressive matrix of UK laws surrounding medical negligence requires extremely detailed (and not always medically enlightening) investigations, followed by adversarial courtroom proceedings which often take years to come to a judgement, before brain damaged children can get the financial support they need. Even then, there is great unfairness in the system whereby children who are the victims of negligence get large sums of money from hospitals and their insurers, while children who have an identical disability but where their injury is 'natural', or cannot be proven to be the result of a mistake, get nothing. It is the authors' view that the replacement of this system with a proper, fair compensation scheme, together with a 'no-blame' investigation which focuses on what can be learned from openly admitted mistakes, is long overdue – indeed, it should be a model for practice elsewhere in the Health Service. A welcome by-product would be that less money would go to fruitless litigation, and potentially more to damaged children or to improving health care.

Storytelling

Various storytelling techniques – ranging from straightforward capturing of 'what happened' (along the lines of after action review), turning the messages to be learnt into a story with key characters that fire people's imagination – have been used by a variety of companies to extract 'truth' out of complex sequences of events, in an effort to learn from them.

The authors have had mixed experiences with storytelling – our considered view is that organizations that are used to more 'way out' or 'creative' management tools and techniques can gain benefit from these techniques. More generally, however, our view is that a focus on more traditional methods (which certainly include conventional debriefing, after action review, and, of course, case studies) tends to play rather better with most managers and workers – and can generate equally powerful (and certainly more easily measurable) results.

Analysis of stories – organizational myth and legend – told around the organization can be very enlightening: stories about big bid wins, or about brutal chief executives, reveal a lot about shared underlying beliefs. They can help us understand what the consensus view in the organization is about, what sort of things are most valued, and what is or is not acceptable behaviour.

This extends to metaphor – the following story emerged in a workshop conversation with a customer. It has not been possible to verify the initial source, but the story itself says a lot about how the employee viewed her own organization's culture:

Start with a cage containing five apes. In the cage, hang a banana on a string and put stairs under it. Before long an ape will go up the stairs and start to climb towards the banana. As soon as the ape touches the banana, spray all apes with cold water. After a while, another ape makes an attempt with the same result – all the apes are sprayed with cold water. Then turn off the cold water.

Now if another ape tries to climb the stairs for the banana the other apes will try to prevent it even though no water sprays them. Now remove one of the five apes from the cage and replace with a new one. The new ape sees the banana and tries to climb the stairs. To his horror, all of the apes attack him. After another attempt he is again attacked. He knows now that if he attempts to climb the stairs he will be assaulted.

Next, remove another of the original five apes and replace with a new one. The newcomer goes to the stairs and is attacked. The previous newcomer takes part in the punishment with enthusiasm. Again, replace a third of the original five apes with a new one. The new one makes it to the stairs and is attacked as well. Two of the four apes that beat him up have no idea why they were not permitted to climb the stairs, or why they are participating in the beating of the newest ape. After replacing the fourth and fifth of the original apes there are no longer any apes that have been sprayed with cold water. Nevertheless, no ape ever again approaches the banana. Why not?

Because that's the way it's always been around here.

Culture, custom and environment

Such stories tell us about the impact of culture and the environment on personal behaviours and performance. So far, the focus has been getting the best from individuals – but there are few workplaces where individual performance can be examined in isolation from the wider team, workgroup, or business unit. So what are the issues associated with mobilizing knowledge in the richer environment of the organization – how do culture, custom, and the wider business environment impact on people?

Culture has been described as 'the way we do things around here' – and there is an element of truth in that definition. But it fails to take into account that people are exposed to and participate in many different cultures – and can change 'mode' and move between them with ease. So we need to consider that in addition to the influences described so far, the various multiple cultural influences that an individual is exposed to will also play a large part in forming and influencing beliefs and behaviour.

The biggest influence on all this is belonging: within the workplace, each typically feels a sense of belonging or attachment to one or a number of groups, each with their own, perhaps slightly differing, shared beliefs or views of the world, which in turn may impact the behaviour of the group members. For example, an employee – say an engineer or an accountant – is part of a workgroup, but may also be a member of a professional organization that has its own code of conduct.

But social influences go deeper. We may have lived in another country, say, Sweden or Italy, countries which in turn have their own social norms/shared beliefs that impact on behaviour. A classic example is London's 'sandwich at the desk' culture versus Paris's long lunch. People working in a local manufacturing company will likely find a 'different world' awaiting them if they worked in a global marketing company.

Many such examples can be described, but the underlying message must not be forgotten: it is highly likely there are certain behaviours that are heavily ingrained in each and every workplace, and these may be restricting the effectiveness of knowledge sharing. Recognizing which can and which cannot be changed is an important distinction for the leader of a mobilizing knowledge initiative to make. The academics Johnson and Scholes created the model shown in Figure 4.2 which attempts to categorize the various cultural influences impacting on people's behaviour.

Changing these cultural frames of reference will likely be out of scope of any knowledge management project! But it is important that the influences are understood and taken into account. However, within the likely scope are certain aspects of 'culture' that the project could likely change. The tool Johnson and

Figure 4.2
Cultural frames of reference. (Johnson and Scholes 1999. © Pearson Education Ltd. Reproduced with permission)

Figure 4.3
The cultural web
(Johnson and Scholes
1999. © Pearson
Education Ltd.
Reproduced with
permission)

Scholes describe for analysing these areas, they called the 'Cultural Web' (Figure 4.3).

There are many uses we as KM practitioners can make of the Cultural Web: one is to audit what is currently valued in the organization (behaviours, accomplishments, characteristics); another is to help define the ideal future state of the culture that the project aims to encourage.

In using the Cultural Web as an audit tool, each 'bubble' represents an aspect of the business that informs the 'paradigm' – essentially the shared belief system and 'culture' that is experienced by people at work. A paradigm, by its very nature, is somewhat invisible: it's the working climate, the air breathed, the implicit backdrop to a thousand daily decisions. Using the Cultural Web as an audit tool is a powerful way to make explicit this backdrop, gauge what is useful and can be built on, and identify potential problem areas for action.

A 'first pass' Cultural Web audit might look something like Table 4.3.

Table 4.3 is intended to be a generic example, but in a few of the points, expresses something of the process that ICL went through in the mid to late 1990s. The actual KM project components included development of an intranet site, and a reworking of the office accommodation into open plan (the first private office to go was that of the chief executive – a fairly dramatic symbol that change was coming, and a warning to

Table 4.3 Examples from a Cultural Web audit

	Current	Future/ideal	Desired impact on paradigm
Power structures	Information access is controlled by IS function	Knowledge and information access available to all and owned widely	Use of knowledge seen as crucial to long-term performance – major change
Organizational structures	[Out of project scope]	[Out of project scope]	No change
Controls	Key performance indicators (KPIs) are driven by MIS systems, with a focus on backward-looking financial information	Wider range of KPIs, 'Balanced Scorecard', the knowledge sharing skills/practice of people appraised	Management gain wider understanding of how knowledge impacts on innovation and the future of the company; workers made to focus on their personal contribution – major change
Rituals and routines	Knowledge-sharing rituals restricted to monthly internal communications and email	Many rich new knowledge-sharing rituals, especially for project staff; new sofas near coffee machine; more mobile working	People work in a new way and clearly see their roles as knowledge workers – major change
Stories	How big deals were won; how 'bad' the old boss was	Same sorts of stories, with greater emphasis on the role of knowledge sharing in winning new business/qualities of a good boss	Story content will change as the internal perception of the business changes – slow building change
Symbols	Individual offices; knowledge is power	Open plan offices with meeting rooms and sharing spaces	Democratization and recognition of the importance of the knowledge worker and the new role of management as facilitators – major change

middle management not to try to frustrate it). Appraisal systems were also modified to include questions such as: How can you demonstrate that you have shared your knowledge?

This has just been a brief look at culture, a fascinating and wide subject area. What we hope to convey is the large number of influences that exist which affect behaviour, and that by starting to understand them, a project can better plan for them and influence them.

Skills and competencies

One would expect the team driving the KM programme to have particular specialist skills in their particular areas of expertise, and that the organization would be supportive in their personal and professional development. But what of the general run of staff who are not knowledge and information specialists? Well, it follows from the notion of 'change' and from Golden Rule #2 that if people are being expected to do things differently, then they need to have the skills to achieve this. Skills associated with a mobilizing knowledge programme that *all* knowledge workers need to have can be grouped under two main headings:

- Information and technology literacy
- 'Knowledge' literacy.

Information and technology literacy

We've touched on this topic before – the need to ensure that people within the workforce have the appropriate skills to access and make sense of the right information to do their job. But this is not as simple as it sounds: even something as straightforward as email can pose difficulties.

One customer had had an email system for many years, but saw an unexpected quadrupling in email traffic in the space of 18 months. This took those responsible for the systems by surprise: there were many reasons for it, but partly it was a matter of email culture (as well as a huge opening up of the institutions they dealt with externally). But there was also a large measure of poor practice: many people copied attachments sent when it was possible to link to single files on servers, and so on. The 'email jungle' was growing to such an extent that many individuals had more than 70 emails per day, taking hours of time just to process. The impact on the infrastructure too was dramatic: most people don't know that with many email systems, a 1 Mb file emailed to 10 people uses up ten times 1 Mb in server space.

The answer was to give people new skills in email use: training them to think before using 'CC', to tag emails 'For Information' and 'For Action' in the subject header, and to learn to use Inbox filtering tools to categorize and prioritize mail. Life isn't perfect now: but what was an exponential growth curve has finally dipped. Such measures are only valuable, however, when sufficient people adopt them: training just 10% of the workforce will have little impact – change will only happen when a majority of people have adopted the new thinking.

Beyond email – or even appropriate web browser use – there are many different information competencies: for example, in the civil service and some areas of the private sector, skills in filing and records management protocols are vital. Both public and private sectors need staff skilled in database search queries, or in setting up personalization options for information 'pushed' to them from news feeds or other sources.

Poor change management has resulted in technology tools being added to people's desktops without ensuring that either the correct information management skills and disciplines are in place, or that people have the technology skills to use the tools to their full potential. A knowledge management programme represents an ideal opportunity to revisit investments like these, and properly exploit them to deliver the value they were intended to bring in the first place.

Knowledge literacy

Only people *know* things ... anything else is information. Knowledge literacy, then, is much more concerned with knowing 'what you know', and knowing appropriate ways to share and communicate it – we will discuss these areas in depth in the following section on sharing, collaboration and community.

Skills auditing process and remedial action

So how are the skills gaps in organizations to be uncovered? The standard approach, a skills audit, is based around formal competency frameworks. This can work fairly well, though the criteria used will need to be fine tuned to focus on the types of knowledge work found within the business.

Most large organizations have specialists whose job it is to manage personal and professional development, and a part of their role will be to ensure that this development effort matches the needs of the business, so getting knowledge and information skills onto their agenda is very important. Indeed, input from human resource and training specialists is important at many points in development and delivery of a KM programme, having input to elements like measurement and appraisal as well as skills and competencies.

When it comes to addressing skills gaps of individuals, there are many different approaches, including traditional, formal training in a classroom setting, and 'buddy' schemes where people watch others at work, learn by doing things themselves, and asking questions. There is also increasing interest in 'e-learning' – leveraging packaged or network-based software (often quite sophisticated in its approach to assessment and revision), backed up by email facilitation by a trained tutor (of the sort being pioneered by Learn Direct in the UK). Up until now, this sort of training has mainly been embraced to build basic computer literacy or basic skills in standard software packages. However, the ideas are now being exploited for more KM-specific skill sets, and the potential to combine this approach with improved induction schemes is being explored, and piloted, by a number of UK organizations.

Sharing, collaboration and community

Knowledge management professionals speak a great deal about 'fostering knowledge sharing' and 'improving knowledge exchange' – but it is often unclear precisely what they mean by this. This confusion is compounded by the emphasis in many quarters on software tools – that somehow by publishing documents or storing them into a system, they are somehow automatically shared.

In the authors' view, the capture of information (in databases, in document repositories, or by other means such as in discussion groups), and access to this information once published, is very important – but far more important are the dynamics of information and knowledge – how people assimilate it, how they exchange and combine it and make new thinking out of it.

The knowledge-friendly workplace

It has taken a long time for workplace design to catch up with the idea of knowledge work. In the days of Frederick W. Taylor – who provided much of the thinking that helped drive the highly evolved factory practices of early last century embraced by Henry Ford and other industrialists, and was essentially the first management consultant – factory workers weren't expected to know very much – they were told (or shown) what to do, and got on with it.

This sort of environment would, on the face of it, seem to be very inhospitable territory for knowledge management thinking – but rather surprisingly, a real knowledge management revolution was in precisely this area. Naturally, it didn't come out of Taylorist thinking: instead, it came out of Japan – from the practice of *'kaizen'*, or often translated as 'continuous improvement' but also having the meaning 'organized improvement'. In a practice that, prior to the 1980s, would have been frankly impossible in the heavily unionized, 'us and them' workplaces of the UK, workers were encouraged to talk among themselves to solve problems. To discuss barriers to efficiency, problems with particular processes, tools, or approaches – and they were respected for their input, both by having their thoughts and ideas listened to and acted upon, but also by being empowered to think and act for themselves.

The importation of 'continuous improvement' ideas to first US and later European management thinking was what begat the Quality Management movement in the 1980s – and began the West's slow climb to match and even exceed Japanese levels of productivity, efficiency, and quality.

Perhaps this reading – though certainly true in the UK and US – is slightly unfair – after all, the German economic miracle, and the extremely high productivity levels found in post-war Scandinavian and Dutch workplaces, were no accident, and involved worker participation at all levels in the management process. But it proves a point: if we return to our definition of a knowledge worker as being someone who knows more about how to do their job than their boss does, then knowledge work is everywhere nowadays, not just in white collar, air-conditioned offices.

But white collar offices too have been slow to change: the lack of available meeting rooms in building after building simply demonstrates how lacking management responses have been to changing work patterns. There was a time when 'work' for most office staff meant showing up at 9am, sitting at a desk, perhaps attending a few formal meetings, and going home at 5pm. The biggest part of the day revolved around paperwork (and later email). That has changed enormously: tolerance (in some cases, active promotion by employers) of mobile or home-based working, plus increased reliance on team working (including virtual teams – not located in a single building – and cross-functional teams from different workgroups and specialisms) has led to an explosion of hot-desking, and a need for far more informal meetings (with a consequent requirement for more small meeting spaces).

Few organizations have gone as far as they might have done in attempting to understand this change and reflect it in workplace design. The wonderful British Airways headquarters building in Heathrow – with its mix of sharing spaces and 'quiet' rooms built around walkthough thoroughfares – remains highly unusual. An important element of the mobilising knowledge programme in pre Fujitsu Services ICL was the so-called 'New World' office accommodation programme, whereby offices were systematically remodelled with far fewer, mostly 'hot' desks (about 30% fewer desks in some cases) but many more meeting rooms, quiet rooms for solitary working, and comfortable meeting spaces near coffee machines. Coffee and tea were also made free. The message was that you don't come to work to answer email – you can do that at home or at customers' premises – you come instead to do what you can uniquely do at work: meet with and talk to other colleagues, discuss work and exchange information.

But there remain many bosses sceptical of this: the authors know of several senior civil servants who remain hostile to the idea of even part-time mobile or home working (even though it might save their staff up to three hours per day in travel) because they feel a need to be in 'control' and able to directly supervise staff. This demonstrates a real lack of trust – and may say quite a lot about the organization's overall culture – but such attitudes are hard to criticize in isolation from the more general picture.

It also demonstrates a somewhat antiquated view of what we mean by 'work'. One of the authors recalls working in a Sunday newspaper office close to deadline on a Saturday evening. The editor was known for his ill temper and by this time on a Saturday was aware that the time had passed for his own role in decision-making, and that getting the paper out was now the responsibility of the subeditors in the production team. At some point, minutes from first edition deadline, he came out of his office and shouted at the chief subeditor: 'Put your people to work. Look, there's a man over there reading a book'. Despite the deadline pressure, there was general hilarity when the retort came back: 'It's not a book – it's a dictionary!'

There is a serious point here – that an antiquated view of work can be harmful to the business. In the old scenario, how many of us would feel comfortable sitting reading a magazine (even a specialist journal) at their desk, while our boss was watching? Yet if the same article was thrown up on screen by a search engine, it would count as research. Middle managers have to be made aware that their expectations have impact, and that their directions to staff need to take account of the new realities of knowledge work. Sitting at a desk all day answering email demonstrates that a staff member has been present, but it doesn't necessarily demonstrate true commitment or engagement, and certainly does not guarantee that any proper knowledge work has been done.

Some organizations are more 'ready' than others to cut people loose – particularly ones where performance management, measurement and appraisal systems are more evolved than others. In this context, middle management play a pivotal role: by embracing new ways of working, and focusing their efforts on enabling and empowering individuals in their teams to stretch their own personal boundaries, they can help the organization deliver on their people's potential. Equally, this powerful group can potentially block change across the board: at one customer, when consultants raised the issue of hot-desking during a knowledge management workshop, noting that this might involve removing managers' offices to replace them with meeting rooms, they were pointedly told that the last facilities manager who suggested this lasted precisely one week in the post. This group was not about to pass up the few remaining perks of power for benefits they couldn't bring themselves even to imagine.

Not all organizations are forward-looking or even open to discussion on these sorts of topics. Yet organizations that fail to grasp the necessity for providing the right conditions for knowledge work – and for the informal knowledge and information sharing that goes along with 'social' practice in organizations – are placing themselves at risk.

The spiral of innovation

Beyond the design of the workplace is the wider notion of collaboration and sharing – and the impact that this in turn, has on the organization's ability to renew itself through innovation. Some of the most interesting work in this area has been done by a pair of Japanese academics – Ikijiro Nonaka and Horotaka

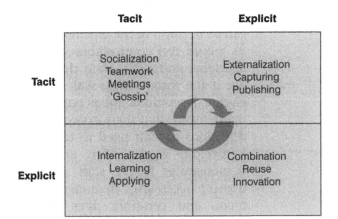

Figure 4.4
The Spiral of Innovation
(adapted from Nonaka
and Takeuchi 1995)

Takeuchi – who analysed the wider systems that delivered '*kaizen*' within Japanese companies, and extracted a theory of knowledge exchange and innovation that aims to illuminate the dynamics of knowledge within a collaborative environment.

The 'Spiral of Innovation' matrix (Figure 4.4) has become something of a totem in knowledge management circles, as a model for demonstrating the interaction of various knowledge-related activities, it provides some useful insights. It is based on the premise that there are two kinds of knowledge – tacit knowledge and explicit knowledge, tacit being knowledge held by the individual 'in their head', so to speak, and explicit knowledge being knowledge that was somehow captured or written down.

As stated in the introduction to the book, our view is that the tacit–explicit distinction is somewhat erroneous: we believe view is that 'knowledge' exists only within people, and that 'explicit' sources are simply information of greater or lesser relevance to an individual who needs to carry out a specific activity. We see knowledge management as concerning itself with the dynamics of information and knowledge – how people interact with information, make it their own, put it to use along with their own personally held knowledge, and create new information. As this is the focus of the matrix, it is a useful tool in analysing how knowledge flows around the organization.

It is worth explaining each of the four processes as they highlight ideas and examples that are useful when mobilizing knowledge, and when looking to incorporate them in our design of the new reality.

The matrix spiral is based on the notion that information and knowledge are exchanged or transformed in various processes.

Process 1: socialization

The process begins in the top left quadrant with the sorts of knowledge-related activity we have just been discussing: teamwork, meetings (formal and informal) and general gossip and chit-chat. Occasions for knowledge exchange through 'socialization' are all over the workplace, from staff briefings to working lunches – and initiatives to foster it include the sorts of environmental change (quiet, comfortable meeting areas and more coffee machines) we have been discussing, plus things like away-days, internal conferences, get-togethers of staff from different geographies, or residential training. Xerox devised an entire programme just to enable their engineers to get together to share 'war stories' about recalcitrant equipment . . . money well spent in their estimation as it proved the most efficient process for sharing.

Networked collaboration tools such as chat rooms (for online work) or discussion boards (for offline, time-shifted communication) can be deployed to enable text 'conversations' as a way of knowledge exchange although with some limited success. Research suggests that trust plays a huge part in how well online transmission can work, and this takes a long time to build within virtual groups that are not cohesive, and seldom meet face-to-face if at all. There is a lot of anecdotal evidence to suggest such conversation seems to work far better with people who already know each other.

Process 2: externalization

The next category focuses on the process by which knowledge is externalized – written down or otherwise expressed in some concrete form. This, along with the next process, combination, is where the majority of technology-led knowledge management efforts have been focused, things such as:

- First generation customer relationship management or contact management systems – capturing data about customer transactions, structuring this into some kind of 'story' or picture of the customer, and occasionally attempting to capture knowledge and insight as to customer's motives and intentions.
- Databases of expertise – schemes such as BP's 'Connect' system (adopted by many other companies including Fujitsu)

whereby a searchable database is created listing not just job title and contact information, but also volunteered information such as CVs and lists of interests, qualifications and expertise.

- Document management systems – built around formal organizational processes to capture documents that become a matter of record. There is a clear distinction between this kind of 'for the record' document management, and more loose 'document sharing'. Document management, works hand in hand with records management, as found in the Civil Service and also in law, accountancy and pharmaceutical firms, as well as key record-keeping departments (such as HR) of most large corporates. These may feature full version control, 'imaging'-style capture of incoming paperwork, and a robust classification system created with the goal of eliminating all, or most, paper filing.

- Document sharing systems – more loose, usually intranet-based, systems where staff are encouraged to publish documents. Increasingly these are built around communities of practice (which we'll come to in a moment). In government circles there is a push to formalize them and tie them into records management. An issue for both intranet and internet-based systems is the notion of roll-back; in a public or legal enquiry situation it may be important to know 'who knew what' or had access to what at a certain time. This is not possible with most current intranet tools.

- After action reports, storytelling or 'knowledge harvesting' techniques – increasingly, a variety of techniques are being used to capture 'tacit' knowledge and make it explicit in some form, whether by formal reports, structured or unstructured interviews, or by some sort of storytelling technique.

The two big issues associated with these are **context** and **trust**.

The main difficulty when writing down information is that it takes on a life of its own. Consider how many political rows there are over 'leaked' documents that can be read in a certain way, but when the full facts and context are known, there is often little real controversy. For example, an otherwise identical document advocating, say, closure of half of the rail network, would have quite a different significance when presented as a submission from a radical think-tank than it would if prepared by a transport minister's policy adviser. A certain amount of context – prior knowledge – can be necessary if documents and information are to be properly understood. This prior knowledge might relate to a particular audience or at a particular moment in time, or to technical knowledge that may make it unintelligible or downright misleading to a layperson.

This possible misinterpretation has an impact on trust – individuals are understandably reluctant to publish information that they consider sensitive or which has a particular context. It is this lack of trust that is often the primary cause of individuals' resistance to the publishing of material that might be useful to others. It is one of the assumptions of knowledge management that the making explicit of personally held knowledge is a 'good thing'. So how can this issue of context and trust best be addressed?

One approach has been to reduce the size of the potential audience. Early intranets, almost as a point of principle, chose to broadcast their entire contents to the whole company (or at least to the whole division or business unit that they were created to service). More sophisticated approaches have been to introduce 'communities of practice' around publishing tools.

Many organizations have some form of communities of practice anyway – be they formal groupings (engineers, salespeople) or more opt-in kind of groups (people interested in a particular business area or developing market, for example) from across various business divisions. Formally providing support for these informal groupings – by, for example, providing forms-based tools (no HTML expertise required) to quickly and easily build an intranet presence, with built-in content management. This can be a powerful way to encourage the sharing of knowledge and information.

ICL's second generation of its intranet was launched at the start of 1999 and was completely built around the idea of communities: providing the same tools for functional business units as for virtual communities of practice. It proved a great success, with the 50 or so communities that were part of the original set-up quickly becoming more than 500 communities within a year, and the majority of ICL's then 19 000 staff participating in multiple groups. Communities ranged in size from as few as 15 participants to 4000, with most settling around an optimum number of 100–200. By the time of ICL's full merger with Fujitsu in spring 2002, 500 items of new content were being added to the site every week – not an avalanche, but a steady stream of fresh, and (importantly) volunteered content, much of it high quality.

From this experience, we have drawn up a few rules associated with communities:

1 They need to be self-administered – otherwise the central overhead is too great (a year after construction, the entire staff complement for ICL's intranet operation was two people, both primarily focused on new features and future development).
2 That administration process must be extremely easy and quick, without special skills required (ICL community administrators spend, on average, between a day and two days a month on housekeeping, something easily fitted in alongside their main role).
3 There needs to be a gatekeeper – to manage the entry of new members, including welcome, house rules etc. Some communities may need a wall around them (a group of people working in a customer account where there is sensitive customer information, for example).
4 There needs to be an owner – senior enough to request resources (administrator time) and be a figurehead for the group. This needn't be a management figure, it could simply be a distinguished practitioner of some kind.
5 There needs to be payback for publishing – some kind of visibility or feedback. There have been experiments with payment (air miles), content rating (star ratings beside articles), and links to measurement processes – but one of the most common forms of recognition (and generally powerful enough to encourage people to participate) is a weekly or monthly list of new content circulated to group members (and to members of the management team where appropriate).
6 It's OK to 'lurk' ... it's not a requirement to participate heavily – though people who use material taken from the community site should be encouraged – at least to notify or thank the owners.
7 Don't just think virtual – face-to-face elements can be important too. ICL and later Fujitsu's 'Mobilizing Knowledge' community, holds a physical meeting of a subset of its 150 members every two months or so, where members present to the group on the KM work they are doing with customers, and seek input. Sometimes software vendors are also invited to present or demonstrate on new technologies. In a poll conducted among the group, the personal networking element and opportunity to hear about people's experiences came way above accessing content as the main drivers for participation.

Process 3: combination

Access to community-based and other published content leads us to the next category: combination. This is defined as an individual, using the knowledge he or she personally holds, combining it together with knowledge already expressed in some form – documents, presentations, web content – to create new material, both building on the existing knowledge and also developing new thinking.

Combination is the process behind the main **outputs** of knowledge work: the sales proposal, the presentation to a customer, a marketing plan for a new product or blueprint for a factory layout.

So how can we best support combination? The main elements here are the quality of tools: networks with decent performance, desktop tools (email, word processing, graphics, specialist applications) that do the job well (with appropriate training where needed). The aim of proper infrastructure design is to enable workers to get stuck into the job of thinking, analysing and delivering the outputs of their work, not get hung up on how to use the tools to operate the technology.

So far we have outlined the first three processes of innovation:

- knowledge is exchanged and shared via a process of 'socialization'
- some of this knowledge can be written down and made explicit – 'externalized'
- this 'externalized' knowledge provides a useful information source to create new and better outputs – the process of 'combination'.

But how do workers acquire and integrate new knowledge? This brings us to the final box – internalization.

Process 4: internalization

Internalization is defined as the process of individual learning, with that individual integrating and coming to fully understand and attain a level of knowledge on a particular topic. This involves a bringing together of existing personally held knowledge; new information gathered or used during work; and learning from the experiences of trying to put that information to use in a particular context.

With this process come the sort of rules of thumb – heuristics – that individual people develop to help them make sense of the world, and to carry out tasks efficiently, that sometimes get codified into working practices.

Internalization is a process that occurs within the individual – a process of learning – that also has parallels for the organization as a whole. Organizations, too, need to learn to absorb new information about the external environment, make sense of it, and take appropriate measures given the changing circumstances.

Support for internalization at the personal level should include providing the circumstances where individuals can make sense of their learning – allowing them to answer questions such as: 'what happened?', 'what was supposed to happen', 'why was there a difference'. In reality this may be through providing 'quiet spaces' or by creating time-sheet codes for 'follow-up' after certain activities.

From an organizational perspective, the ability of a company to ask and truthfully answer these questions will be a key determinant in coping with a changing world: this is why the idea of a learning organization – one which tolerates and learns from experimentation at the margins of its business, and looks beyond the immediate industry boundaries to what is happening at the periphery of its field of vision – is such a powerful driver for many forward-looking companies.

Seeing the spiral

And so we come full circle. Internalized knowledge is shared with others via the socialization process, and the cycle begins anew (see Figure 4.5). The vision is an intriguing one, and certainly reflects some notion of truth as individuals experience it in organizations.

The model is not without its critics, however, particularly those who see how a spiral of ever-increasing knowledge might work in, say, a Japanese company (which was the focus of Nonaka and Takeuchi's original work) where individuals stay with the same company for life, there is an open culture of sharing, and the way to 'get on' is to play the company game. In western countries, where the average duration of employment with a single employer is falling fast and is currently between 4 and 8 years, and there is huge and growing use of outsourcing personnel, consultants, contractors and other 'temporary' staff with little commitment to the knowledge base (or indeed the

Figure 4.5
Dimensions of knowledge creation – how it can grow (adapted from Nonaka and Takeuchi 1995, p. 57)

Individual ⟳ Group ⟳ Organizational ⟳ Interorganizational

long-term existence) of the companies they spend their time working for, it becomes easy to see how this spiral might break down, or never get going in the first place.

However, the model is one of the first attempts to uncover the dynamics of knowledge exchange in the enterprise, and whether it is complete or not, the insights it presents can still be used to help provide some framework for the sorts of knowledge-sharing initiatives outlined in this section.

4.1.4 Business processes

The importance of process

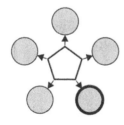

Business processes are the things that we all follow at work – the daily actions, activities and tasks that take up our energy and time. The way people perform these has an impact on how satisfied, or unsatisfied their customers are, and how much of a difference those individuals make for their own organizations and, indeed, for themselves. In a major way they affect the way knowledge is mobilized around the organization to add value.

The following are a couple of formal definitions of what a process is:

> *A sequence of steps which adds value by producing required outputs from a variety of inputs.* (British Quality Foundation 1998)

> *A series of actions, changes, or functions bringing about a result.* (Dictionary.com 2002)

The improvement of business processes should be at the very core of knowledge management, with the goal of doing things differently and better. Designing the new reality must have a process redesign element – getting people to look at the way things are currently done and asking – can we do this faster, at

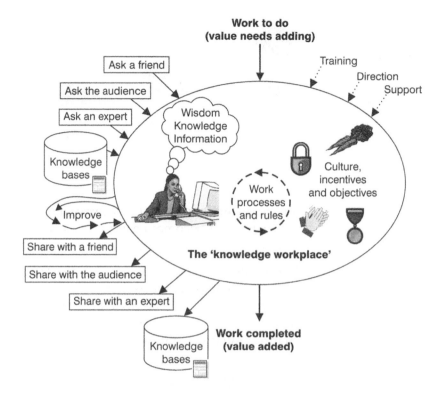

Figure 4.6
The knowledge workplace (developed by Trevor Howes and Tony Clack)

less cost, can we improve the quality, should we be doing this at all, and are there things we do not do, but should?

The 'knowledge workplace' was introduced in Chapter 3 and is shown again in Figure 4.6 for reference.

At the centre of the workplace are work processes, performed by people who may be supported by some technology. These people would have received varying degrees of training, direction, and support to help guide their actions. They will also use their own knowledge in performing the work.

The work will either flow to them, or they themselves will initiate work that needs to be done. In trying to complete the work they may ask friends, a wider audience, or specific experts for advice. They may also use paper and electronic systems to find what they need. In doing their work they may also improve the information and knowledge – for example, by adding what they have learnt from their own experiences. So as well as completing the work, they may also share this new found knowledge with friends, a wider audience, specific experts, or record it on paper or on electronic systems.

The knowledge workplace is where a cycle of work constantly flows, where the individual can add value and contribute to the wider community of knowledge.

At the centre of all this are the core business processes – both those things that are 'formally' known to be done and also knowledge sharing and other informal actions that may be carried out. It is important to realize that in a knowledge management context, when we talk about processes, we include both informal and formal types. An example: a customer of one of the authors had separate teams performing accounting work across seven different locations, each sharing a building and working closely with their own customers. When they reorganized the teams into a single centralized location, they redesigned the formal processes to cope with the changed accounting information flow, but they also had to take into account that the informal chats where key knowledge was passed between themselves and their local customers' would no longer happen. Acknowledging this helped them put in place other ways of meeting with their customers, keeping the relationships going and ensuring that important informal information exchanges still continued.

This example echoes the message in our Golden Rule below:

> **Golden Rule #4: Process change leads to improved performance** – Organizations need to build in new processes and routines through job redesign, to ensure knowledge capture and reuse, and to establish and reinforce desired behaviours and activity.

There are many ways in which performance can be strategically improved to meet the pressures on the organization. For example, there will almost always be some form of competitor out there that is working to gain your customer's attention (even in government, for example, there are competitors for central funding). By better managing or reducing the costs of performing processes, any new competitors will have to be very efficient from day one if they are to compete. Working in unique and special ways can help your organization be 'different' from the competitors, making it difficult for competitors. In addition, the organization may want to 'be the best' at doing a certain thing – this may be by having very close customer relationships, or by producing or providing specialist goods and services. By being the best and constantly innovating, the competition will again have difficulty in competing against your organization.

These can all be achieved by improving the formal and informal processes that the people in the organization follow.

Tesco, the leading UK supermarket, has focused on its supply chain (from product development, supply, storage, and sale) not just to drive down cost but also to gain control of the quality of products. The flow of information between all those involved in the supply chain, and the exchange of knowledge between people, is key to keeping control, but also in looking for innovative new ways of working.

Any process effort must take place with the vision and strategy clearly in mind. The process needs from knowledge management are particularly focused on the information flow and interactions of people with knowledge. We now need to understand the different knowledge management processes that must be borne in mind when designing our new reality.

Looking at key knowledge processes

In the previous section we outlined the 'Spiral of Innovation' that enables knowledge to be shared and improved, with a view to encouraging innovation. There are a set of 'knowledge processes' proposed by Gilbert Probst, Steffen Raub and Kai Romhardt (2000) that can be useful to help understand how efficient an organization's knowledge processes are currently, and assess the future potential of specific improvements (Figure 4.7).

People tend not to carry these processes out in quite such a structured, logical or disciplined way as presented in the questions below, but they are outlined below in such a way for ease of representation. In designing a new reality one should ask the questions:

- Do people perform all these processes in the organization?
- Are they supported with adequate and appropriate technology?
- Are individuals encouraged to carry them out, or do things discourage them?
- In order to meet our needs and mobilize knowledge, what should be happening?
- What supporting technologies or information sources will help?
- What leadership or people areas will help them be carried out?
- Are feedback and control processes needed to keep everything in balance?

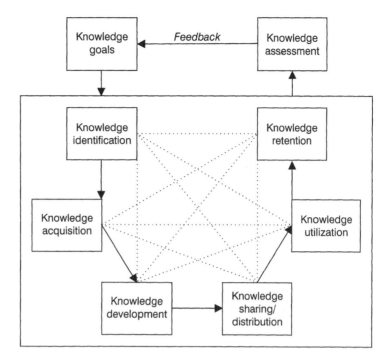

Figure 4.7
Building blocks of knowledge management (Probst, Raub and Romhardt 2000, p. 34)

The processes show knowledge creation as 'knowledge development' where it builds upon identified and acquired knowledge, which is then shared, utilized and retained. Also shown are feedback processes where the performance is assessed against the knowledge goals of the organization. This allows a constant check to be maintained on the effectiveness and efficiency of the processes, a very important aspect of any process work.

As an example, a team developing a new IT system may have some **knowledge goals** – to foster best practice and ensure all the key requirements of the users are incorporated in the design, and to help future projects to learn from their experiences and progress.

When starting the project the project manager and team will identify what sorts of information and knowledge will likely help them (**knowledge identification**) – this could be any of the knowledge types identified in Chapter 2. The team will then seek out the information and get it for the team (**knowledge acquisition**). This might include requesting identified 'experts' to join the team, or finding previous documentation and gaining permission to use it. The team will now be ready to move on with the project and start developing the new system.

During the work people will have ideas and discover useful ways of doing things (**knowledge development**) and will likely share this with other team members and interested parties (**knowledge sharing/distribution**). Once the knowledge is shared then people will start using it to move the IT system development on (**knowledge utilization**). The knowledge at the end of each project stage will be captured on an intranet, written up as 'knowledge bites' for new projects, or incorporated into training material for IT staff (**knowledge retention**). Also at the end of each project stage the project is reviewed to see if it is meeting its original knowledge goals (**knowledge assessment**). It may be that different experts may need to be involved, or other knowledge types would help out.

Only a basic flavour of these knowledge processes can be gained from such a simple example, but it assists with initial assesment of what important knowledge and information business processes exist in the organization.

How to analyse processes

The approach to business process analysis must be pragmatic and focused on meeting the requirements, and constraints, of each specific situation. People within the organization will have the experience and knowledge of what currently happens, and most significantly what is important. Involving them in the analysis is therefore essential if any change is to be successful.

Knowledge processes are at the heart of how the organization works, and will be impacted on by all of the other key KM areas (leadership, people, technology, and information). Designing the new process reality can be a complex job, but as mentioned previously, the benefits to the project and organization can be enormous. Our experience shows that many of the 'off-the-wall' and 'silly' ideas that are raised during the first set of meetings will set the scene for the level of improvement likely. We find such improvement ideas should be captured in an 'opportunity log' that can be used throughout the project to capture gaps, weaknesses, inconsistencies, duplications, as well as general improvement opportunities. This log will be a vital source of ideas when redesign should take place.

Deciding on the type of process changes will help everyone understand how radical and risk-bearing the task will be. There are many different types of process changes, ranging from the

Table 4.4 Different types of process change

	Continuous improvement	Process redesign	Radical business change
Cost	Low	Medium	High
Scope	Local	Local→ far reaching	Far reaching
Scale	Small	Medium	Large
Risk	Low	Medium	High
Return	Low	Medium	High

continuous and low-impact to the radical, high-risk and high-reward type. They are known by many different names, but the main categories are shown in Table 4.4.

Continuous improvement tends to, as its name suggests, be a continuous activity carried out within an organization. Capturing ideas from employee suggestions, or introducing changes as the demands from customers alter over time, are both examples of this.

Example: A medium-sized corporate hospitality company regularly set aside money to implement changes suggested by staff. A percentage of any resulting financial savings, and profit from extra business won, was used for staff bonuses and a few 'party' nights throughout the year. As a result staff tended to talk more about what could be done better after events for customers, improving knowledge sharing, learning, and organizational performance all at the same time.

Process redesign activities tend to be part of a project that challenges old ways of working and may recommend changes running across all our key enablers. The brief is typically that some problems need to be addressed and the 'end-to-end' processes (logically related processes that may start from one end of the organization and pass through many departments) should be looked at for wide-scale change opportunities.

Example: A city council wanted to improve the way it dealt with customers when approving disabled car parking passes. It had previously charged customers £2 for an administration fee which was non-refundable, even if at the end of the process they were refused a pass. There was resistance to this among customers. The reason for the charge was that the processes at each local office in the community for checking and handling the money were complicated and time consuming. After a process review it was decided to handle the authorization at a central location, with redesigned forms that clearly placed more of the data gathering responsibilities onto those applying. The administration fee was also scrapped. The result was a reduction in 'confrontations' faced by local office staff regarding the administration charges, and fewer forms rejected due to incomplete information.

Radical business change projects tend to have all parts of the organization as possible areas for change. The focus is typically on designing and implementing new and changed processes that significantly improve the value delivered to customers. The organization is then restructured around these processes. This could mean new physical locations, IT systems, roles, and a whole new culture being required to ensure the new processes are performed in the optimum manner. These projects tend to be substantial programmes – the scope, scale, and variety of the changes require a number of parallel projects to be coordinated together. Risk and reward will both be high – and organizations do not enter into such changes lightly. Significant and compelling pressures must be facing organizations who need to make wide-scale changes for survival or to grasp highly attractive opportunities.

First Direct, the phone and internet bank, is a classic example of such a move – where an existing financial institution created a new bank with no branches and offering 24-hour customer contact. The central idea was a change in the value delivered to customers through new processes and interactions with customers. Achieving this required the traditional banking processes to be turned on their head and made ultra-customer friendly. With the new processes developed, the call centres, new roles, and IT systems had all to be created to support them. The needs for sharing and gaining customer and system knowledge were driven by the new ways of working, forcing people to behave differently.

For knowledge management the most common types of projects are those closest to continuous improvement and process redesign. It is unlikely that the drive to gain and share knowledge better will result in radical business changes of the scale described.

During the information and knowledge process analysis, some process information should be captured. A template for basic process information required has already been introduced, and can be found in Appendix 3.

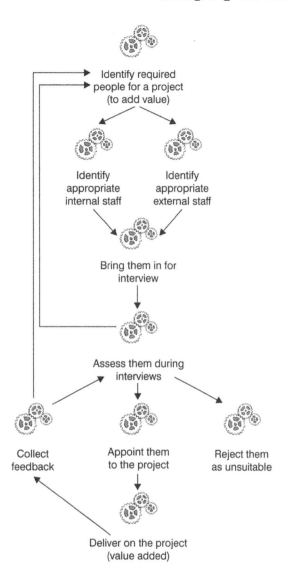

Figure 4.8
Staff recruitment for a
project – an example
process

It is also important to capture the flow of processes, and the information they use, consume, and produce. Figure 4.8 is a simple example of the process for recruiting and using people on an IT project.

By mapping out the key processes that currently happen it is sometimes obvious where improvements can be made. But what we also need to understand is how do people in the organization fit into the process picture? People at work tend to meet and chat and share knowledge, as well as perform their work. The updated Figure 4.9 shows these people, each with their own specific knowledge performing the processes. The dotted line

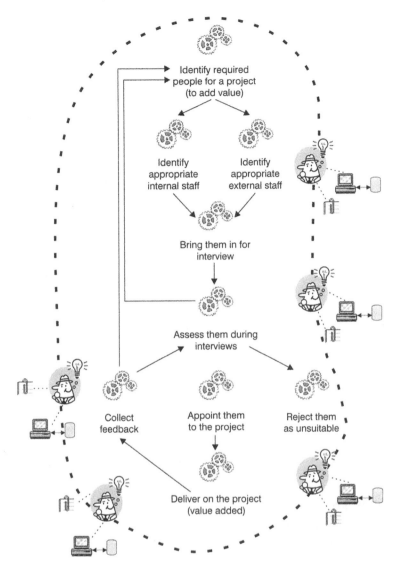

Figure 4.9
Staff recruitment for a
project – with roles
and community

also highlights the community that they form – sharing and building knowledge during formal and informal interactions.

It is precisely these interactions that can make the difference between a process that is average, and one that is exceptional. Over time, as experience and knowledge are gained and shared about the process, then cost, time, and quality should all increase, and the process itself should adapt and evolve to changing needs. If these people were stopped from talking to each other and sharing their knowledge, then not only would the organization suffer, but the satisfaction of work would diminish for everyone concerned.

Whether these processes involve tangible objects, some kind of manufactured goods, for instance, or concern some aspect of provision of a service, part of the work will involve the use of data and information. This may include pricing data, stock location, facts about the product or service – and also knowledge (what is known to the employee about the product or service, about how to deliver it, background knowledge about the customer etc.).

An awareness of the knowledge and information issues surrounding a business process is essential. As part of this exercise an analysis of the information produced by the processes (such as invoices, a project plan, or an operational IT system), in addition to the formal and informal knowledge processes, will be required. A more informed analysis of the processes will enable additional strategic improvements to be identified.

Knowledge and information types revisited

In Chapter 3, we introduced the idea of using knowledge types to help identify possible benefits. These types are shown in Figure 4.10, and here we will revisit them in a process context to generate further ideas for improvement. Getting the right

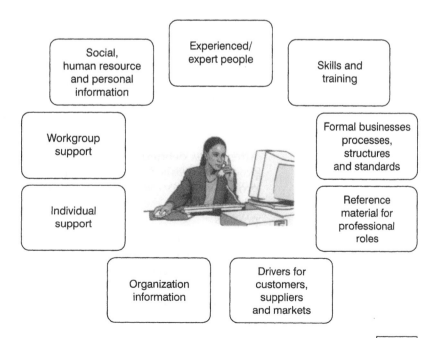

Figure 4.10
The nine knowledge types (developed by Trevor Howes, Jack Kenward and Tony Clack 2001)

Table 4.5 Knowledge need examples – process and outcomes

Knowledge type	Example process	Example outcome
Experienced/Expert people	Periodically, each person should enter details into a log that states a description of projects worked on, skills used, level of knowledge held (1–5), and a 'willingness to use' (1–5), so that people enquiring can understand 'who knows what' – the forming of a directory of expertise	Easier access to people with specific knowledge; better exploitation of existing knowledge and experience
Skills and training	A process where people must enter details into a log (perhaps as part of a directory of expertise) after they receive training	Easier access to people with specific skills; better exploitation of training
	A process where people are required to share a 'tip' from a conference or event attended	Better value from spending on events
Formal business processes, structures and standards	The availability and publicizing of 'easy to follow' organizational and project process and role descriptions.	Increased knowledge of how to do things – reducing uncertainty and increasing conformity. Increased clarity of each person's official responsibilities – know who to go to for formal requests
	After action debriefing process established following project stage reviews; case study process at the end of projects	Learning captured from projects before it gets forgotten
	Project start-up process – project manager required to spend time on search for relevant material from similar past projects	Project managers start to apply the lessons from previous projects to new ones – less risk, quicker start-up

Table 4.5 Continued

Knowledge type	Example process	Example outcome
Reference material for professional roles	The availability of 'best practice' reports, templates, and examples. For example, project management help files and templates	Increased standardization of information captured, saved 'reinventing the wheel'
	Access to professional journals online	Allow people to maintain currency of skills and understand what changes and improvements elsewhere may be useful in their work
Drivers for customers, suppliers and markets	Access to customer/supplier websites and annual reports. Also recording what priorities are driving customers/suppliers from visits and after meetings	Ability to understand better the culture, goods and services and changes in customers to enable more empathic relationships
Organizational information	Descriptions of all the goods and services offered, who by, and case studies to be available simply to all	Reduced induction time, especially for sales; less searching time; and improved customer communications
Individual support	A 'questions and answers' template should be created for the different roles and projects to guide advice and tips in response to common problems/concerns	Less uncertainty for new joiners and new to project staff. Sharing and helping each other will help build a community spirit
Workgroup support	'Job folder' creation and maintenance process introduced for roles with high turnover; becomes a key knowledge asset at induction time for new staff	Less knowledge lost when people leave, new staff become more efficient more quickly
Social, human resource and personal information	Voluntary posting of personal details, interests and pictures	Allowing people to be more individualistic and understand more about their colleagues

balance of changes across these knowledge types will enable the project to be confident that all major areas have been considered. Confidence in the end result will also increase by using a structured way to generate improvement ideas.

Table 4.5 is a more detailed delve into these areas, with example processes and outcomes for each knowledge type.

Process knowledge-type analysis using these nine types might include some of the Table 4.5 examples of knowledge processes and outcomes that could co-exist alongside the work processes.

There is significant scope for better knowledge processes to be built into many business activities. In addition, the very establishment of a consistent number of areas should help deliver the wider change in behaviour identified in our Golden Rule #4.

Golden Rule #4: Process change leads to improved perform-ance – Organizations need to build in new processes and routines through job redesign, to ensure knowledge capture and reuse, and to establish and reinforce desired behaviours and activity.

Each organization and group will have their own ideas as to how things have been improved, and likely they will also have 'disaster stories' when similar things were introduced and did not work! Listening to such stories and learning the lessons are invaluable when planning the changes and understanding pitfalls to avoid, and wider project risks.

Knowledge management and Business Process Reengineering

It has been repeatedly stressed throughout this book that it is hugely valuable to be able to recall the past and to learn the lessons from past experiences. Focusing on process is not a new activity, but what has been a more recent development is the notion of examining a process end to end, ignoring the implications of the current structure of the organization, and rebuilding an entirely new process that is more efficient (and often leading to organizational change as a result).

This activity has often been given the label Business Process Re-engineering (BPR) and is akin to the 'Radical Business Change' model described above. In the early 1990s, this discipline emerged as a significant new tool for improving business performance. In terms of delivering knowledge management consultancy, the authors have been involved in a number of BPR projects – adding knowledge management insights when processes where being reworked.

However, there have been very few BPR projects which start off with the goal of increasing value from knowledge – in fact, large-scale BPR projects have reduced radically in number in recent years as companies have gone back to more incremental approaches (the exception has been in the implementation of e-business, which does offer opportunities for radical streamlining of processes).

From a mobilizing knowledge perspective, then, continuous improvement via changes to process is a key area of focus: using process redesign techniques to consider how information is produced, consumed, absorbed, stored and accessed, and then to bring about improvements in the efficiency of these processes. But this is not, by any means, always part of a BPR exercise.

The original creators of the BPR method, Michael Hammer and James Champy, wrote in 1993:

> *The reality that organizations have to confront is that the old ways of doing business simply don't work any more. In today's environment, nothing is constant or predictable – not market growth, customer demand, product life cycles, the rate of technological change, or the nature of competition.*

What they were stressing is that an organization should never rest, but always be adapting. What they specifically focused upon was process, and its role in delivering value. By looking at any organization's processes, there would likely be significant drift from the most effective and efficient ideal. However, they argue that opportunities for improvement would come not just from the realignment of processes, but that developments in information and communications technologies would require new types of processes, structures, and relationships to be brought into being.

This was the thinking behind the early wave of BPR. Today, however, the focus has shifted from 'pure' process change (combined with a technology deployment) to a more people-focused approach that recognizes the importance of individual and organizational learning, and the key role that non-process elements (people's individual interactions, which cannot be defined in process terms) play in organizational performance:

The organization needs to be seen not as a stable hierarchy, but as an adaptive, continually changing learning organization, capable of benefiting from the variety of knowledge, experience and skills of individuals through a culture which encourages mutual questioning and challenge around a shared purpose or vision.

(Johnson and Scholes 1999)

In the early 1990s, those applying BPR techniques often focused on business processes and technology to the detriment of the softer, human dimensions. This sometimes led to drastic cuts in staff numbers, while many roles were redefined, and new operational measurements introduced: a focus on a fixed number of key performance indicators became the mainstay of many organizations. What this ignored was that in many companies, the 'loose' or subjective nature of many organizational processes, and the freedom to exchange knowledge, was a core (and essential) business competence, a competence accorded little importance during these early programmes.

Creativity and innovation tended to take a secondary priority, as staff were shed if they were seen as not directly adding value to what were defined as core business processes. Individuals with vast amounts of personally held knowledge were forced out, and this knowledge (together with significant potential for creativity) was lost – a significant (and often ignored) impact of change, while staff who remained had to deal with the loss of many colleagues and friends.

During 1995 two books tapped the need for a more holistic approach to business performance improvement, focusing on the value of knowledge. These were *Wellspring of Knowledge* by Dorothy Leonard-Barton and *The Knowledge Creating Company* by Nonaka and Takeuchi, which we have already discussed earlier in this chapter. Though coming at the topic from very different angles, they both attempted to re-evaluate the importance to an organization of the knowledge and creativity of individuals, concluding that it is how the companies managed this creativity that was the key to sustained competitive advantage. To a large extent, these authors began to redefine the debate: no longer could experienced staff be seen purely as surplus to requirements today, without much thought for tomorrow.

Hammer and Champy themselves also identified weaknesses in the BPR method they were central in developing. Champy's 1995 book, *Reengineering Management – The Mandate for New*

Leadership, even started with a first sentence of 'Reengineering is in trouble'. He highlighted that his earlier work focused almost solely on operational processes, giving little attention to how the people in organizations should be organized, inspired, deployed measured, and rewarded for value-adding work. Hammer's (1996) follow-on book, *Beyond Reengineering – How the Process-Centred Organization is Changing our Work and our Lives*, has Hammer also stating that he was wrong with the approach – by promoting the radical nature of reengineering, other factors had been ignored, especially the softer, people-focused perspective and the loss of organizational knowledge during change:

> *In the aftermath of reengineering, business leaders discovered that they no longer understood how to manage their business.*
>
> (Hammer 1996)

BPR then, as an approach, does not have a hugely significant relationship with mobilizing knowledge, but it does now at least recognize that the key to success is to incorporate people and knowledge to the core of a change programme. Through the process and knowledge-type ideas introduced, we can learn from past examples of BPR and be wary of the bad reputation it gained for not being 'knowledge friendly'.

To summarize, business processes, or the work people do, are responsible for adding value for customers, the organization, and the individual. It is critical that the knowledge contribution is appreciated and any new reality should include a number of 'knowledge processes'.

Business process modelling and improvement techniques can be hugely valuable in creating and reinforcing good knowledge-sharing behaviour, but 'pure' BPR – especially on an enterprise-wide scale – needs to be tempered by an appropriate focus on the personally held knowledge and skills of individuals, in order to lower project risk and deliver the potential benefits.

By changing the processes, you change what people focus upon, and this is an opportunity to improve organizational performance through the mobilization of knowledge.

Golden Rule #4: Process change leads to improved performance – Organizations need to build in new processes and routines through job redesign, to ensure knowledge capture and reuse, and to establish and reinforce desired behaviours and activity.

4.2 Stage 3, part 2: Technology and information/content

4.2.1 Technology in context

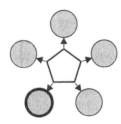

At the risk of being glib, knowledge management technologies are about *delivering* the right *information* to the right *people* at the right *time*. This statement is oft repeated – but what does it mean? In our view, it can be understood as the following elements:

- *Delivering* – this potentially involves multiple formats, including web pages, databases, documents; multiple modes of access including mail delivery, web search and 'agent' or 'push' delivery of personalized information; and multiple channels – desktop and laptop PCs, hand-held devices, and data-enable mobile telephony services.
- *Information* – this is relevant data, structured information or documents, filtered according to role or preference, and pitched at an appropriate level for the context inhabited by the user. We make a distinction between information and 'content', which is a word particularly (but not exclusively) associated with Internet or intranet publishing.
- *People* – increasingly not just employees, but also the wider community of people and organizations that communicate with the enterprise such as customers, suppliers, partners and other stakeholders.
- *Time* – recognition that different information technologies have a different time basis, and as such are appropriate for different purposes (e.g. document management systems and web pages – interactive and instant at the point of delivery; email or news/discussion groups – essentially 'time-shifted' or asynchronous; structured databases and online chat – instant and 'online').

As we have repeatedly emphasized, only *people* can *know* things – everything else is just information, and knowledge management is primarily concerned with how people interact with this information. In this context, if leadership, people and process are the *levers* for mobilizing knowledge in an organization, then technology and information are the *enablers* – crucial elements of infrastructure and support systems which need to be in place if the potential of the organization to maximize value of what its people know, and of its information assets, is to be realized.

The approach we take in this book recognizes that the success of any technology implementation is largely governed by people's willingness to use technology-based tools. When it comes to efforts to mobilize knowledge in the organization, workers must be able to be persuaded to modify their behaviour, so that they can make the most of their personal knowledge, by putting it to effective use within the workgroup, to develop new skills and ways of thinking – to make the most of better access to knowledge and information possessed by others, and managed within the enterprise.

The backdrop to this, the essential prerequisite and a primary opportunity for today's organizations, is the raft of knowledge management technologies which have developed in relatively recent time. To help create this new collaborative environment, systems need to be developed over time to support people in the way they work:

- Providing secure storage of both structured and unstructured information in a variety of formats.
- Enabling easy access to data, information and expertise.
- Making it easy to share information with and get information from other people.
- Searching, filtering and ranking information from the individual's perspective, to help that individual make sense of what data and information might be at his or her disposal.
- Providing 'intelligent help' to assist people to exploit available data, information and knowledge.

Going beyond our initial definition, then, the purpose of KM technologies is to support the creation, delivery, management (including presentation), and retrieval of information. This information is typically corporate in nature (policies, procedures, news), but may also be specific to users in their particular role within the workgroup.

One way to categorize the complex and interdependent elements above is to classify knowledge management technologies into three essential elements around which this chapter is based:

- **Access** is the foundation: dependent of course on the basic IT infrastructure (desktop and network services, servers and user directory architecture), in KM terms the focus is on access to:
  - key repositories (such as underlying information stores – file storage, databases, mainframes/legacy systems), and
  - appropriate applications (such as basic content creation tools – typically Microsoft Office applications Word, Excel

and PowerPoint; content management systems and work-flow; and content delivery through portal and personalization tools.

- **Discovery** concerns itself with search, retrieval, structuring, aggregation and presentation of information, the interface to the rapidly growing information jungle that people in most organizations have to somehow navigate.
- **Collaboration** is about working with other people to productive ends – tools for sharing information or interacting in some way. At their simplest, this includes internet-type newsgroups and discussion forums, and chat. Email also comes into this category, along with groupware tools (similar to, but usually more sophisticated and integrated than, normal internet tools) and a growing raft of specialist collaborative applications.

Unfortunately the available knowledge management software products don't neatly fall into these categories: the business, information and technical requirements which underpin enterprise-wide document management, for example, cut across all three. But in terms of defining how people interact with technology, these are useful categorizations and we will use them here to examine the issues and opportunities associated with each.

Before doing this, however, we need to consider our starting point: the stage of evolution of the organization. The challenges posed by the Year 2000 'Millennium Bug' (how quaint that sounds now!) gave organizations an opportunity to raise their standards across the board: most organizations, large and small, are running 'modern' desktop and server infrastructures now, and there have been significant efforts to migrate data and applications from aging proprietary systems to new arrangements, including data centres (giving significant potential for new data analysis tools to be deployed), while new technologies for integrating legacy mainframe applications offer similar potential to unlock data and information previously inaccessible to most of the enterprise.

But there remains a substantial gulf between the potential of today's technology and the ability of organizations to exploit it. One of the hot topics in the aftermath of 'Y2K' is *infrastructure exploitation* – making better use of the tools and infrastructure that is already in place. In knowledge management terms (focusing on behaviour) this makes a great deal of sense. But it would be foolish to stop looking for new tools and new ways to deploy them within the business – exploitation activity needs to be carried on in parallel with exploration of new tools and technologies that might be deployed to help the business achieve its objectives.

4.2.2 The audit process

The appropriate way to begin with our exploration is with a knowledge technology and information management audit – a fairly wide-ranging (though, of necessity, high-level) exercise that seeks to uncover the particular knowledge-related technologies deployed in the business, assess how they are used, and determine the main issues facing the business. The precise approach will vary according to circumstances, but our three headings are a useful starting point.

Some of the following phrases may be new to you, and explanations are provided later in the chapter.

1 Access and infrastructure

1.1 What sort of information does the organization support?

    (a) What's centrally owned and managed (e.g. document management, performance and management information systems, customer databases, email infrastructure)?

    (b) What's departmental (e.g. local records, team documentation, project records)?

    (c) What's local (e.g. locally stored email, shared drives)?

    (d) Are local and departmental file stores actively managed in any way beyond straightforward backup?

    (e) Are local and departmental file stores linked to document or records management systems in any way?

    (f) If there are any proprietary information systems in use from the desktop, how easy is it to get information in and out of them?

    (g) How well do proprietary systems and other back-end elements interlink and exchange data among themselves?

1.2 How is this information supported and managed?

    (a) Are their issues with accuracy/relevancy?

    (b) Is there formal ownership of this information?

    (c) Is approval required for contributing/publishing information, and how is this managed?

1.3 Are there any issues regarding access to information outside the organization's core information system, such as:

(a) Remote access by staff with laptops? If so how satisfactory is this and does it support current business needs?

(b) Access by staff via hand-held device or laptop? Are bandwidth/security protocols adequate but still sufficiently flexible to allow reasonably productive use of information?

(c) Access to information by partners/suppliers (via extranet).

1.4 What are the key content creation tools in use (e.g. Word, Excel)?

(a) Are skills in these considered to be adequate?

(b) If non-standard, is this a barrier to sharing and dissemination?

1.5 Does the organization have what could be described as a 'portal'?

(a) If so, is this front-end access to an integrated system, a 'home page' linking out to different 'sites' on a variety of infrastructures around the enterprise, or a mixture of the two?

(b) Does the system have transactional capability to allow users to interface with back-end systems (e.g. personnel system to notify change of address)?

(c) How is information delivered to users (do they have to seek out and search for information, or are there 'agent', 'alert' or other 'push' systems in place)?

2 Discovery and information management

2.1 Does the organization have an intranet?

(a) If so, how many intranet sites does the organization have?

(b) How easy is it to publish on the intranet?

(c) Are their issues with dated or erroneous material?

(d) How is it kept up to date/by whom?

(e) Is there formal ownership of material?

(f) Is approval required for publishing and how is this managed?

2.2 Does the organization have a content management system to manage intranet publishing?

> (a) If so, how many people can/do use the associated publishing tools?
> (b) Is there an approval process built in (workflow)?
> (c) Does Web content have a 'lifecycle' including automated deletion?
> (d) What sort of metadata is associated with published content?

2.3 What sort of search tools does the organization have?

> (a) How easy is it to use the search tools?
> (b) What sort of indexing of content is done?
> (c) Does this extend to other information repositories such as file stores?
> (d) Is there a classification system or taxonomy in place for published material?
> (e) How easy is it to use this system, and is it possible to bypass it when publishing material (e.g. as raw HTML)?

3 Collaboration and expertise

3.1 Does the organization have universal access to email?

> (a) If so, is there a single integrated address book?
> (b) Is this integrated with other directory information such as phone numbers?
> (c) Is coping with email volume seen as a problem (by users, by administrators)?
> (d) Do people send large attachments through the email system, or do they link to files in public folders, shared drives or document management systems?

3.2 Is there a database of skills/expertise available?

> (a) Is this openly accessible, or restricted to managers?
> (b) Is participation voluntary? If not, where does the content come from?

3.3 Does the organization use a groupware suite such as Lotus Notes?

> (a) If so, how are databases/data sources managed?
> (b) Who does the database development (in-house team, local 'clued-up' users, external developers)?

(c) Are there constraints on deployment of new databases?

(d) How are things like data integrity and 'end of life' of databases managed?

(e) Are groupware collaboration tools (such as shared calendars, discussion groups, online chat, whiteboard tools etc.) in use? If so, who is using them, and for what?

3.4 Are there any other 'collaborative knowledge management tools' such as whiteboards, video or audio conferencing in use?

(a) If so, who is using them, for what, and to what extent?

(b) Are outputs stored/shared or dumped after use?

What should emerge from this process is a fairly clear and accurate snapshot of the organization, though of necessity it will be an incomplete picture – for any very large organization, it won't be possible to quickly move to anything like a comprehensive 'log' of information sources and uses (for example, one customer organization recently completed an exercise to create an information asset register – this took several months, logged literally thousands of sources from external news feeds to document repositories and groupware databases, and it still hasn't delivered a strategy for managing it all – though they are working on it!). Nevertheless, the learning gained from such an exercise is invaluable when it comes to feeding into the strategy process – uncovering which areas are going well, which require additional support, which have been neglected, and which are the most promising new areas and issues for intervention and development. Indeed, taking a fresh look at an organization's information systems from a KM perspective can provide useful insight, and it can help focus the overall IT strategy on the specific information needs of the business.

Some surprising findings may emerge – one organization of just 5000 people found that fairly lax controls on development in Lotus Notes had left them with more than 11 000 different Notes databases – more than two for every user. It was estimated that more than half of these had fallen into disuse – but it wasn't clear precisely which half. Equally, it wasn't known how many of these were used for things like contact details, and how many times these details had been captured and stored in different places around the company. For all the relatively low importance of the individual databases concerned (at least to the enterprise as a whole) the overall impact in terms of information policy for the organization was substantial.

Another organization had more than 400 'intranets' – ranging from stand-alone 'this is the team' workgroup-driven sites created in static HTML using a basic editor such as Microsoft FrontPage, to more sophisticated sites which had been set up by business units using external designers and databases of content. An effort had been made to create a directory of 'home pages' and at first glance it looked as if the organization was a fairly progressive one. But behind the scenes it was actually a nightmare – no common standards (whether of page design and feel, technology, or information), extremely basic search tools that 'missed' most of the published content, and no ownership of content post-publication (which meant that content could not be trusted to be current and relevant). Needless to say, the whole concept of 'intranet' had a fairly poor reputation in that company – it was associated with unmet expectations, as users had consistently failed to find what they were looking for. This is an extreme example – but parts of this story are fairly typical in organizations where information technology strategy has struggled to match the growth and change over the past decade – an all-too-common phenomenon when the rate of change facing both public and private sector organizations has been accelerating rapidly.

It should be noted that there is one commonly used information audit approach that we specifically don't recommend: the 'knowledge map'. The authors believe that while it can be useful to map out some of the main information flows when analysing business processes (whether at the macro level – across the value chain – or at the micro level in working to improve specific processes within the business), and certainly worth pulling together a list of 'approved' information sources into some kind of information asset register, it is a pointless exercise to attempt to map out all the knowledge and information within an organization, and attempt to show the links. As the KM pioneers Thomas Davenport and Larry Prusak say in their 1997 book *Working Knowledge*:

> *Organisations contain such a vast amount of knowledge, that mapping it would be a futile endeavour.*

4.2.3 Moving forward – the technology opportunity

For most organizations, the output of the knowledge technology and information management audit should contain few surprises: after all, information management and IT management are long-standing disciplines with their own specialisms (database administrators, librarians, systems architects, and so on), and managers are usually aware of strategic issues bubbling away, even if their daily routine is focused on keeping the existing show on the road with limited resources. But the temptation to say 'yes, we know about all this' should be avoided: an audit exercise, which will certainly have an element of documenting 'known problems', also provides an opportunity to step back and view the overall picture: listing the particular problems, noting particular strengths, teasing out the opportunities, making connections that might not otherwise be apparent. This is where the use of consultants can add particular value: fresh eyes, not constrained by knowledge of internal politics, can open up new thinking, or articulate, codify and corroborate what managers 'know', but find hard to gain consensus on when it comes to budgets and business cases.

This section focuses on how to identify and build on strategic opportunities for KM, basing the approach once again on our three dimensions of knowledge and information technology: access, collaboration and discovery. As we suggested previously, the boundaries between these categories is somewhat blurred – the degree of overlap is quite significant. Something of this is expressed in the Figure 4.11. This is, of course, only one of a number of possible ways to map out the essential elements of KM technologies: but the degree of overlap (especially where all three come together) demonstrates that it is quite hard to unpick some elements from others.

Prior to 'Y2K', any discussion about the 'access' component of knowledge management technologies would have looked a little different to today's discussion: as a side-effect of protection against the 'Millennium Bug', legacy systems were overhauled, migrated to new environments, or replaced, wholly new desktop and server infrastructures were created, email and internet access rolled out universally across organizations, and local and wide area network arrangements reviewed.

That is not to say that IT infrastructure is now perfect, or that there are no challenges remaining: in a drive to improve service and cut costs, many organizations are investing in enterprise management tools (to make control and maintenance of the IT 'estate' easier and gain wider benefits, for example by automating software updates such as virus protection); user administration and directory systems are being

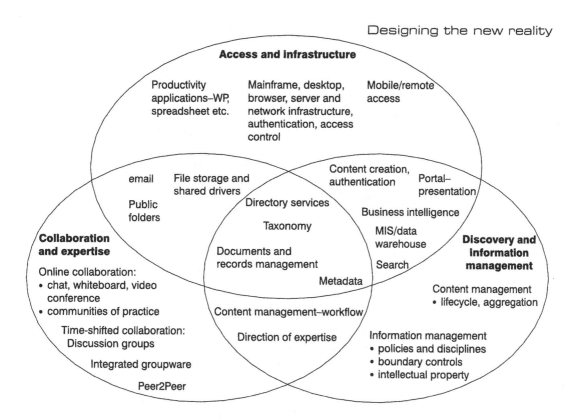

Figure 4.11 The three dimensions of knowledge and information technology

updated and unified (an important enabler in efforts to implement content personalization, as we shall discuss); while the issue of vastly increased support for remote or mobile workers continues to be a difficult one. Practical, usable, portable devices and the mobile telephony or wireless network infrastructures needed to support them (GPRS, Bluetooth, etc.) have been slow to become available and even slower to mature into reliable business tools. But as time passes, the infrastructure discussion moved increasingly beyond the basics to more elevated concerns.

Before 2000, the issue was universality of access: get basic tools (word processing, spreadsheets, relevant applications, email, internet, intranet) out to all workers who needed them. Now, with this infrastructure in place, discussions are much more likely to focus on how it is used, maintained, and exploited for business benefit.

But with all this focus on the basic infrastructure, some things have been slow to change. For most organizations today, the majority of documents are still located either on local hard drives, or on file systems, such as NT, UNIX. The shared network drive is still by far the most common document repository for individuals or workgroups who need to share files. The most common alternative, the sharing of files through email attachments, is even less satisfactory – mailbox sizes for every user of more than 100 Mb are now common-place, and without a viable file-sharing alternative, pressure to continually increase mailbox limits this can only grow. Expanding data protection or industry regulatory require-ments – which are only beginning to catch up with the issues surrounding digital records – may force firms to retain infor-mation in their archives almost indefinitely and are another driver for a more coherent approach in this area.

While they do have an impact on the shape of any mobilizing knowledge programme, the most pressing infrastructure issues (networks, desktop design issues) are beyond the scope of this book. What we will focus on are the issues that are either KM-specific, or essential prerequisites whose imple-mentation has significant impact on the success of the overall KM effort. We will deal with the following in turn:

Access and infrastructure:

- Directory and meta-directory services
- Taxonomy and information classification
- File storage and document sharing
- Document and electronic records management
- Metadata and search
- Intranets and the role of the portal.

Discovery and information management:

- Search and content aggregation
- Content management – lifecycle and workflow
- Management information systems, business intelligence and data warehousing.

Collaboration and expertise:

- Email use
- Document sharing – from email to public folders to communities
- Directories of expertise
- Collaborative tools – synchronous/asynchronous.

Access and infrastructure

Directory and meta-directory services

With such a focus on the human elements of KM throughout this book, it may be surprising to begin consideration of KM technologies with such an apparently dry and mechanistic topic: but it is no exaggeration to say that the degree of sophistication with which KM technology tools can be deployed hangs largely on the directory facilities implemented by the enterprise.

Directories are the tools by which organizations manage their user base – the individual usernames, passwords and permissions associated with each user, and increasingly the details of the hardware and software that these users have access to. Managing this 'identity' information is a far from straightforward function, especially when managing systems with a large number of users, logging on to many different servers, widely dispersed geographically across wide area networks with complex 'trust' relationships controlling who has access to what.

Information about applications, people, hardware and software is scattered all over the organization – and is continuing to proliferate. Some of it is stored in conventional directory services – but the majority of it tends to be found in custom databases or in the data files of proprietary software. Identity management becomes an issue when organizations want to start to better manage the overall 'IT estate' (introducing organization-wide enterprise management to reduce the cost of IT support, for example). But there are other situations when it becomes important:

- Secure authentication and log-in – global directories need to be in place to underpin services such as 'intranet self-service', where users can update personnel records or book travel arrangements. This also applies to e-commerce roll-outs.
- Single sign-on – this sits a step below secure authentication but the goal is to put an end to username, password and access problems across different platforms and networks. This is considered a must when introducing personalization of content delivery via a corporate portal.
- Global email – particularly in merger situations, bringing together disparate organizations into a single email address book, and presenting a common face to the outside world, which can be a real challenge

As each additional layer of complexity is added – a new system to manage, a new network application deployed – the number of places identity information is stored increases. The ideal situation – a single directory designed to contain all available information about devices, users and networks, which is at the same time the central authority for network security – remains a pipedream for most companies, constrained as they are by the limitations of ever-changing organizational boundaries and hard to maintain legacy applications.

There is no silver bullet for this situation but companies such as Novell (with recent releases of Novell Directory Services) and Microsoft (with Active Directory) have been busy introducing so-called 'metadirectory' tools that reach out across networks, providing connectivity to enable sharing, synchronization and integrity checking of information across standard directory applications (for example, running X.500 or LDAP protocols), and custom databases and legacy systems.

The issue of managing identity information in organizations goes beyond a strictly KM brief, into areas regarded as the province of network architects and systems designers. But the importance of having one single version of the 'truth' when it comes to information about the people in an organization is critical to much that a KM programme seeks to provide: from an integrated email and telephone list, to personalized content management, to an enterprise-wide directory of expertise, it can't easily be done without a solid global directory foundation.

Taxonomy and information classification

Directories enable us to manage the user base of the organization – and the infrastructure they depend on – in an integrated, organized and structured fashion. Taxonomies fulfil a similar role for information – providing a single, logical and coherent structure. At its simplest, a taxonomy is a structured set of categories – a little like a dictionary, or perhaps a thesaurus (though even that is not quite a complete analogy). Arguably the most 'visible' and consequently best-known taxonomy is the one that drives Yahoo.com – a multi-nested forest of information, which attempts to provide a classification of the world of information accessible from the World Wide Web.

The point of any taxonomy is to make distinctions between categories down to a point where this is useful (in terms of enabling people to store something in the right place, and then find it again), and no further: a well-designed taxonomy is not about splitting hairs for the sake of it – it has to reflect the world view and experience of the organization concerned, to reflect how people's brains work (hoping to avoid a potentially paralysing, large-scale corporate version of the 'lost document' syndrome commonly found in home-grown, domestic filing systems: does the stub of the credit card bill you just paid get filed under V for 'Visa card bill', B for 'bill', C for 'credit card bills', or P for 'paid'? Thank heavens that most domestic filing doesn't have sub-folders!). In creating a taxonomy, it is important to gain an understanding of how information is generated and used within the organization, learning to anticipate how users are likely to attempt to find things, and perhaps most importantly, gain knowledge of the many ways in which users associate information and form them into shared mental categories.

Taking Yahoo as an example, we end up with something similar to Figure 4.12.

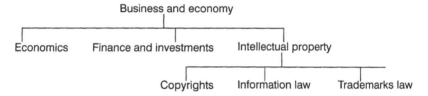

Figure 4.12
Example of a taxonomy

This is a truncated example, but demonstrates that the divisions in Yahoo's view of the world are somewhat arbitrary. In terms of corporate taxonomies, the nested Yahoo example is particularly relevant as it demonstrates the 'use' of taxonomies: taxonomies are not technology *per se*, but are used to provide the underlying data structures used by intranets and document management systems. The data structure itself is just a text file – no clever technology needed – but the applications to which it is put can be very sophisticated.

The burgeoning interest in taxonomies has come about as organizations grapple with improving ways to enable users to find information, using a variety of approaches from browsing to advanced search. Taxonomies tend therefore to be used for one (or more) of the following:

- As *corporate taxonomies* – often the replication or evolution of former corporate or departmental paper filing systems, carried over or built upon to become the classification structure for new electronic systems such as document management or intranet-based document repositories.

- To support *automated indexing* of documents and web content in document management or intranet repositories, or on specified other repositories (including internet sites) defined as useful sources.
- As the structure created or woven by *automatic categorization* software.

Corporate taxonomies

Most organizations, large or small, have a schema for filing paper information – the organization-wide one is often supplemented by schemas created at divisional or business unit level, and these are often the basis for the creation of a new taxonomy for use in information systems. One advantage of starting with the ready-approved corporate model is that they reflect the existing knowledge and information base of the organization – and therefore have significant value in their own right as an important information asset. The down side is that opportunities may be lost to sort anomalies, address departmental silos, or create a structure that is perhaps less tied to the organizational structure, leading to fewer problems if the structure should change (a frequent occurrence in most organizations). Depending on the how this corporate taxonomy is used, it may be possible to use it to browse the information filed or stored according to the taxonomy structure.

The difference between a filing system and a taxonomy is that the taxonomy is virtual: in a filing system, a document needs to physically reside in a specific file (requiring multiple copies for multiple files if more than one location is thought necessary). A piece of content may reside in a specific folder on a specific server, according to the taxonomy – but this would be a fairly unsophisticated way to go about things. Instead, the taxonomy classification can be added to the document's *metadata* (the data record containing information about the document – this will be discussed later) and so retrieved through searching that record. In this way, multiple classifications are easily possible).

Automated indexing

One of the ways that search engines work is to parse the text of documents (and sometimes to use shape recognition to parse graphic elements too) and to index text for retrieval when specific keywords are entered by users. Some more advanced search engines use taxonomies to help categorize documents in appropriate places – they can be programmed, for example, to recognize from a group of, say, aerospace technical terms to classify a document as belonging to a particular aerospace specialism, even though the word 'aerospace', or even the word for the particular aerospace specialism, never appears. This is achieved through careful matching of the taxonomy to a thesaurus of specialist language. Advanced automated indexing of this kind is extremely powerful and increasingly accurate – the only down side is that it is time-consuming and expensive to set up, and only really worthwhile for large organizations with large-scale information management needs.

Automatic categorization

The key to this technology is a process of automatic categorization: the system, though using a variety of clever algorithms, is able to make sense of a subset of information in order to create an outline taxonomy (consisting of navigation structure and category names – this bears a strong resemblance to an empty website). Some technologies also build an apparent awareness of context based upon 'training': administrators or developers spend time asking users questions about particular information, establishing and inputting information about 'what is', 'why', and 'how' relationships, which again, in turn, creates an outline taxonomy.

Enthusiasts of automated categorization insist that every-increasing automation of this process is the ultimate future for taxonomy development: using automated linguistic analysis technology to summarize and categorize text, and ramping up speed and scale by carrying out federated searches across multiple databases, leading to rapid processing of large volumes of content. The goal in all of this is higher levels of consistency and ever-greater speed.

Others – the authors among them – view this with some scepticism, having experience of projects where automated taxonomy software was thrown out in mid-course and replaced with technology based on 'normal', i.e. human-generated, taxonomies. Conventional taxonomies do require greater user input and a higher degree of user awareness, but our experience is that the productivity potential is substantially greater when deployed correctly.

One thing is certain, though: automated technologies, when perfected, will certainly have the edge over manual methods in terms of cost, and over time, the technology will only get better. But in our view, it isn't there yet.

File storage and document sharing

Far from the rarefied world of automated taxonomies is the humble departmental or workgroup file server or shared network drive. Usually 'local' (either in a physical sense of sitting under a desk in a particular location, or belonging to a particular, localized group of people) the G:\ (or H:\, J:\, K:\ or L:\ drive. . .) is the workhorse of information sharing in most organizations, providing backed-up personal storage for individuals, electronic folders for 'common' or regularly shared folders, and a repository for sharing documents locally among a defined group of people.

There is great affection for the shared drive – but it has some severe limitations:

- Documents are identified only by their physical 'place in the hierarchy' and their filename – it is possible to search Microsoft Office documents by the rudimentary 'metadata' stored in document properties. In most situations no one really fills it in – while the content inside the files is locked away from desktop search tools.
- The 'free use' concept of the shared drive often means that no individual is responsible for tidying up – with a result that after a period, it can get clogged up with files and folders – about many of which nothing is known (especially if left behind by someone who has left the organization).
- They are 'local' or departmental in nature and often tied to the physical office in which they reside – network permissions may not be easily obtainable to enable sharing outside the charmed circle of local users – or not possible at all if security restrictions across network domains are strictly applied.

Much the same criticisms can be made of other related document-sharing technologies: for example, public folders (a Microsoft Exchange technology accessible via Microsoft Outlook) may enable wider sharing than with a local workgroup, but the other issues still apply, while email (with all the problems of waste of bandwidth, multiple storage of files, and lack of version control) is not a satisfactory long term or large scale answer for document sharing.

So what is the future for the shared network drive? We believe it still has some life in it yet, and any workgroup level mobilizing knowledge initiative should certainly expend some effort on examining its function for the group, and in establishing some housekeeping rules and responsibilities (as well as providing training in its use).

But there are, increasingly, alternatives, whether in the form of 'collaborative' KM solutions which have a records and document management component (such as Open Text's Livelink suite), or in tools designed specifically for the purpose of making the shared network drive obsolete, such as Microsoft's SharePoint product set. We have, on the whole, been avoiding discussion of particular products in this book (largely because the KM software market is so vast, with many products overlapping). However, SharePoint is worth a mention as it is aimed primarily at the workgroup and departmental marketplace, with particular tools for rapid taxonomy development based around categories and metadata, and the ability to point to and index pre-existing content repositories such as shared network drives and public folders, enabling sophisticated search capability to be deployed across this pre-existing document-based content, while new document contents can be categorized according to the taxonomy. It is our view that SharePoint (or Livelink, or some similar technology) is without doubt the future of departmental information sharing for many organizations (and, since basic workflow tools to handle approval for publication are built in, may even provide sufficient functionality for many 'for the record' document management needs too).

Document and electronic records management

Organizations have always had a need to store documents and maintain records: whether, in the public sector, to meet the guidelines set out by the Public Records Office, or in the private sector, to meet statutory obligations in the areas of finance, tax or employment legislation, or to protect themselves in contractual or intellectual property matters. This is not a new phenomenon, and certainly existed even in the days of paper – the authors know of one government department which has to bear the cost of three large central London buildings which are used for nothing but filing of paperwork (kept for a minimum of seven years, some categories much longer than that), while another keeps its older records 200 miles away in Yorkshire. Fewer than 5% of documents are ever looked at again after being sent for filing – but as you never know which 5%, they all have to be kept for the time allotted.

Several elements have come together at once to drive both private and public sector firms to push towards all-electronic records and document management:

- The cost of big city office space – this makes keeping paper files an expensive business.
- Universally accessible, high-quality infrastructure in the wake of Y2K – this wasn't available in the past to the same extent.
- Coming legislative changes: in government, Freedom of Information, and in both public and private sector, changes in data protection law.

People often confuse technologies designed primarily for information sharing – mainly intranet-based tools – with document management systems. The distinction we would employ is this one:

- Document management is designed 'for the record' – documents are version controlled, authenticated, and stored according to a suitable corporate taxonomy. The degree of control extends to check-in, check-out processes and frequently to 'workflow' behind the scenes which might specify a process of authoring and approval. The intention is to store the document under strict controls for formal, official or legal purposes. Full-blown document management systems also often have 'imaging' capability.
- Document sharing is intended as altogether more loose – the intention of 'publishing', to make material available either to an immediate peer group or to the whole organization. Many of the same controls need to be in place – workflow to manage approval, taxonomy to manage classification – but the degree of formality of the process can be much less – and the process of managing the document record much more straightforward.

Historically, the distinction has been fairly straightforward in that document management has been traditionally 'owned' by industrial-strength, proprietary systems, while document sharing has been limited by often fairly basic intranet publishing capability. However, with technologies such as the SharePoint product set – which brings many high-end features to the workgroup and enables easy integration with existing intranet content sources – coming along, and intranet integration capability beginning to be integrated with more traditional, formerly client–server-based document management products such as FileNet and Meridio, the landscape is changing.

The issue of records management in conjunction with document management adds an additional layer of complexity. The 'file' record may encompass information about many different documents – perhaps drafts or versions of an original (all of which – or a selection, depending on the set-up – may continue to be accessible). The record contains information on what 'file' a document belongs to – the file being a virtual entity with a taxonomy categorization applied, that links up related documents. But records management doesn't just apply to documents – it is becoming a very important element of web content management too, storing information about content version and delivery.

Records management issues have come to the fore in this area because of the increasing importance of corporate intranets in decision-making, particularly in the public sector. With paper folders, it is relatively easy to track back and find out precisely what information an individual had access to at a particular time of day when a decision was taken. However, with traditional, HTML-driven intranet-based delivery of information, it isn't possible to be clear on precisely what information was at an individual's disposal – even if regular 'snapshots' of the status of the intranet are taken, it is not always possible to be certain a particular piece of information was either present or missing. New advances in records management – storing a record of all intranet content changes, with the possibility of recreating the site as viewed by any given individual at a particular time – are beginning to make this kind of roll-back a reality. This is not just relevant for public sector bodies: in a contractual dispute with, say, an extranet partner, it could be important to demonstrate precisely what information was published at what moment. This is an important consideration for anyone looking to move forward with intranet technologies.

Beyond content-management-related records, organizations need to keep a wider, more traditional set of records of business decisions and transactions to meet the demands of the organization's accountability, and to service their own information needs. A record is evidence of an activity or decision and demonstrates accountability. Such records are created by the day-to-day work in the organization; and they need to be captured, managed and preserved in an organized system that maintains their integrity and authenticity, retaining their value as retrievable corporate records.

The following is a summary of the typical requirements for electronic records management:

- capturing, storing, indexing and retrieving all elements of the record as a complex unit, and for all types of record
- management of records within class categories or filing structures to maintain the narrative links between records – i.e. at the file/folder level
- storage of record-level metadata including retention and disposal rules
- integration between electronic and paper records
- secure storage and management to ensure authenticity and accountability, including support for legal and regulatory requirements – preventing change to content
- appraisal and selection of records for preservation and transfer to a permanent archive (or in the case of government, the Public Records Office)
- management facilities for the systematic retention and safe-keeping of records
- migration and export of records for permanent preservation without loss of information.

While there is overlap between the characteristics of electronic documents and electronic records, the key difference is that electronic records are documents which have been captured into a corporate classification and filing system, retain the links between documents, and are subject to business rules on retention and disposal. An electronic record management system must preserve content, structure and context of the electronic records, and must ensure that records are 'registered' and that authentication procedures and audit trails are put in place. This will in turn permit these records to be used as legal evidence, improve corporate accountability and assist organizations in meeting the requirements of internal and external auditors.

Many organizations require both electronic document management and electronic records management. These are closely related functions, which are rapidly converging, as corporate records management becomes a mainstream application. They may sometimes be found in a single integrated software package, supporting the management of electronic information in different but complementary ways.

Metadata and search

Metadata is information about information. A familiar example of metadata is the front cover of a book, containing the book title, author, publisher, and perhaps the ISBN number – simple metadata which tells the reader about the book. Other metadata might include the abstract – the 'blurb' on the dust jacket or the back cover – and even the table of contents. If this were to be translated to the electronic arena, then a metadata record of the book's content might include all of these things, in addition to other (electronically collectable) information such as file format, file creation date, and last modification date

So what's the difference between electronic records and metadata? Partly purpose, though in some aspects, perhaps, there is no distinction: although electronic records have a life of their own as a unique and valuable information base, they *are* made up of 100% of metadata, that is 'data about data'.

Some documents allow metadata to be incorporated into their structure – we have already described the tag fields accessible via a Word document's Properties box, which contains various author-editable metadata – room for a full title (not constrained by filename conventions), subject, author's name, and various boxes for category, keywords and comments. (Word also collects a variety of non-editable metadata such as creation and last edit dates.)

Just about all other electronically generated documents also have some kind of metadata attached, sometimes editable: for example, HTML documents can have ⟨meta⟩ tags attached, to provide indexing tools with information that doesn't appear in the text. A standard set of metadata fields – the Dublin Core – has been defined, which can be used to provide the right format for metadata in many different contexts, from page design information in XML documents to information about performers in MP3 files. XML – Extensible Markup Language – is a much more structured document format than HTML, built around metadata which can potentially be used to specify not just how to control how the data in the document should be presented (as with HTML's markup tags) but also how the data should interact with other data in the viewing application.

In a KM context, the role of metadata is twofold: to assist with content management from creation to delivery, and to assist with search. Metadata's importance in search primarily revolves around use of keyword and taxonomy information – for example, metadata may allow us to distinguish between an article *by* Bill Gates and one *about* Bill Gates – an important distinction.

One final issue involving metadata involves some tools that are starting to become effective – and used to good effect on some technical and academic repositories. Auto summarizing generates (with minimal human intervention) a summary or précis of a document, that gets inserted into metadata fields and is made available as a useful abstract when presented to a user following a search. This technology is closely related to developments with automated taxonomy and machine interpretation of natural language. While human-generated summaries or abstracts clearly remain significantly superior, this technology has significant potential in making sense (and improving availability) of existing large archives of content, where there is no cost justification for revisiting of the archive by a human editor.

Intranets, personalization and the role of the portal

It has taken us a long time in this chapter to arrive at a discussion of the role of intranets. This is because, at this level of magnification, the intranet itself begins to disappear. What we see instead are its components: search tools, taxonomies, content management systems, document publishing tools – and portals.

Portals are primarily concerned with the presentation of information to users. The challenge – and the promise – of the coming generation of corporate portals is to simplify access to information and application functionality, within a single environment that is totally transparent to the user. They are the 'top level' of any corporate intranet, sitting above applications access, content management, search, and all other functionality.

There was a period around 1999–2001 when company intranets almost went out of fashion – in large part because the early adopting organizations that initially implemented them failed to reap the business benefits they anticipated (as promised by their promoters in the early years of web technologies). But it is apparent that since that time, the notion of the corporate portal has returned with a vengeance. In large part, this is due to significantly improved technology (particularly off-the-shelf tools) – and also to (as we have previously discussed) the revamped and standardized desktop and network infrastructure forced on organizations by Y2K, which companies are increasingly looking to exploit for financial return. But it is also due to an increasing realization within organizations that technology alone is not the answer to anything – rather, the business fit, the detail which goes into the implementation, and the focus on change management all need to be in place, as well as a solid business case, before any money is spent.

With the rise of the 'knowledge economy' (which certainly didn't go away in the downward stock market following the bursting of the dot.com bubble), the baseline of corporate value has expanded from a focus on bricks and mortar to an emphasis on intellectual capital, with a commensurate need to make organizational information and personally held knowledge more *visible*, more *measurable* and more importantly, more *manageable* – all tasks well suited to next-generation intranet technologies.

The knowledge economy debate has led to a progressive redefinition of the value of corporate information, and an acknowledgement that collecting and analysing data (the old function of information management) is only the first step – the real step forward comes in enabling and empowering people to use that information *effectively*. Such an approach becomes increasingly necessary as organizations increasingly come to rely on consolidated information for strategic (as well as just tactical) decision-making, which means getting this information to end users in an easy and timely manner becomes critical to company success. In today's fast-moving business climate, organizations that don't have the capability to learn from, and respond rapidly to, changes in the external market environment, stand little chance of long-term survival.

So what is the role of the portal in this trend? From a user perspective, portals appear to be just another kind of home page, albeit in more sophisticated form. But the technology driver for portals comes from rather a different angle: frustration with the limitations of the standard desktop and conventional graphical user interface, which hasn't changed in its base conception since the launch of the first Apple Macintosh in 1984 – the desktop metaphor remains the same (though obviously expanded in functionality). By desktop, we mean more than the start-up screen in Windows, with its groupings of folders and application icons. Behind this sits a raft of separate applications, functions and data processes, different servers and services, and, through email and web technologies and various collaborative tools, interaction with the world outside the enterprise. Any task which needs access to information sources, transaction-based services (such as forms to fill out), communication, or content creation (usually done in Office applications) requires workers to be quite skilled in using a whole raft of different tools and services scattered around their working environment. The challenge – and the promise – of today's generation of corporate portal is to simplify these processes, providing a gateway to services and information that works intuitively within a single environment that is totally transparent to the user.

So, out of all this, have we a definition of the portal? Here's ours:

> A tool that provides the individual worker with personalized access to, and interaction with, information, applications and business processes relevant to their role in the organization – a gateway to corporate knowledge and systems.

This definition is, of necessity, a little broad. What we have seen is that many vendors have jumped on the portals 'bandwagon' – the common thread in the emergence of portal products being to take a basic intranet solution and expand the range of services accessible from within it, while at the same time offering the ability to hide from the users the complexity of information processing (from disparate information sources) which lies behind. The result is a more or less unitary view of corporate information.

The term 'portal' had a life in the early years of the Web – the first real one was Yahoo, which in the beginning was no more than a collection of listings categorized by theme. Faced with the challenge of alternative technologies based on smart search – first through Alta Vista, then by Google – Yahoo's offering is now much more sophisticated, but is still essentially a collection of links (based on the Yahoo taxonomy).

The eventual model for corporate portals came some time later – as organizations (many owned by publishing companies, used to managing rich sources of specialist material) attempted to set up commercial stall on the World Wide Web with a portal (or gateway) into specialist material, both local content and relevant links. Areas of interest from wristwatches to world music got their own 'portals' of variable quality. What was almost universal here, though, was the lack of sophistication in content management.

What arose out of this – applying to both publicly available web content and to the first truly functional corporate intranets –

were the first off-the-shelf portal software products. For our purposes, 'real' portal solutions began as server-based tools using web-based presentation to offer **content aggregation:** this is the display, organization and presentation of information within the portal, usually accompanied by a basic **search** engine which allows the user to search for information within the portal environment. At this level, **personalization** consists of aggregating information for specific workgroups (either within business units or cross-organizational 'communities of practice'). Some solutions added lightweight **business process functionality** (simple forms with actions associated), commonly through the use of scripts.

Second generation portal tools (now mature technology) began to focus on **integration** with multiple content sources, providing a greater level of business process functionality via access to traditional information applications through portal components. Second generation tools also offered a more sophisticated search capability (often based on detailed taxonomies) to serve context-based queries. This is all supported by a robust framework to develop functionality around 'portal components'.

Figure 4.13 is useful in describing how this functionality (across both first and second generation portals) works in practice.

Figure 4.13
Portal dimensions
(Knight and Azar 2002
– reproduced with
permission of *KM*
Magazine)

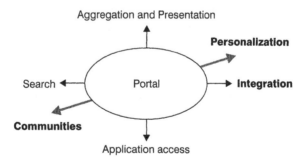

The 'compass' points on this grid define the essential features of a corporate portal:

- Content aggregation and presentation – single view of multiple sources
- Application access (including business process functionality)
- Search tools – pointed at multiple courses
- Integration – with a range of sources across servers, platforms networks etc.

Beyond the compass grid there are additional dimensions, labelled as running across both **Communities** and **Personalization.** This is where the role of portals moves beyond technical considerations into providing support for mobilizing knowledge between people across organizations. The 'compass grid' feature set – Aggregation, Search, Integration and Applications access – may provide employment and entertainment for technical specialists – but real business benefit lies across the other axis.

The 'Communities' axis determines the social and cultural context in which information is used. Activity on this axis will determine, in large measure, whether the portal will meet the needs of the business. There are questions to be asked here around motivation to contribute, access and reuse information, maintenance of content, and overall culture of involvement – whether people in the organization expect to dip into an information repository and find information (structured or unstructured) without putting anything back in, or whether the culture is a more dynamic one of involvement, participation, and sharing of personally held knowledge and expertise.

Likewise with 'Personalization': where the culture of participation is high, personalization can be focused on quick access to relevant, commonly used, information sources and tools. We believe personalization has been misunderstood to some extent. Role-based personalization, where not just content but application services are tailored to individual need – is, in the authors' view, where most benefit is to be gained preferable to individual customization in most cases. Although the tools exist to allow individuals an infinitely customizable working environment, we do not believe that there is a push among individuals for extreme flexibility in presentation and access, nor is there a strong business case for it (indeed, lack of business motivation and the amount of training required to enable effective use of such features would appear, for the moment, to work against too high a level of individual personalization or ability to manipulate presentation within the user interface).

Discovery and information management

Search and content aggregation

We have established that aggregation is a key technology element of a portal. Aggregation – bringing together content from multiple sources – is primarily a function of search (whether that search is one knowingly generated by the user, or is the result of the user clicking a link that triggers a search for available content relating to that link). In most organizations, information is spread over multiple systems and formats.

Today's more advanced search tools are able to connect through interface software into remote repositories, and understand content within them through a variety of 'filters' for different content formats. Usually the connecting is done by linking to a repository and identifying metadata fields which can be pointed back to the system hosting the search tools. This allows users to run searches across the new repository, concurrent with searches across existing repositories (what users are really doing – though this is hidden from them – is searching for information through an index, which is a map containing metadata of content alongside key words from the various repositories). The ability to search across multiple repositories means that the user never needs to know the physical location of any of the content he or she wants to access.

Search technologies have evolved considerably from simple 'and, or' type queries to the more advanced queries. Types of queries normally found can be categorized into four groups:

- Keyword
- Boolean query
- Context search
- Phrase search.

Keyword

Keyword searches operate on document metadata (often in conjunction with the taxonomy classifications) to deliver content which has been tagged with a particular marker.

> *Example*: search for keywords 'Budget, 1997' might deliver content about Gordon Brown's incoming budget after the Labour Party's first election victory – but only if the document or content item had been either categorized under an appropriate heading, or had the correct keywords applied when the document metadata was assembled or saved.

Boolean

Boolean is the oldest kind of query and harks back to a past where search and discovery technologies were driven primarily by academics (mostly mathematicians). Boolean search is most useful when searching free text, where content can be added, excluded and refined by adding the operators 'and', 'or', 'not' etc.

Example: search for 'cats' not 'dogs'.

This will bring back any content containing the words 'cats' and not 'dogs'.

Example: search for 'The cat jumped over the moon'.

This will bring back anything to do with any of the words in the sentences

Context

A more advanced form of searching – based on use of a thesaurus which recognizes that words used in the search but not in the content of a document may have an equivalent meaning:

Example: search for 'President of USA'.

This might bring back content containing information about something along the lines of 'George W. Bush, elected in 2001' – the phrase 'president of the USA' might be mapped to the names of various incumbents to achieve this result.

The quality of context-based search is dependent on the comprehensiveness and accuracy of the thesaurus, and the configuration of keywords – this is what determines how 'clever' the search engine is. The configuration is based on complex logic embedded in the system to determine probability of words occurring in different contexts, and stemming techniques used to breakdown meanings of sentences and words.

Phrase search

Again based around free text search, phrase search specifically looks for a set of words precisely expressed in a document:

Example: search for 'The cat jumped over the moon'.

Will bring back a document containing only this exact sentence match.

When setting up search engines, it is important to consider how the users are likely to utilize them to find information.

However clever your taxonomy (which might allow browsing) or your metadata (which allows clever use of keyword searches), users on the whole are most likely to use free text-based searching – or perhaps phrase queries if they are moderately advanced users. Successful use of search is partly a matter of familiarity – getting the users to feel confident about technology and what it can do for them – and training. Our experience is that some of the worst complainers in organizations (about the inability to find things on intranet or document management systems) are people who have not been shown how to use search tools properly – quick coaching even in something as simple as Boolean rules can help these individuals to be much more productive.

Content management – lifecycle and workflow

If portals are about aggregation and presentation of content at the point where the user needs it, then content management is about creating, storing, processing and maintaining that content behind the scenes.

Key aspects of content management include **lifecycle management** (from creation to publication to expiry) and **workflow management** (focused on submission, approval and renewal) that were once mainly the concern of organizations in the publishing business, but are now an area of focus for all organizations seeking to capture, classify, make available and (most importantly) reuse or repurpose information content created by staff. There is also the issue of **repurposing**: managing the translation of content between different formats, appropriate for delivery in different contexts, and on different devices or platforms.

Figure 4.14 shows how portals and content management are interrelated: while 'Translation' and 'Search' exist as independent applications sitting across both categories, it is fairly easy to split out most of the roles of a portal (whose primary role is to provide the user interface for 'consumption' of information) and content management (primarily concerned with production and management of content).

Lifecycle management

The principal role of content management is managing the lifecycle of content. In our experience of analysing why first generation corporate intranet projects have often 'failed', a

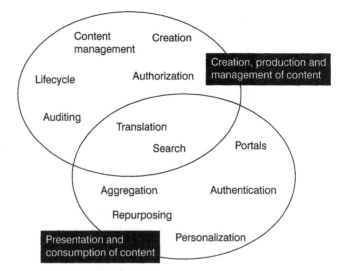

Figure 4.14
Content management
and portal alignment
(Knight and Azar
2002)

consistent reason given by users why the system hasn't
delivered benefit is unreliability of content: specifically, problems with multiple versions, inconsistency in availability (only
turning up a portion of documents or articles known to exist),
and most importantly, the amount of out-of-date content they
come across.

In the early days of HTML, every page was coded by hand:
HTML tags were inserted into text files specifying heading styles,
font sizes, and graphics placement. As the language of HTML
grew more complex, editors such as Microsoft FrontPage and
Macromedia DreamWeaver emerged to enable this process to be
carried out by editors and designers without the need to directly
create HTML code (using HTML-style sheets, for example, to
ensure consistency of display). This contributed to an explosion
of content and a variety of ingenious solutions – the majority of
them home-grown – to automate the page generation process,
often combining use of 'templates' into which content is put for
display/playback, and content databases. For text, these databases were mostly relational; for graphics and streamed sound
and video, object-oriented databases (which store content as self-
contained objects) were preferred.

Modern off-the-shelf content management products follow the
principles derived from these early systems, and use a variety of
methods to take raw content – funnelled in from automated data
collection systems or online news feeds, created through
standard desktop authoring tools, or input via forms on the
browser – and manage the whole life of that content through

amending and acting on the metadata associated with that piece of content.

For example:

- A news feed sends raw text (ASCII) via a comms link into a receiving content management application – that text is parsed and metadata (such as content tags or creation date) separated from the news report to create a tagged item – that item is then made available to the personalization system in the portal – and delivered as content via an appropriate display template to users whose profile requested it. Otherwise it is stored, indexed and made available to all users via the search interface, and expired or archived after a set period.
- A component in a portal displays the latest sales figures to the user – the content management system behind the scenes manages the interface to the system that collects or calculates that data, delivers it to the portal, and expires it after a set period or when new data is available.
- A worker publishes a document to a 'community of practice' site on a particular topic. The worker does this by posting it via a web form, simultaneously giving it a classification under the corporate taxonomy. Once entered, the document and its related metadata (including this classification) is indexed and made available for search to those people with appropriate permissions to see it. The content is visible for a period and after a set time, an email is automatically sent to the author asking if it is still current (if the author has left the company, a mail can be sent automatically to the content administrator). The user can either authorize it for republication, or ignore the mail, at which point it is automatically deleted from the system after a given period.

It can be seen from the above examples – and there are many more scenarios that could be outlined – that the range of tasks carried out by content management systems is substantial, and that the number of external points of contact can also be considerable. We earlier used the phase 'off-the-shelf content management products', but the reality is that unless requirements are extremely basic, any content management product will require considerable work to integrate it with existing systems. Having said that – the potential benefits, in terms of reduction in effort to publish and maintain content, and in the integrity and currency of content available – are also very substantial. No serious intranet is possible today without a functional content management system to control the content lifecycle.

One new feature which is beginning to be found in content management systems is records-based auditing functionality (as mentioned previously), giving the ability to track not just who published what at what time, but also who has accessed content, and what content was on view at a specific moment – a form of 'rolling back' to previous versions which up till now has proved difficult (indeed, impossible in most configurations).

Workflow management

Tied closely into content lifecycle is workflow. One of the problems with the 'traditional' method of building intranets is the problem of approval – the person who authors content is not necessarily the person who has to approve it, and it may be someone different again who has responsibility for ensuring its publication in a given form or style.

There is often considerable focus on workflow within full-featured document management systems – many have tools which enable quite a complex document generation, collaboration, approval and publication process (either using external workflow tools, such as the ones present in Lotus Notes, or using third party or proprietary software).

Workflow – though generally less sophisticated – is also an important element within content management systems. Generally, approval is the main process (sometimes achieved using simple scripting), using lists and rules (e.g. 'only one has to approve', 'or all have to approve in list'). Notifications are often sent by email and/or within the content management system itself. Workflow tools may also be used to help manage the content expiry process as outlined above.

Repurposing

While the main 'presentation layer' tends to reside with the portal software, content management systems may have a role to play in delivering appropriate content to non-standard devices. Although slow to get started, demand is quietly building for delivery of content to a range of mobile devices, such as mobile phones (through Wireless Access Protocol or WAP pages), Palm devices (though rudimentary plain text internet browsers with some limited graphics capability) or Microsoft WindowsCE-based devices with fairly full-featured web browsers incorporating colour, image and sound such as Compaq's iPaq.

None of these devices is particularly high powered at the moment, and they are also bandwidth constrained in terms of the speed of the telephony or wireless signal they can accept (at least until 3G mobile technologies become commonplace), and all make use of various server-side technologies to tailor and reformat content, which is delivered to the various devices in the form of templates (content is formatted using a variety of templates, each of which can be created for specific devices).

At the moment, much of this is still done by hand, though some vendors (for example, Cisco with its Content Transformation Engine provide this functionality through a bolt-on 'black box' approach). However, it is expected to get easier in the near future if, as expected, demand for these sorts of services continues to grow, as organizations make greater use of the potential of mobile devices.

Management information systems, business intelligence and data warehousing

Organizations gather and process vast amounts of data – on individual projects and transactions involving customers, on the activities and performance of staff, and on the flows of funds around the organization and between the organization and customers, partners and suppliers. Turning this into management information for decision-makers has long been a crucial role of the IT or IS department.

Both the variety and complexity of data and information collected – to say nothing of the volume – have increased vastly in recent years – making it progressively harder to get hold of the right information for decision-making. Although the issue of management information has traditionally been seen as a purely IT question – and certainly, the issue surrounding set-up and management of very large-scale mainframe financial systems or data warehouses are beyond the scope of this book – the question of 'use' puts the issue of management information firmly in the arena of mobilizing knowledge.

Beyond summary reports generated by financial systems – cash flows, customer numbers etc. – additional information sits in all sorts of places around the business – most commonly in personal or workgroup spreadsheets or databases. A range of new, relatively easy to implement business intelligence software (such as the toolset supporting the Microsoft Data Warehousing Framework) allow individuals to interact directly with data contained across these individual repositories – supporting decision-making by:

- Manipulating the presentation of data, using graphical devices, colour coding and sorting/filtering capabilities to identify and plot trends that might otherwise be very hard to spot, as well as visualize relationships between data sets.
- Create summary data, then 'drill down' into relevant fine detail.

The sort of effort required to bring together locally held historical business data, data warehouse information, and other operational data that may be being collected but not fully integrated into existing systems, can be fairly substantial – but a useful spin-off is that it helps build an integrated, consistent view of the business. However, as the principal beneficiaries of this sort of system are generally managers and people at the 'top' of the company, it tends to be fairly easy to make the business case as they can usually visualize the benefits without any difficulty.

Business intelligence tools are often deployed as part of Balanced Scorecard introduction – automating the collection, collation and presentation of Balanced Scorecard data.

Collaboration and expertise

For those with little experience of the topic area, the term 'knowledge management' tends to mean one of two things: intranets, or (if they have been paying a little more attention) sharing and collaboration tools. The theme of this book is that the goal of any mobilizing knowledge initiative is changing how people structure their time – and one of the main changes that any initiative needs to bring about is to improve collaboration and sharing. In this section we discuss the principal tools to help support and enable this improvement.

Email use

Email is all-pervasive these days – but very few organizations do it 'right'. Used correctly, email is the number one collaborative tool, perhps the most useful communications method in the organization. However, used badly and it becomes an anchor holding up production across the board. Carry out an audit of the main knowledge and information problems facing most organizations, and email comes out at the top of the list: people who have to cope with floods of the stuff, an average of 75 to a 100 emails a day in some organizations, taking hours every day to manage.

You can have too much of a good thing. Email overload has come about because people have embraced it so enthusiastically. Can't get someone first time on the phone? Send an email. Need to broadcast a request for help (or to show your superiors you are working hard)? Blast out an email to a large group. Need to send out a large document for comment? Send it out as an attachment, not forgetting to CC: anyone who you think might be interested.

And the problem is growing: one government department, which was no green field site, having already been using email for 4 years or so, experienced a disturbing quadrupling in email volumes within the space of 18 months – on top of which mailbox sizes grew even faster as the size and frequency of attachments sent exceeded even the growth in the volume of mail. The cause remains a mystery, but is likely to be a coming together of a number of factors, not least the coming on stream of a universal address list enabling email access to the whole department, along with greater familiarity with email due to growing home Internet use in the period, and introduction of a document management system that was accompanied by a push to avoid the use of paper documents where possible. All good things: but the overall impact on the department was substantial.

It is possible to turn the email tide – but best practice has to be rigorously enforced. We list here some best practice which, if followed, can start to 'hack back the email jungle' as one customer rather dramatically put it.

Mailbox size

Sensible limits (we suggest 50–60 Mb) have to be set and enforced, with people given the option of storing mail locally in offline personal mailboxes, or burning it onto CD. This has the double effect of reducing pressure on mail servers, and also sending out a psychological message that people's own behaviour in not observing email discipline is partly the cause of any problems they may be having.

Attachments

Some mail systems have the capability to use 'smart' attachments – where only a single copy of a file is maintained – but in the vast majority of cases, mailing a 1 Mb file to ten people results in 10 Mb of mail for the server – few people are aware of this and most will moderate their attachment use if told. If a document management system is in use, make it policy to send just a link to the master document on the system – that way, the link will be to the current version, and over time there is potential to save huge amounts of bandwidth as people go and seek out the document only if they really need to access it.

Categories and headers

People will be more productive if they can filter mail according to priority. We suggest that organizations make it mandatory to begin a message subject line with a word which describes the kind of mail being sent, for example: FOR ACTION, FOR DISCUSSION, FOR INFORMATION. As well as providing useful information to assist the reader, it also helps the sender to be clear on precisely what the message being sent is intended to achieve. It may be relevant to require other header information to be included: for example, company name if it concerns a customer or supplier, or surname if it concerns an individual. The subject header should always be used as an explanation, rather like a newspaper headline.

Urgent! flag, use of CC: and Reply to All

Use of the Urgent! flag should be discouraged, and people trained to think hard about the number of recipients they are sending mail to. CC: – which means 'carbon copy' – should be used carefully, in particular, staff should be asked to consider whether the 'category' above applies also to the person marked CC:. Individuals should be urged to consider when to use 'Reply to All', particularly in response to large mailings: after one organization's mail system was brought to its knees by a number of people getting into a 'discussion' following a mass mailing, indiscriminate use of 'Reply to All' was made a disciplinary offence.

Use of filtering and other mailbox tools – and common sense

In the authors' experience, simply creating an email policy and publishing it (or even broadcasting it) will have little effect in impacting behaviour, and significant gains can be anticipated only once a substantial number begin to change their ways. For that reason, organizations suffering from email sclerosis should consider a training or education programme which all employees (including senior managers) will be required to attend or participate in, where these guidelines and practices (and the reasons for them) are taught, and where individuals can learn other tips and tricks like use of mailbox filtering tools to help sort out urgent from low-priority mail (this might also be a chance to formalize principles for use of other, little-used technologies like use of personal and team online diaries or calendars). Finally, it might also be an opportunity for individuals to learn some common sense email rules such as don't assume that responses must be (or will be) immediate, and, perhaps most important of all, don't necessarily use email instead of the telephone or a face to face conversation – only use it when it is the best and most appropriate way to communicate.

Document sharing – from email to public folders to communities

We have covered the various technologies associated with document sharing and publishing in some depth – however, it is worth a brief comment on the human aspects of this. The most basic document sharing tools – email, shared network drives, and public folders – all have more or less the same plusses and minuses. The plusses mainly centre on ease of use, while for email and public folders (though not for shared drives, where there may be permissions restrictions) there is near-universality of access. The down side, as we have discussed, is lack of available metadata and search tools and problems associated with trust (version control, risk of being out of date etc.).

When designing technology solutions to this problem – whether these are based on a document management model, or on intranet-based document sharing – the human dimension should not be lost sight of: there are substantial barriers to encouraging people to publish documents, primarily trust ('people will misunderstand or misuse what I've created'), motivation ('what's in it for me?') and practicality ('I like the idea but I don't have the time').

Whether the solution is in building trust by encouraging people to join communities of practice of like-minded individuals, or allotting specific diary time for knowledge sharing, document-sharing technologies – however sophisticated – will fail if these issues are not addressed.

Directories of expertise

We began this section on KM technologies with a discussion of directory services – the component that underpins the entire IT network by pulling together and sharing identity information about people, devices and systems that use the network.

Directories of expertise are, in some ways, the opposite of this: the focus with directory services is on supporting the infra-structure to make its management easier, while directories of expertise are focused on assisting the user. Despite this, directory services are nevertheless the starting point for the development of most directories of expertise. There are two places where correct information about people working in the organization is absolutely essential: the payroll system (some-times run jointly between finance and human resources and so often including things like address and date of birth informa-tion), and the IT system user directory. Tying these together to enable a single interaction to effect change across all relevant systems is often an early goal of any meta-directory project.

If this is the starting point, then a directory of expertise is beginning with a firm foundation: it knows who the members of the organization are, and it knows their contact details (certainly email, often home and mobile phone number and home address – or at least workplace location).

What comes next is entirely dependent on the needs and the culture of the organization. In consultancy companies, for example, an individual consultant's utilization is the corner-stone of measured performance – and the ability to perform is directly related to the skills and experience that consultants can sell themselves on. Hence most consultancy companies have, linked into forward diary systems, a skills and expertise database which is used by resource managers and those leading delivery projects to resource incoming work. Extending this to something published organization-wide is seldom a problem in such a culture – for example, ICL's 'Connect' system, shortly before its merger with Fujitsu, was entirely voluntary, yet had contact and skills information for more than 12 000 employees. On the other hand, some organizations might face resistance: one of the authors made a recommendation for a similar (though much less ambitious) system for a section of a secure government department (in a part of the organization where such a system would not have had any security implications, and could potentially have saved a great deal of money enabling them to find internal expertise, rather than hiring consultants to solve their problems). The reaction was surprising: the culture would be extremely hostile to publishing people's skills and qualifications, as those managing teams would be embarrassed if they were less qualified than their staff. (Remember our definition of a knowledge worker?)

The technology underlying such systems is seldom sophisticated – a simple database, perhaps linked to the main directory containing contact, job title and business division information, with fields available for skills and experience (either in list form or linked to a CV), and possibly also for photograph and a small amount of personal information. The database is linked to an intranet and enabled for web publishing – all very straightforward.

While particular implementations need to be created specific to the organizations they are intended for, our belief is that a directory of expertise of some form – unlocking 'who knows what' within organizations – is an ideal starting point in any mobilizing knowledge programme, a 'quick win' that (assuming no substantial cultural barriers) is essentially without any downside.

Collaborative tools – synchronous/asynchronous

If building information and knowledge sharing is one of the main goals of mobilizing knowledge, then one of the others must be fostering collaborative working. The majority of knowledge management technologies – from email to document publishing – are designed around collaborative working processes, or at the very least, to help individuals learn from and benefit from the experiences of others.

It follows that the final part of our investigation of KM technologies should focus on collaborative tools – the specific technologies that enable groups of people to work together. We can divide collaborative tools into two main groups: **real-time** (or synchronous) technologies, and **time-shifted** (asynchronous) technologies – reflecting the time element of KM that we outlined at the opening of this chapter.

Real-time

Real-time collaboration is what happens when a group of people get together in a room to create a solution or solve a problem. There is no substitute for face to face contact – as demonstrated extremely graphically in a British Airways television advertisement that was aimed at boosting transatlantic travel, which contrasted the experience of two UK bid teams, one who had sent a printed proposal to a US client and followed up with a phone call ('Lovely pullout', said the client) and another group who paid the customer a visit (the client's comment: 'Let's get down to business').

But what happens when that group can't be physically together? Then we can use a variety of solutions to help them get around the reality of distance. These might include:

- Audio conference
- Video conference
- Whiteboard-based technologies (often in conjunction with audio/video conferencing)
- Online chat
- Peer2Peer.

Audio conference is the default choice for the majority of collaborations – easy to organize (services can be set up with a phone call and a PIN number) and easy to participate in (minimal new skills required). The down side of this – as with most 'real-time' technologies – is the absence of a record of the meeting (though, as in face to face meetings, someone can be asked to keep a note).

Video conferencing has never quite taken off, despite the hassles involved in travel. There is no doubt that it works most efficiently among people who already know each other (it's impossible to establish warmth with new people over a video link) but it has its place, despite continuing infrastructure issues impacting on availability and performance. There still isn't a satisfactory and cheap method of providing mass video conference access: large 'group to group' suites are expensive to kit out and operate; ISDN videophone technology requires infrastructure most companies don't have, while H.320 'webcam'-based technologies are best used one to one, and are limited by network constraints. Those running networks aim to meet service levels designed for handling documents and email, not streaming audio and video.

Attached to some bespoke video conferencing systems – and able to be used in audio conferences thanks to companies like Placeware – **whiteboard** tools are becoming more common as a way of sharing documents and presentations among a dispersed group, who are happy using hand-held or speakerphone for the main meeting, but require presentation capability. Again, best used within a group where members are familiar with each other. A useful element to these systems is the ability to provide an online 'space' where meeting notes and presentations can be allowed to remain for a period after the session. Custom applications are no longer required for these sorts of sessions as services are now offered over internet links by companies such as placeware.com.

Online chat or 'instant messaging' provides a quick and immediate solution to conferencing, better than email for very quick discussions that can be carried on without even lifting the telephone. Useful in situations where colleagues know each other and also know that they are all likely to be sitting down to discuss something at the same time. Limited by the stilted nature of typed discourse, which can never be as quick or fluent as verbal conversation.

Peer2Peer is in its infancy as a KM technology but had a brief moment of fame following the growth of the music-sharing service, Napster, and the myriad of peer2peer services that sprung up in its wake. Peer2Peer enables services like instant messaging and file sharing (whether music or business documents) to be carried out independent of the 'hub' – the network server – and in many cases independent of any network security constraints. Some peer2peer providers, such as Groove.com, have provided some slightly more business-focused tools, but the potential for development of this technology in the future by some of the mainstream players is significant but as yet unrealized.

Time-shifted

The ultimate time-shifted conversation is the letter – written at a time chosen by the writer, sent off to be read at a time chosen by the recipient, who can then write a reply if they so choose. Email emulates this – though the nature of its instant delivery has led to the expectation of a vastly speeded-up process. We have already discussed email in some detail, but there are other important kinds of time-shifted collaboration, notably:

- Discussion forums or newsgroups
- Serendipity.

Discussion forums

The phenomenon of mass participation in newsgroups or web-based discussion boards has been one of the major surprises of the internet era – a relatively low-tech, text-based form of communication which nevertheless has proved a lasting success. An important issue is self-election – users choose to participate in forums that interest them, and they may 'lurk' (read but not post) for a considerable period of time before they feel sufficiently clued up about what is going on to join in. Another important element is the time-shifted nature of the forum – people post when they have the time, read when they have the time, but the forum (if it has critical mass) continues. A great deal can be learned from internet discussion boards when it comes to building communities of practice within organizations – the principle of self-election and no-coercion to publish ('lurking is OK') must be paramount.

Serendipity

Tools like Orbital's Organik provide functionality that watches what you do – indexing the words you write and the documents and web pages you read – and makes recommendations as to material that might interest you based on its own database of content on the local network and/or on the World Wide Web. While the writers of this software promote it as a major way to capture and exploit 'tacit knowledge', the authors remain somewhat sceptical of its general usefulness, except in circumstances where users sit at their PC and write or browse all day – surely a minority of knowledge workers! While it might be an interesting tool to play with, our view is that knowledge management efforts (and budgets) are far better focused elsewhere.

| 5 | Making it all happen |

5.1 Stage 4: Implement the new reality

In previous parts of the book we have worked through the various elements that go to make up a mobilizing knowledge project:

- Understanding the drivers – external and internal – pushing the business to get greater return on its knowledge and intellectual capital.
- Conducting various types of audit to understand the particular issues facing the business in the area of knowledge and information, and take stock of the company's preparedness for change.
- Creating a vision – looking forward to a desired future for the organization in which the value from employees is maximized, and from the information created, collected and accessed by the organization as a whole.
- Developing a high-level strategy – stating the major areas within scope and how the organization should move forward.
- Producing a benefit-driven business case – to understand the more detailed priorities within the strategy, and to gain funding and commitment to detailed design and implementation.
- Considering the role of the levers and enablers – leadership, people, process, technology and information – and gaining an understanding of the part each might play in mobilizing knowledge within the organization.

5.1.1 Getting started

Preparation for the implementation stage will have begun in Stage 3 (Designing the new reality) – helping to build consensus, allowing people to try new approaches and learn in a safe way, training in knowledge management and change, and working within cross-organizational teams.

There will typically have been outline planning on how the knowledge management changes will be managed into the organization. Identifying any issues and blockers and incorporating them into any change management, communication, and education plans as appropriate. Possible change management issues have been described in Stage 3 and they will continue to be relevant throughout.

But what actions should an organization undertake to get started with the implementation of the detailed designs? One important thing to remember is that every company is already doing knowledge management: every organization is already creating, storing, using and sharing information, and in any sizeable company there will already be a significant number of people – from dedicated librarians and administrative staff, to specialists in the generation and manipulation of management information – who are already employed to work with the company's information and ensure it meets its needs to support the knowledge work going on. It would be a serious mistake not to involve these people, harness their enthusiasm, channel their efforts into helping build the vision, and where possible to put them to use as champions for a new approach to information and knowledge.

Even so, there are very few companies, even with a cast-iron benefits-based business case and top-level support, that elect to go for a 'big bang' approach. Far more common is a 'KM-by-stealth' approach where many small 'fires' are started – a pilot here, a small-scale roll-out there, which can later be brought under a common umbrella and used to generate case studies that in turn can be deployed to build understanding and awareness of the potential of a KM approach.

In the authors' experience, it matters little whether these projects were initially conceived under the KM banner, under some other banner (quality or process improvement initiative, e-business or CRM programme) or no banner at all: the important thing is to show that by paying attention to the way knowledge and information flows between people and systems, efficiencies or other business benefits can be achieved that are significant and potentially replicable in other contexts (or at least contain some elements that can be learned from).

A vital step, at the start of a knowledge management initiative, is to bring together like-minded individuals to be involved in the more forward-thinking projects, and to undertake some kind of activity audit – a list (it needn't be complete) of relevant projects where information and knowledge are to the fore. This might include database projects, software trials, e-learning initiatives, intranet or content management activity, or staff development efforts involving secondments or debriefing work – right across the range of knowledge-related activity. Most importantly of all, an effort must be made to identify knowledge-related pilot project activity and make sure the participants are included in the conversation.

5.1.2 Pilots and innovation

Regarding pilots – these truly are the lifeblood of innovation. We have previously discussed the characteristics of 'living' (or at least, long-lived) companies identified by Arie de Geus (*The Living Company*, 1997). As well as more expected characteristics such as being financially conservative and possessing a strong corporate identity, he also noted that most had gone through the experience of fundamental transformation, and had also gone through what he described as 'historic organizational learning in the process'. As a result, he noted that they developed another vital characteristic: the ability to anticipate change, through sensitivity to the marketplace and to the wider cultural, technological and business environment. This was achieved by being tolerant of 'experiments at the margin' – not always geared at immediate profit, but providing learning through doing and by giving people free reign to think in depth about what the future might hold.

We have already mentioned the latitude given to 3M employees to spend time on pet projects – what we haven't mentioned is the staggering statistic that in 2000, 40% of the profits of the 3M corporation came from products that didn't exist in 1995. Quite how this was achieved is a remarkable story in itself – but we have the genesis of it in its policy of toleration of 'non-productive' work. This is the thinking behind our Golden Rule #5:

Golden Rule #5: Organizational learning leads to organizational success – Organizations can only survive and prosper by learning from the business environment, and putting that learning to practical use by responding to it in some way. The capability to do this learning well is what distinguishes successful companies from also-rans.

In other words: pilot, learn, pilot, learn, pilot . . .

The starting point of any KM effort then is not a strategy: it is more important to start by doing something that is intended to make a difference at local level: a pilot, a small-scale project, an experiment based on 'what-if' thinking, and to start to ensure that those efforts are joined up in some way (or at least are in communication with one another where cross-fertilization – knowledge exchange – can occur). Once some results have been achieved – or at least some learning has been recognized and formulated in a coherent way – the next step is to case study.

5.1.3 Case by case

It is the authors' view that the well-prepared case study is, without question, the No. 1 tool for building support, underpinning a business case, and educating key individuals to the potential for knowledge management within their organization. Nothing succeeds like success, and regardless of how good a case can be made for a proposed activity, nothing beats getting up and telling the decision-maker or budget holder: 'We did it previously over here and this was the result'. Nothing comes close as an aid to helping decision-makers visualize the future, and nothing is more important in the toolkit of a knowledge management evangelist in building stakeholder support.

A good case study is not hard to structure: three questions are good enough, and the answers to them needn't be lengthy and convoluted:

- What problem was the business/workgroup/team facing?
- What was done about it?
- What was the outcome?

It is not important to directly answer two more, implicit, questions: 'What can we learn in general terms from this?' and 'Where can we apply this learning?' These are not formally part of a case study, although they can be introduced to great effect when they are presented and used as a source of ideas for projects.

Those in the organization and familiar with the pressures faced will be able to infer these questions from the case study content. Therefore, it is not important to make them explicit, when the danger is to make them too specific and easy to dismiss as being not relevant.

The preparation of case studies does cause problems for some organizations, largely due to misunderstanding their purpose. A case study is not a project report: it's not a 'for the record' activity (though it may come to form *part* of the formal record). Equally it's not a chronological log of events. Rather, it's a slice of learning from the project – a story (whether of 'good news' or shades of grey) that captures the nub of events. Technology companies regularly case study their successes, whether for presentation as part of sales support materials for a customer, or – an effort usually run by the marketing department and done with the maximum possible gloss – for turning into briefing materials for journalists so that they can create their own versions of events. The writers of these case studies tend to be professional journalists themselves with an eye for a story and some skill in eliciting the juicy quote – ideal when you want to create a positive message, but without the particular baggage of formal advertising. As we have mentioned before in the book, some companies including Fujitsu Services are also beginning to use journalists to document internal case studies, with the aim of being better able to carry out the internal marketing work required to make successful projects visible and to win approval to carry on the good work.

5.2 From pilot to programme

We covered some of the background to getting started with knowledge management in the very first section of the book – we know there are very few 'green field' sites (hence the need to make an effort to list out all relevant activity). We assume that initial efforts will incorporate most of the following:

- Audit of knowledge and information related projects
- Pilot projects, with an effort to learn from them
- Case studies, to make concrete that learning and help build buy-in.

This is the necessary backdrop to implementing a knowledge management strategy, or as we term it – 'mobilizing knowledge'. The following tells the story of one customer that moved from a myriad of knowledge-related projects to a more strategic approach. The experience provides a wealth of learning points on ways to approach implementation.

Case study

The UK Department of Health employs 5500 staff. Its mission is to promote the 'health and well-being of people of England', and its biggest job is to run the National Health Service which, with a million staff, has the largest payroll in Europe (though in operational delivery it is a very fragmented organization, divided between the various functions of general practice medicine, hospitals, and other health-related services and institutions.) Aside from its NHS responsibilities, the Department is also responsible for policymaking in the areas of Social Care – things like health services for the elderly – and for Public Health policies aimed at promoting health and preventing disease. However, these unique elements aside, in many ways it is a typical government department, spending its time on creating policy, supporting government ministers, and handling enquiries from MPs, researchers, academic institutions and the general public. The political element is important: regardless of which government is in power, health is always a political hot potato, with the sheer difficulty of effecting change in the vast, complex and interdependent edifice that is the NHS wholly unappreciated by the media, reflecting widespread public demand for improvement to the service and a reversal of perceived decline over some decades.

By any standards, and particularly in UK government, the Department has effective IT systems, with Lotus Notes and a Microsoft Windows and Office desktop available to all staff. In addition, there is a universally accessible intranet, an electronic records and document management infrastructure, and remote access arrangements for mobile workers. It has also been an innovator in the knowledge area: for example, it was first in government to roll out a ministerial briefing system. This collates information about more than 90 official policies – updated daily where appropriate – which is now being emulated by other departments and was the inspiration for the 'Knowledge Network' – which will initially be a pooled briefing system linking the Prime Minister's Cabinet Office with more than 20 Departments, with potential for helping deliver the 'joined-up government' (coordinating policymaking across Whitehall) promised by the incoming New Labour administration in 1997. But despite this, the Department had been looking for better ways to leverage its information infrastructure, principally in an effort to deliver on various 'e-government' initiatives:

- First is the Modernizing Government agenda – the framework which defines a series of deadlines for delivery of services electronically to citizens and business.
- In addition, there are Freedom of Information initiatives. Britain is in the process of introducing American-style freedom of information legislation. But research from Ireland – where such legislation was introduced earlier – has show that it immediately has a heavy impact on staff and systems, as civil servants struggle to use systems to search for now publicly available information using tools not designed for this purpose.
- Finally, there is a move to more evidence-based policymaking. This is associated with faster, wider consultation, issues of identification of experts, verification of evidence, and improved sharing and collaboration, often outside the boundaries of the Department – a challenging agenda, requiring departments to be both wider in their consultation, and faster and more responsive to change.

Clearly, there is a huge knowledge component to all of this. But where would one start?

In fact, the Department started more than two years ago when it commissioned a project called KLIMT – which stands for Knowledge, Learning and Information Management Toolkit. The goal was to create a methodology for 'doing' knowledge management at workgroup level – setting out a step-by-step process that workgroups could follow.

'Toolkit' doesn't mean software – KLIMT is a set of materials, containing workshop exercises, workshop frameworks, assessment questionnaires, technical white papers, best practice guides, and templates for planning, measurement and reporting. It is designed to be used at a workgroup level, and is structured into four parts or phases:

- Introduction – This is about education and awareness of the issues. There are materials to 'sell' the programme to managers, then to begin the process of bringing knowledge issues into awareness within a specific group (typically 15–40 people).
- Assessment tools – A set of resources structured around a workshop that aims to enable a group to assess the gap between the availability and usefulness of knowledge assets, and the sort of requirement they would have to improve efficiency.
- Action and planning tools – a set of resources, again structured around a workshop, aimed at informing and supporting an initiative to tackle the most serious issues identified by the group.
- Measurement and benchmarking tools – tools aimed at enabling the group to measure and report on progress, and capture ideas and best practice.

From its inception, KLIMT was not aimed at helping introduce new technologies. Rather, effort was centred on enabling people to make better use of knowledge assets and tools already in use by the workgroup, and on the most important element of all – behaviour. KLIMT requires groups to look at how they interact with each other as individuals, and how the group interacts with the wider world.

The project began with the intention of giving it to groups to 'do' by themselves. However, the learning curve was found to be too steep – it was unrealistic to expect managers to properly understand knowledge management simply on the basis of reading some material. Also, using this approach there was limited opportunity to share best practice between groups – an important aspect of the project was to find ways to improve knowledge sharing across the Department.

The answer to this was facilitation by the centre. The centre would provide facilitation (for the pilot groups, this was provided by ICL (later Fujitsu Services) consultants who also developed the materials). This increased the resource requirement but ensured that the process was properly conducted.

Overall, KLIMT has been successful with pilot groups, and not surprisingly there are a number of recurrent themes:

- There is the issue of induction – problems of new staff finding it very hard to get started and become productive in a new role.
- Allied to this are issues related to staff turnover, secondments from external organizations for short periods, and a lot of movement of staff within the department – the loss of organizational memory is an issue.
- Also an issue is contact information, accessing people and expertise both inside the department and outside.
- Knowledge and information management skills were an issue – many staff felt they did not have all the skills they needed to get the best from the tools at their disposal.
- And finally information overload – too much email, insufficient filtering of material, and the need for better search and retrieval.

Now these issues apply to many organizations – but one of the benefits of the KLIMT approach was that it enables plans to be drawn up at workgroup level to address some of the specific issues affecting organizational performance, with feedback (through the facilitators) to the centre.

For example, part of the remit of one pilot workgroup was to collect and process statistics on a particular topic, and answer questions on this body of data from academics and ministers' aides. The group had computer systems in place to access data after 1986, but before that, the period from 1947 to 1985, the data was held on paper in 12 large filing cupboards. The group had low morale and high staff turnover – the head of the group was the longest-serving member of staff at 13 months' service. It was decided, as part of the KLIMT process, to do something about this, and team members were allocated to collate the most important data from these filing cupboards and put it onto the Department's external internet site. This effort took four people a number of weeks to complete, but the end result was to remove one of the more joyless tasks altogether from the workload. Staff, no longer burdened with sifting through this paperwork, began to find themselves with more interesting and challenging work to do. Morale improved, and staff retention with it.

KLIMT was not the only knowledge management initiative in the Department. Work was being done in various business units – for example, a directory of expertise in an internal consultancy group (the one which discovered the 'missing' Russian speaker), while other pilot projects, involving storytelling or debriefing/'knowledge harvesting' were also taking place, particularly in the regional offices who manage the relationship with the NHS. Separate knowledge management work was beginning to be done in the NHS itself, most notably around best practice in the hospital admission and after-care processes for common surgical procedures. Back in the Department, efforts were continuing on plans for external contacts databases, freedom of information infrastructure, ongoing work in electronic records and document management, and for a revised intranet on a communities of practice model using elements of personalization.

As a result, it became clear within the Department that some kind of coordinated effort was required, to provide a holistic approach, and help assist with questions such as prioritization, costing and resource allocation. A group was formed – the 'Knowledge Management Board' – to bring together those involved in KM initiatives across the Department and develop a knowledge management strategy.

Bringing a strategic view to KM projects is exactly the role of the five-stage model – to recognize that wherever a project or programme may be, a vision and strategy should underpin it, and a benefit-driven case should focus the effort. We shall leave this case study now, and return to it at the end of the chapter.

> **Golden Rule #1: Be crystal clear on the expected benefits** – Always have a business case that details the agreed benefits that the knowledge management initiatives must deliver. Progress towards their realization must be properly managed and measured.

5.2.1 Ownership

All individual projects should have proper ownership in terms of resource allocation and project management, while beyond that, overall programme ownership is vital if the aim of coordinating KM effort and building critical mass is to be achieved.

As we briefly touched on in the introduction to the book, roles and responsibilities fall roughly into three categories each of which has different implications in terms of delivery. Which implementation approach, or any combination, is most appropriate will depend on the circumstances of the organization and project, and the authors find the most pragmatic and low-risk approach is the most successful:

- Top-down
- Bottom-up
- Business unit.

Top-down

Golden Rule #3 states: *Nothing happens without leadership.* By top-down, we mean the responsibility of the 'centre' or 'top' of the organization to provide both leadership and resources to effect change. Also provided by the 'centre' (though be aware that definitions of 'top' and 'centre' vary widely from organization to organization) is infrastructure, be this technology or things like organization-wide processes, project management methodologies, or supporting human resource frameworks (training policies, appraisal systems), all of which might need fine-tuning or even outright overhaul in the light of knowledge management principles.

Bottom-up

Golden Rule #2 states: *People's behaviours must change for the long term.* Real change – and real improvement – happens only when people do things differently. There is more on change management – which is mostly about getting people to change what they do and what they think – to come later in the book. But ultimately, the goal must be to change, in a variety of ways, the behaviour of every member of every workgroup – and this can be achieved only by changing how they think about their roles, responsibilities, and the personal knowledge they hold and use as part of their daily activity. The KLIMT process at the Department of Health was an innovative approach to this challenge – giving workgroups the tools to examine what they do and how they might do it better.

Table 5.1 Typical implementation grid

Priority	Project by business area	Timeframe	Ownership
	Leadership/accountability		
Milestone	Appoint CKO	Short term	Top-down
Prerequisite	KM projects audit	Short term	Top-down
Milestone	Formal adoption of KM strategy	Short term	Top-down
	People, skills and HR		
Main project	Revamp appraisal process	Medium term	Top-down
Pilot	Knowledge harvesting in ops	Short term	Bottom-up
Potential	Wider knowledge harvesting initiative	Long term	Top-down

Role of the business unit

The role of the 'middle' is a bit harder to define, but since in most organizations a high degree of management control (for instance, allocation of budgets, staffing levels, even some policy decisions) is devolved from the centre of the company to business units and divisions, then there is a leadership role to be exercised here too. Significant thought needs to be given to how to bring on board the senior managers who now inhabit this level of the business, and who have both a significant part to play in implementation, and also much to gain from the potential for improved efficiency, effectiveness and innovation from KM activity.

If we use the above as the basis for the design of the implementation programme, then we have three main dimensions: business area, priority, and ownership. Table 5.1 is a typical ongoing implementation grid that shows how these might be put together.

It is possible to turn this sheet into a GANTT chart, which will give an overall view of the programme based on timeframe.

5.3 Programme design – additional considerations

The task of formalizing the KM programme is a multi-layered one, but beyond the factors already considered, there are some other considerations worth exploring. Further people-related considerations regarding change management and resistance to change are also provided in Appendix 4.

5.3.1 The art of the possible

The first question to ask is: 'What will be possible in each proposed area?' – in other words, what sort of scope will be appropriate for any change. It can be useful to use a common format for expressing programme objectives, to help enable benefits, costs, and risks to be described clearly. A common way for stating objectives is to use the SMART criteria (Figure 5.1).

Figure 5.1
SMART criteria for
balanced objectives

S   Specific
M   Measurable
A   Agreed
R   Realistic
T   Time-related

Specific

There must be no confusion as to what is to be changed, and it needs to be possible to tell afterwards that things have changed – so specific criteria have to be set out.

Measurable

In addition, it must be measurable whether the specific criteria outlined have been achieved or not. For knowledge management initiatives this can be an especially challenging task. Help is given to do this in 'From strategy to action', Chapter 3, p. 64.

Agreed

It is no good having IT professionals – or worse, external consultants – to fix project objectives. Those who will own the responsibility for carrying them out must have 'Agreed' them. Engaging the hearts and minds of the owner(s) is essential if proper motivation and commitment are to be forthcoming.

Realistic

The significant risks and assumptions must be uncovered if those running the project are able to state with confidence that the objectives can realistically be achieved.

Time-related

Most goals can appear 'realistic' over a long timeframe – so the length of time available to meet the objectives must be clear and apparent to all: objectives must therefore be 'Time-related'.

5.3.2 Postscript – Department of Health

We left the story of the Department's knowledge management efforts at the point where they were just about to develop a comprehensive KM strategy, the first to be formally adopted by a government department. The work was conducted over a period of two months, coinciding with a major review of the structure of the Department to refocus it on delivery of changes in the NHS, and this key driver was put at the heart of the recommendations.

What emerged for approval by the board was a list of more than 20 projects over a three and a half year period – ranging from a revamp of enabling infrastructure (revision of information management approaches and a new roadmap for intranet development), to process change pilots and small-scale experiments with 'knowledge harvesting'. From a top-down perspective, formal responsibilities for KM in the Department were allocated, while from a 'bottom-up' perspective, a major revision to KLIMT was authorized to reflect some of the changed priorities uncovered in the strategy development exercise, including better links into exploitation of the office information systems infrastructure, to e-learning initiatives, and better mechanisms for capturing and learning from the experiences of participating workgroups. The KLIMT process is now the formal mechanism for delivering knowledge management awareness, practice and skills at workgroup level throughout the Department.

Reaping the rewards

6.1 Stage 5: Never rest – realize the benefits

We ended the previous chapter with the implementation underway: having analysed the need, built the vision, created the business case, and designed the programme, we then focused on the task of moving things forward. As we have described, a typical KM programme is a picture of complexity – an infrastructure project here, some process improvement there, a variety of interlinked dependencies and political agendas. Along the way is the potential for a myriad of setbacks: unexpected budget constraints or shifts in business priority, software that doesn't work, and implementations held up by dependencies outside the control of the programme manager.

In all of this, those driving the mobilizing knowledge effort need to keep in mind the end objective: realizing the business benefits identified at the outset in the initial business case. For this to be achieved, the benefits must continue to be actively managed.

6.1.1 The art of benefits management

When we discussed development of a business case in Chapter 3, we noted that it was unlikely (though not, of course, impossible) that chief executives or other senior managers would ever be interested in knowledge management for its own sake: rather, any interest or willingness to entertain a mobilizing knowledge programme would be contingent on promises of clear business benefit that mapped fairly precisely to top-level corporate goals. In order to prepare and present a compelling case for action, it was necessary to gain an understanding of the most compelling corporate objectives and challenges – and to articulate the tangible benefits that mobilizing knowledge would help meet.

It follows that during the design, development, and implementation phases there must be a continual focus on business benefits – those running the programme must keep in focus its ultimate rationale. One way to do this is to ensure that the 'quality management' activities of a project – the various review processes – must be tailored to assess progress against the agreed measurable benefits – ensuring they are not lost sight of, and to prevent the programme's emphasis from drifting over time.

For example, in the PRINCE2 project management methodology, the mechanism for project review and measurement of success utilizes a 'quality plan'. For a KM project, it is important to ensure that the monitoring and review of promised benefits should be incorporated in this plan. The PRINCE2 methodology also has a project start-up process, which provides an opportunity to spell out anticipated benefits up front during the initial start of a project, in addition to assessing progress during the stages of the project through quality reviews.

It may be necessary to go beyond this, however. In these sorts of formal methodologies there are mechanisms for reviewing progress towards expected benefits – but an effort should also be made to ensure that they are visible to everyone on the project, and all activities should be tested against them: spending time and effort doing things that do not contribute to the expected benefits will likely be a waste of energy and resources. The role descriptions of team members should include explicit statements of benefits expected from their efforts up front.

Standard practice, and one used by the authors, is to provide descriptions of the expected deliverables to each team member (PRINCE2 calls these Product Descriptions). These clearly spell out what is required and how its quality will be tested. Acceptance of any deliverable will involve checking if it will deliver the benefits originally defined, asking the team 'Is it going to meet the quality expected?' Having clear descriptions of the expected benefits visible in meetings and workshops focuses everyone's attention – anyone in the room can then stop the meeting and question if the subject under discussion is helping us to realize these benefits? – if the answer is no, then we quickly move on. It is often the case that mini discussions around the displayed benefits start within meetings and workshops – people need to continually remind themselves and check their understanding of the situation – testing the formally expected outcomes and comparing them to their own expectations.

Part of the difficulty, of course, is a conceptual one related to scope and scale: it may be relatively easy to ensure that the specific deliverables of a project (e.g. a documents repository, a new process for publishing) are achieved – but what about the softer side: how can we guarantee that an end result – better customer service, say – can be delivered from a programme that is riddled with interdependencies, some of which may not be under the full control of the programme manager?

This is where those running a KM programme need to be creative – and also to be sternly focused on fine-tuning of the implementation until the benefits are realized. Here we also return to the role of case studies in documenting and publicizing success stories, demonstrating to the organization that benefits are both achievable and worth striving for. Another element of standard project management methodologies – the communications plan – can be used to help address some of these aspects – communicating the larger goals, making the most of successes along the way, building recognition of individual and group achievements, and generally helping consolidate the gains.

Over time the corporate drivers and the ways the organization might benefit from knowledge management will change. The map of benefits produced for the business case must be updated to reflect the changing priorities of the organization: where possible, this should be captured during Stage 3, where assumptions about the future (and the role of leadership, people, process, technology and information in that future) are laid bare. Sometimes, significant organizational changes will be made unexpectedly – in which case, those running the programme must make the effort to realign what they are doing with the big picture emerging in the organization – otherwise some 'new broom', who hasn't been party to the discussion in the past, is likely to come along and question: 'Why the investment?' It is vital to be able to answer and precisely define what value is being added and in what way, and what specific corporate objectives are being supported. The map of the benefits we defined must live throughout the project, and beyond, ensuring not only that the benefits continue, but are continually seen to be adding tangible benefits. Reminding us of the first Golden Rule:

Golden Rule #1: Be crystal clear on the expected benefits – Always have a business case that details the agreed benefits that the knowledge management initiatives must deliver. Progress towards their realization must be properly managed and measured.

6.2 Managing risk

Managing risk is another core project management discipline that is highly relevant to a mobilizing knowledge programme. Many project risks are specific, and have been discussed in the preceding chapters, for example particular risks associated with technology implementation such as unforeseen development problems or dependencies on infrastructure upgrades. These are the bread and butter of project and programme management – and in conjunction with the focus on benefits, form the main workload of the individual in charge of delivery.

But there are also some higher-level concerns: here we outline some of the more substantive business risks – the major pitfalls facing an organization attempting to get better value from knowledge and information – and propose some ways to mitigate. We list these as follows:

- Continuously improve or fall behind
- Change grinds to a halt for lack of commitment
- The longer you wait, the harder it gets
- No leader, no progress.

6.2.1 Continuously improve or fall behind

A horse never runs so fast as when he has other horses to catch up and outpace (Ovid)

Innovations, improvements, new tools and new ideas arrive in a steady stream, as the thinking and experience driving knowledge management, information management and process improvement continues to grow and advance. As a result, competitor organizations are likely to be continually improving what they do in a constant battle for performance advantage. It follows that continuous improvement – reflecting on current practice, learning from mistakes, and finding ways to exploit that learning – must be a key element in any mobilizing knowledge programme. Building in such organizational learning is hard work – though the tools and techniques outlined in previous chapters, as practised by a growing number of organizations, can surely help.

But there is also an opportunity to look outside the organization and learn at the 'macro' level, in addition to the 'micro' improvement gained through quality efforts. Monitoring and comparing your organization with best practice in other organizations through benchmarking studies, and by using the EFQM (European Foundation for Quality Management) excellence model, enable a better understanding of areas for improvement.

The EFQM framework is divided into nine criteria, grouped into Enablers (the top-level processes in the organization) and Results (what these achieve). The framework has been around since the early 1990s, and has been adopted by many organizations to help redefine internal and external customer relationships and processes. One of its many benefits is a clear-cut list of definitions – what do we mean by a 'process', a 'customer', a particular indicator. In particular, it has been used successfully to help meld together disparate organizations after mergers or acquisitions – providing the framework for a 'new' business rationale from which all parties can work towards a shared understanding.

From a KM perspective, we have on occasion been invited to bring together the EFQM model and our own KM strategy framework – at the same time being asked to formulate our KM thinking in the same sorts of clearly defined terms as the EFQM model proposes. As a consequence of this work, we have come to the view that from a KM viewpoint, the disciplines are highly complementary: where the EFQM model provides a framework of *what* needs to be done, the disciplines associated with a knowledge management approach (leadership, people, process, information and content) addresses *how* this might be achieved. In organizations where EFQM is already embedded in business practice, we have found that a combined approach delivers fasters results and greater operational efficiencies. The EFQM model is intended to be used such that it becomes a single enterprise-wide framework, particularly useful as we have already stated, in post-merger or in business transformation situations.

One of the primary benefits of joining the EFQM 'club' (www.efqm.org) is access to a raft of benchmarking data on a very large variety of performance indicators, plus the opportunity to compare performance with similar organizations in the same or related industry sectors – an extremely useful and powerful resource.

Combined with internal efforts to improve efficiency, use of benchmarking becomes an important component of companies striving to become a 'learning organization'.

Golden Rule #5: Organizational learning leads to organizational success – Organizations can only survive and prosper by learning from the business environment, and putting that learning to practical use by responding to it in some way. The capability to do this learning well is what distinguishes successful companies from also-rans.

6.2.2 No commitment, no change

Change gets off the ground only if there is a compelling business case, arrived at by an individual change leader (or more likely a group of leaders) through examining the realities of the business environment, and convincing their peers and superiors within the organization of the need for change. In the process, significant reasons for change must be clearly identified and discussed with those affected, and the benefits identified for moving forward. A typical subtext would read: 'we must change, we must do it quickly, and this project will provide a way for doing this'.

This business case may win acceptance at the beginning of the project – but despite the commitment of a core team, the KM programme may subsequently run into problems: for example, senior managers might forget the point of the exercise, and the KM project is targeted in a round of budget cuts; or despite continued formal buy-in from the top, it may become increasingly difficult to get support from business unit managers whose cooperation is required for pilots, case studies or roll-outs.

What can the KM change leader do in these circumstances? In many ways, the answer is similar to the difficulties associated with benefits management: keep the end goal relevant to the business, and make sure that the 'big picture' is known and communicated to all.

A useful tool to foster and embed the need for change is the 'burning platform' analogy:

> To those affected explain that the platform you are currently standing on (the product, service or working practices of the relevant part of the organization) is on fire and there is no way of putting this out. All efforts have been made to find a solution but we must now move to a new platform if we are to be safe. What the change programme will do, with their help, is to create this new safe platform, and construct a strong bridge so everyone can move over to it. This will not be easy or simple, but it is essential if the team is to survive.

It is fairly easy for an initiative to run into trouble: at the start of the project there may be resistance from groups of staff or from managers who might feel threatened by potential changes in the culture, organizational structures, processes, systems, or rules; alternatively, there might be friction from unforeseen difficulties which stop or hinder people from joining in.

One example from a consultancy group is the difficulty in getting the go-ahead for a simple change in time recording systems and rules to allow 'knowledge sharing' or 'knowledge write-up' as a valid activity. In such a structured environment where people are strictly measured on their use of time, not having a timesheet code, or 'budgeted time' marked out for knowledge-sharing activities led to mass non-participation: this didn't change until there were significant changes in recording systems, involving not only timesheet code provision, but an actual requirement to spend a certain amount of time in knowledge-sharing activity, with a tie-in to the appraisal system. Apart from the KM implications, this should be a lesson to those who set performance targets: be very careful what you measure, it may have unintended effects!

Particular dangers arise when the 'project' is nearing completion – that is, when the 'hard' deliverables are near to acceptance stage. As this point is reached, and the attention of the project team begins to move on to new activities, a real risk arises that the new ways of behaving will start falling away and the old behaviours will creep back in – the changes will not yet have been 'frozen' or embedded into the organization.

This final stage – of never-ending implementation and continuous improvement – is where the real 'culture change' will take place. Until programme elements are complete, any observed changes in behaviour are most likely to have been due to the momentum of the project. If attention and effort is focused on the people involved in the project, they are likely to respond by complying with whatever is requested. When the spotlight goes off, there is a risk that those same members of staff might slip back into comfortable routines established long before the change programme.

This is especially true if when individuals ignore some of the new rules or processes put in place, the infringement goes unnoticed. Without any comeback, they are likely to continue to push their luck and may even try to see what else they may be able to get away with. When confident about it, they will let their colleagues know – helping to spread the rot that quickly begins to set in. One worst case encountered by the authors was when a senior manager refused to participate in new document-sharing processes – a clear signal that 'important' people needn't bother with such trivialities. This compromised the project almost before the roll-out was completed.

It can be difficult for those managing the change project to prevent something like this, unless they have been delegated authority, or have a direct line to top management. We discussed earlier in the book the opportunities for putting to use natural 'knowledge brokers', harnessing their enthusiasm for joining people up and sharing information across boundaries: some-times the very opposite of a knowledge broker is encountered, who (through fear or other blockers identified) will resist knowledge-sharing initiatives across the board. Sometimes the only way to ensure a project's success is for these people to move (or be moved) into other areas of the business, or employment elsewhere. If they cannot and will not change, even after open and candid discussions, incentives, the agreement of compelling messages, peer pressures, and leadership messages, then there are few other alternatives available.

The authors experienced such a situation with a manager of an international division who was meant to ensure a new set of communications and management processes and a supporting IT system were implemented successfully. Other things going on always seemed more important than the project, and this apathy was evident in meetings with his staff. He would not turn up for meetings, and when he did attend he not only made it obvious that he did not understand the project, but also openly questioned why it was being done at all in front of everyone. When highlighted to his management they applied pressure as

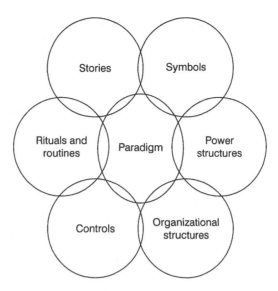

Figure 6.1
The Cultural Web
(Johnson and Scholes
1999. © Pearson
Education Ltd.
Reproduced with
permission)

best they could, until he finally moved to a position in another company.

Such drastic solutions are very much a last resort. In Chapter 4, we discussed use of the Cultural Web (Figure 6.1) as an influencing tool: this should be very much in the forefront of the KM change leader's mind. The goal is to use the various levers – both hard (controls, power structures and organizational structures) and soft (rituals and routines, story and symbol – such as the burning platform) to change the paradigm. It may take a long time, but the goal should be to generate sufficient buy-in that change gains the positive support of the majority, working with key influencers to change attitudes and beliefs.

Sometimes, of course, this isn't possible. One of the authors was involved in a series of roll-outs of new newspaper systems. Journalists, on the whole, are notorious for their reluctance to embrace new technology, and are not renowned for their respect of management edicts either. In the end, after going through the experience several times, it was concluded that the best method was to train all staff in the new system, then come in on a Sunday morning (before work began on Monday's edition) and physically remove all trace of the old system. A brutal approach, but one that utilizes the tremendous focus which journalists have on getting a paper out. The staff were quick to adapt – Monday's editions ran late, but by Tuesday it was as if nothing had happened. But changing attitudes, beliefs and behaviours is much harder than changing IT systems.

Golden Rule #2: People's behaviours must change for the long term – People's beliefs must be affected if long-term improvements in behaviour are to be achieved. You must do more than just 'build an IT system'.

6.2.3 No leader, no progress

Throughout, we have assumed that the mobilizing knowledge programme will have a dedicated leader. As the programme moves beyond project deliverables towards a future of ongoing improvement-seeking, the need for leadership doesn't end: in fact, it becomes even more important as the goal becomes to embed knowledge-sharing behaviours in the everyday working culture, 'the way we do things around here'.

Consequently, the KM programme leader still needs to maintain his or her role as the figurehead of the change: in fact, it is commonly noted that loss of the leader from a delivery programme means the end of the benefits. This can be compounded by the added risk that new leaders who come on board may start to cause disruption, as they do not understand the thinking behind the programme design or the specifics of what has been done. Planning of leadership succession and emphasis on the ongoing importance of knowledge management to the organization are important to maintaining success.

Ongoing leadership at all levels is absolutely critical:

- The leader of the mobilizing knowledge programme needs to work to win over the hearts and minds of those at the top of the organization – which can be achieved only through case studies and a focus on benefits and outcomes.
- That leader needs to work with those delivering the change – the natural knowledge brokers or change leaders in the various divisions and business units to build awareness and commitment at lower levels in the organization.
- Finally, a great deal depends on those lower-level change leaders to drive individual workgroup level change – and once again, the only way to do this is to focus on the personal – answering the question 'what's in it for me?' with a very clear and unambiguous focus on, for example, making life easier and more productive for the individual.

Golden Rule #3: Nothing happens without leadership – Those responsible for running the organization must inspire and encourage all staff throughout the 'voyage of discovery' that is the change programme. Continuing on after implementation to ensure lasting change.

6.3 Becoming a learning organization

6.3.1 Adapt and survive

We have repeatedly discussed the idea of organizational learning throughout this book. The whole idea of the learning organization – developed by Peter Senge (beginning with his book *The Fifth Discipline: The Art and Practice of the Learning Organisation*) focuses on the notion that not just people, but organizations can learn and adapt. According to David Garvin this means:

> *an organisation skilled at creating, acquiring, and transferring knowledge, and at modifying its behavior to reflect new knowledge and insights.*

In other words, what we are talking about is an organization that is not just able to mobilize knowledge in pursuit of end goals, but also uses what it knows to **modify** what it does – constantly evolving and adapting as new knowledge comes to light and as understanding of the business environment develops. It means that the organization is both able and willing to make the effort to understand what does and does not work, and make changes, which could be quite fundamental. Such 'joined-up thinking' – which encompasses everything from quality management to information architecture, to scanning and making sense of the business environment in order to inform both operational and strategic decision-making – is the holy grail of twenty-first century management. But it is not at all easy to achieve (and most organizations – with their silo mentalities and interdepartmental mistrusts and enmities – are not at all set up to bring such thinking about).

One of the issues is that people at all levels in the organization naturally tend to seek out routine and order, looking to master what they do, and fitting in with existing ways of doing things. The challenge is to make learning and adapting a part of the organizational culture – precisely the area of focus we have been discussing in the whole arena of KM.

The link between the learning organization and mobilizing knowledge has been repeatedly made by business gurus such as Senge, de Geus and others. According to Dorothy Leonard-Barton, the learning organization has the following qualities:

- enthusiasm for knowledge
- managers (who) respect and encourage the accumulation of knowledge

- people who are knowingly engaged in building core techno-logical capabilities
- people who are curious
- people who are information seekers.

She also noted:

- Such companies have 'leaders who listen and learn'.

To tie this into our central theme of people and behaviour – mobilizing knowledge around the organization is of little value if people and the organization do not change and improve their behaviours as a result.

Part of becoming a 'learning organization' is to ensure that continuous improvement becomes a part of daily life: the management task is to support individuals in gathering ideas and spotting opportunities, and allowing time for people to discuss and share knowledge. Supporting people to work together, not just to initiate ideas and actions, but to allow them to own and feel proud with the end result.

Within the workgroup or business unit, we should look at 'mini-projects' to help bring this about – using the five-stage KM framework at a local (rather than strategic organizational) level to examine appropriate ways to mobilize knowledge to support continuous improvement. Along the way, there will be change management issues, leadership, people, process, technology, and information will all have a role to play, and plans must be drawn up and implemented. A particular benefit of formalizing continuous improvement in this way – support from the top, with delivery at workgroup level – is that it allows all minor initiatives to have a safe place of high-level ownership, where duplications can be reduced, and knowledge sharing, reuse, and capture all encouraged and supported.

At the macro level, organizations need to get far better at all sorts of organizational learning:

- Tolerating experiments at the margins in processes, technolo-gies and blue skies thinking that may or may not bear fruit one day – this is a key characteristic identified by Arie de Geus of the 'Living Company'.
- When appropriate, mobilizing that learning rapidly. If sud-denly a technology becomes 'hot', it needs to rapidly formalize the learning from those involved in experiments

and quickly bring it into the mainstream. An example is Barclays Bank, which in the late 1990s had four experts in smart card technology. When smart cards suddenly became an issue, it was able to intensify the knowledge of this group to skill up 50 people to similar standards – it had tolerated the 'uneconomic' blue sky activities of the four, but was later able to reap the benefit when the right time arose.

- Sharing best practice across organizational boundaries – getting past the 'not invented here' syndrome. Organizational structure (as well as methods of setting targets and measuring individual performance) has a huge impact on this – organizations who ignore the knowledge management implications when restructuring are playing a dangerous game with precious organizational knowledge.

- Using internal and environmental perceptions to provide input into both tactical and strategic decision-making. All sorts of tools exist for creating business strategy, from scenario planning (envisioning possible futures and plotting a course to exploit anticipated opportunities or mitigate upcoming problems) to Michael Porter's '5 Forces' model (1985) (which analyses supplier and competitor power, and threat of substitute products or new industry entrants, to assess industry or sector competitiveness and attractiveness). The danger is in using these only at annual strategy reviews, and then only in a limited way, organizations miss out on the opportunity for application of continuous learning.

Inability to see the storm coming and deal with it affects many businesses and often leads to their demise – whereas the opposite may also be the case, for example, Shell in the 1980s, which had used scenario planning to calculate the risk of an oil price slump, and prepared for the worst. It was much better prepared (and had much better financial results) than rivals such as BP, which hadn't anticipated the problem and ended up downsizing substantially as a result.

Golden Rule #5: Organizational learning leads to organizational success – Organizations can only survive and prosper by learning from the business environment, and putting that learning to practical use by responding to it in some way. The capability to do this learning well is what distinguishes successful companies from also-rans.

7

Epilogue: Lessons from the journey

As we come to the end of this exploration of the various organizational and operational perspectives on KM, it's time to review the journey so far. As a unitary discipline, it is still very much in its infancy: while we can go far back in time to discussions about the nature of knowledge, and subsequently track the impact and evolution of data processing information technologies throughout the twentieth century, knowledge management as a distinct discipline – in many ways, a synthesis of information management, human resource management, organizational design principles, behavioural science, and other influences – began only in the early 1990s.

The initial wave of excitement principally based on web technologies has long subsided, with ongoing practical work complemented by a growing and increasingly mature academic and business literature analysing the dynamics of knowledge in organizations.

While in this book we have covered these elements, we hope that we have moved forward into what we have observed as a third wave of KM: focused first on practical benefit (how does this activity help deliver on core objectives?, the 'so what?' question, and the link to organizational strategy: how can what we have learned about the dynamics of knowledge in organiza-tions, and the practice of mobilizing it, be put to use in

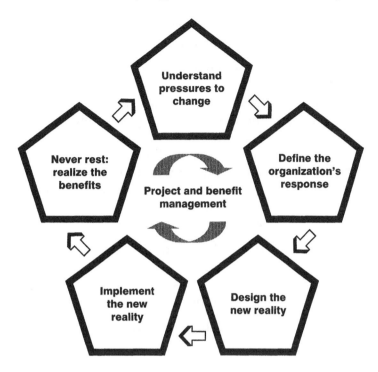

Figure 7.1

The five-stage knowledge management delivery framework

improving overall organizational performance and building organizational learning and memory).

This final section is split into three main elements:

- A review of the five-step framework and the various actions and issues that arise at each stage.
- A review of the five Golden Rules and their significance in implementing and gaining benefit from a mobilizing knowledge programme.
- A look ahead at what the main business issues will be in the early decades of the twenty-first century, and assessing the relevant knowledge implications.

7.1 The five-stage KM delivery framework

The purpose of the framework has been to provide a model that ensures consistency and comprehensiveness in development and delivery of a KM programme. We hoped to achieve this by creating a scalable approach that would be applicable at multiple levels in an organization. Linking up the various KM concepts in a logical fashion to ensure completeness and appropriateness in method and approach.

7.1.1 Stage 1: Understand the pressures to change

Throughout this book, we have repeatedly focused on the fact that mobilizing knowledge is not undertaken for its own sake – rather, effort is undertaken to improve the value gained from knowledge in the organization in order to achieve some specific strategic end. In **Stage 1,** we focused on teasing out those strategic goals – finding out what key challenges and issues are facing the organization, what the overall direction of the organization is, and exploring how better exploitation of information and knowledge can assist delivering the desired outcome.

This is the backdrop to the creation of a strategy for knowledge management – which will make sense only if it derives directly from the vision, mission, goals and objectives of the organization.

The questions any would-be strategist needs to answer are:

- Where do we want to be?
- Where are we now?
- How do we get there from here?

The first of these, 'Where do we want to be?', is driven, as we have seen, by corporate strategy – we need to come to a view about the role of knowledge in supporting the big picture. But while this is the primary concern of Stage 1 there has to be an element of audit ('where are we now?') involved at this stage too, running across roles, culture, processes, content and technology. Every journey has to start from somewhere. The initial linkages made at this stage between the global strategic picture and possibilities for mobilizing knowledge are used in the next stage to construct the business case.

7.1.2 Stage 2: Define the organization's response

In **Stage 2,** efforts move on to the formalization of a KM strategy: in our terms, this means not just a vision statement (important though this is), but also a plan for action, based on a properly argued business case, together with some degree of allocation of resources. To get to this, a deeper audit of the organization's capability in the areas of knowledge and information will be necessary. The development of a business case, though, is crucial to the whole exercise, providing a specific rationale for each element of a mobilizing knowledge programme, together with linkages showing how various elements are dependent on one another and how they combine to deliver the end goals in support of organizational strategy. In Chapter 3, we examined the 'chasm of faith' in depth, and looked at how tools like the Balanced Scorecard and a focus on benefit categories can help us build up a detailed business case.

7.1.3 Stage 3: Design the new reality

Stage 3 focuses on the five 'levers' of change. These areas will provide the meat of any mobilizing knowledge programme – these are the specific areas we have to work with, and any particular mobilizing knowledge project will focus on one or more of these enablers – in strategy terms, answering the question 'How do I get there?'

This is the point where it is necessary to get down to considerable detail about each specific area: focusing on the issues and opportunities available in each of these areas (and leveraging some of the examples outlined in Chapter 4) should provide the richness necessary to construct a comprehensive and effective delivery programme.

The five levers of change are represented in Figure 7.2.

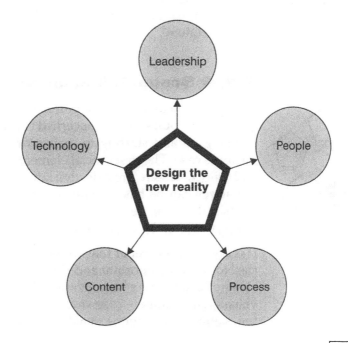

Figure 7.2
The five levers of change to shape the new reality

Leadership: Focusing on the need for, and role of, leaders at every level in the organization, from top-level ownership of the whole programme (with a responsibility to evangelize and affirm the KM message), down to important knowledge broker roles at workgroup level.

People: Only people have knowledge – everything else is just data and information. So there should be a primary focus in any mobilizing knowledge programme on the role of people: skills, behaviour, motivation, reward, attitudes and workplace culture all come under scrutiny.

Process: Business processes exist to add and deliver value to the end customers of the organization. The strategy should make clear the potential for new processes to improve knowledge identification, use, creation, sharing, and recording – all with the aim of adding value at every stage.

Technology: Technology remains a key enabler – though it should never be overemphasized. KM strategy should consider the untapped potential of technology infrastructure, collaboration tools and specialist software, while also recognizing the limits.

Information: The relevance, availability, context, and quality of available information in and across organizations will determine in large measure the success of any mobilizing knowledge programme – therefore any strategy must place significant focus on the management and availability of information and Web-based 'content'.

7.1.4 Stage 4: Implement the new reality

Change is nearly always painful: yet there is no progress without it. **Stage 4** is concerned with implementation – of focusing on and starting to realize the benefits outlined in the business case. The first crucial element is the importance of trials and pilots, which provide the key learning on which bigger initiatives can be based, while at the same time providing case studies that can be used to build commitment and 'sell' the programme to the unconverted.

It is the authors' belief that well-communicated case studies are the No. 1 most important and useful change tool available to any change leader in an organization. People are extremely bad at visualizing change – case studies (especially those done within the same organization) enable people to identify much more closely with the programme, and help liberate their imagination to see possibilities in their own workplace.

Chapter 5 focuses on issues surrounding implementation at the various different levels in an organization, concluding that workgroup level implementation – changing and improving the day-to-day knowledge sharing and use of people, modifying how they go about their daily business – is absolutely crucial if the change programme is to succeed. Other important considerations discussed include apportionment of ownership, setting of project objectives, measurement of success, and the overall shape of the programme.

7.1.5 Stage 5: Never rest: realize the benefits

Stage 5 focuses on benefits management – how to achieve the desired end outcomes through blending a focus on benefits with traditional project management disciplines. This goes hand in hand with the management of risk, both those 'close' to the project (such as development or roll-out slippage or threat to budgets) and more complex threats associated with organizational change. Also explored are the linkages to other complementary programmes such as EFQM implementation, plus issues of leadership and succession planning.

We conclude with a discussion on how KM fits with the concept of the learning organization – the 'joined-up thinking' seen when an organization begins to build the capability to use what it knows to modify what it does – evolving and adapting as new knowledge comes to light, and as understanding of the business environment develops. The building of such organizations means changing the culture to the degree that the people within it are both able and willing to make the effort to understand what does and does not work, and embrace potentially fundamental change.

7.2 Five golden rules

Throughout the book, we have repeatedly referred to the five Golden Rules outlined at the beginning. Given the main themes of the book, there is no need to expand on them here. But they are worth restating in their entirety:

Golden Rule #1: Be crystal clear on the expected benefits – Always have a business case that details the agreed benefits that the knowledge management initiatives must deliver. Progress towards their realization must be properly managed and measured.

Golden Rule #2: People's behaviours must change for the long term – People's beliefs must be affected if long-term improvements in behaviour are to be achieved. You must do more than just 'build an IT system'.

Golden Rule #3: Nothing happens without leadership – Those responsible for running the organization must inspire and encourage all staff throughout the 'voyage of discovery' that is the change programme, continuing on after implementation to ensure lasting change.

Golden Rule #4: Process change leads to improved performance – Organizations need to build in new processes and routines through job redesign, to ensure knowledge capture and reuse, and to establish and reinforce desired behaviours and activity.

Golden Rule #5: Organizational learning leads to organizational success – Organizations can only survive and prosper by learning from the business environment, and putting that learning to practical use by responding to it in some way. The capability to do this learning well is what distinguishes successful companies from also-rans.

The point of these Golden Rules is to keep constantly in mind the key issues that make or break any mobilizing knowledge programme: a focus on benefits and business case, on behavioural change, on leadership, on process improvement to design in knowledge-friendly ways of working to daily routine, and on building in organizational learning.

7.3 Looking to the future: mobilizing knowledge in a changing world

We would like to conclude with a scan of the horizon: our assessment of the business issues that will impact on organizations, knowledge, and information in the future. There are many huge sources of potential change out there – including things like the demographic time-bomb of aging population and low birth rate in the industrialized world, with knock-on effects on pensions, immigration, skills, loss of knowledge and experience, and so forth – that are simply too big to tackle in a volume such as this, but nevertheless have dramatic implications for knowledge and wealth creation in the global and national organizations so many of us work for. However, there are several key topics we consider directly relevant that will increasingly affect an organization's ability to obtain value from knowledge resources – we will examine them in turn:

- Rapid pace of change
- Shift from value chains to value networks
- Mobilizing knowledge in boom and bust.

7.3.1 Rapid pace of change

In the authors' experience there is little worse in a knowledge management project than confusing people as to how they should behave – giving out conflicting messages, and going through cycles of significant changes in a seemingly unplanned way. These cause staff to switch off their attention and ignore the majority of messages. This is called initiative fatigue, and we don't need to wait decades to experience it: in most organizations, it's with us already.

Partly a consequence of 'good' changes in organizations – such as the empowerment of individuals, and increasing reliance on flexible matrix management structures – organizations increasingly struggle to manage company-wide (or even business unit level) programmes such as process change, systems roll-outs or organizational restructuring. At the same time, workers are bombarded with additional demands – quality measures to be met, revised appraisal systems to adopt, new technologies to learn to use, new processes to be learned and integrated – and that's before they do any 'work'.

'Death by initiative' is not very pleasant – and not made any more palatable by the fact that there is often little coordination at the top. In fact, management incentives can often fan the flames – for example, the authors were shocked to find that at one utility until recently in the public sector, planning and strategy managers got bonuses, not on how well the initiatives they created were implemented, but on how many ideas they could think up and get started on. One region we audited turned up 92 improvement initiatives (national ones not counted). No surprise then it was losing money rapidly and starting to grind to a halt.

Such nonsense is based on poor management, and a lack of understanding of how organizations work. Classical management theory – from Adam Smith to Frederick W. Taylor – is based on the idea that organizations are complicated, but manageable – cause follows effect. The analogy is an aeroplane – all its parts are numbered, and it is possible to improve it by changing the engine output or slightly modifying the wing geometry.

But organizations aren't complicated – they are complex, meaning that the relationships are not necessarily known or easy to manipulate. This is more like quantum physics or chaos theory – where large inputs may have little effect, or relatively small inputs very large ones, depending on interactions of currents and thresholds.

So how to avoid KM becoming yet another initiative for people to contend with in the maelstrom of corporate change? What if KM is in competition with other programmes – such as CRM, e-procurement, e-business, organizational development or culture change programmes? Our recommendation is: don't argue. If need be, throw away the KM label. Just make sure that mobilizing knowledge thinking and techniques are built into these other programmes – ensure that when these programmes are designed, due consideration and space are given to knowledge sharing, capture, and reuse, and that the opportunities for organizational learning are written into the goals and objectives of the project team.

Part of the drive for an ever-greater number of initiatives come from increasingly feature-rich and occasionally ground-breaking technology. Businesses are already looking to exploit the next wave of mobile and wireless technology – GPRS, 3G and Bluetooth – which enable devices to transmit all sorts of data at higher bandwidth than now, and more importantly to be 'always on' – no need for expensive dial-up access. Part of the challenge is new pricing strategies – so-called 'M-commerce' that will allow payments to be made via phones and other mobile devices.

At the same time, there are a number of behind the scenes technologies that will make deployment quicker, easier and more straightforward: the development of XML (and its adoption by Microsoft as a standard) will make information transfer (based on standardized metadata) between systems and devices much more transparent – while new software standards such as .Net provide a standardized development environment that should make applications increasingly portable (at least across the range of supported devices, which may not include some of Microsoft's competitors such as Palm or Nokia).

Ideally, we should know by now how to manage organizational change in pursuit of exploiting new information and communications technologies – some organizations do it quite well, but many still do it rather badly. If we remember our Golden Rules, we stand a better chance of delivering on the anticipated benefits.

7.3.2 Shift from value chains to value networks

If technology initiatives in a reasonably static organization are difficult to implement, then it becomes much harder in a dynamic environment. In 1980, Michael Porter revolutionized thinking about how companies do business by coming up with the value chain model: this defined organizations' business into two kinds: ones which directly added value, in a process model (e.g. research and development, followed by materials procurement, followed by manufacturing, followed by sales, followed by distribution, followed by after-sales service), and ones which supported business activity across the piece (e.g. IT systems and human resource management). This was what drove the focus on process change that ultimately led to the BPR movement.

Porter's model is taken for granted these days – but increasingly, organizations don't look like this. Most people are familiar with outsourcing – for example, most IT systems in UK government are now run by specialist outsourcing companies such as EDS and Fujitsu – leaving only a handful of top-level people within the organization to control overall direction and strategy. But in some industries, outsourcing has gone very much farther: in some cases, boundaries between companies and supplier partner organizations have more or less gone altogether.

An example is the Swiss watch industry: some companies (such as Rolex) still make everything from cases to movements in-house (they even make their own oils). But many others including some well-known brand names, manufacture either very little, or nothing at all. They might have some in-house design capability and a marketing and distribution network, but movements are sourced direct from a movement supplier, typically ETA (a Swiss concern owned by the Swatch Group, which also owns Omega), cases, hands and dials procured either from other Swiss or German firms or from the Far East, and the whole lot assembled (usually in Switzerland – a certain value of the watch must be Swiss for the dial to say 'Swiss Made') occasionally in a factory owned by the brand, but most often by a third party. What these brands are selling is design, heritage and image – few buyers are aware of the true provenance of what they are wearing on their wrist.

This story repeats itself around the world: Cisco manufactures none of the internet routers that made its name, keeping only design in-house, and outsourcing component manufacture and assembly. Hewlett-Packard has the No. 1 position worldwide in printers – but manufactures not a single device. And the scale of outsourcing is picking up pace: when Microsoft went into the games market with the X Box it turned to electronics outsourcer Flextronics, which created a custom-built factory in Hungary, two hours south east of Vienna, in which to build it. Meanwhile, Flextronics are moving beyond 'pure' assembly-based outsourcing into services such as 'design for manu-facture' – taking product ideas and outsourcing the R&D to create working prototypes that can be more easily turned into manufactured goods. Manufacturing is becoming a service industry.

As boundaries blur between elements of the value network, all sorts of knowledge and information issues arise. How do companies protect their intellectual property in such an environ-ment? (Patents can be expensive.) How can true partnerships be created and sustained? If firms are looking to outsource, what roles and responsibilities should they retain? What if firms decide they need to bring things back in-house – what danger is there to business continuity from the potential loss of organiza-tional memory as the outsourced departs? (there is a real danger of corporate amnesia concerning how parts of the business have been run).

There are no easy answers to any of this – but with careful boundary management, organizations are making a success of these 'supply network' ventures. But the very issues that arise suggest that very careful attention to knowledge management issues might pay dividends in future, not only for risk management purposes, but for building future success.

Mergers and acquisitions are almost the same situation in reverse: multiple cultures, loyalties, systems, processes, infrastructures, brought together due to a deal typically conducted in secret. The authors believe that one of the reasons that more mergers and takeovers destroy shareholder value is that too much attention is given to the balance sheet and analysts earnings forecasts, and not enough to organizational knowledge. Often, the IT director is the last to find out about a merger – despite the fact that the cost of systems integration (let alone the softer elements such as information sharing and culture) can be enough to delay payback from supposed market 'synergies' or rationalization for a considerable period.

And yet, attention to detail can make all the difference in such a situation. An example is the success achieved by Volkswagen when it took over Czech car-maker Skoda. Volkswagen built a new factory in the Czech Republic, and showed an impressive awareness of the importance of tacit knowledge by bringing in workers from Germany at various levels in the organization to 'show' how it should be done. They were paired up with Czech workers – both had to learn the other's language – and though the Czech workers were officially in charge, they were asked to consult with the German group. The result was that in a remarkably short time – 18 months – the Czech factory was operating up to German quality standards.

7.3.3 Mobilizing knowledge in boom and bust

Knowledge management is a relatively new discipline – born essentially in the early 1990s, when the business world was climbing out of recession. It never had to face a downturn until 2000, when the stock market correction that followed in the late 1990s hit profits hard. Following a period of over-extension for many companies, the crash hit hard, especially in the technology sector, leading to the first substantial layoffs in many years in knowledge-critical industries such as telecoms and electronics.

At the time of publication, the KM community was still coming to terms with this new reality. From a situation of coping with information overload, some companies went quiet – with little on the order books and there was not enough for some people to do. Reduced demand across the board put pressure on margins as firms discounted to bring in business – and the overall impact on revenues was substantial. In such a loss-making situation, whole areas of business fell away rapidly for some organizations

– the imperative for those hoping to stay solvent was to act to maintain cashflow. This added up to pressure to cut costs, sometimes dramatically – leading to downsizing, including closure of whole divisions and retreat from efforts to expand into new markets.

The slump was far from even, however – the UK avoided an 'official' recession, maintaining slow but steady growth throughout the period, and there were benefits, especially for sound, well-managed companies with a solid asset base, well placed in their markets and a vision for the future to take advantage. All of the recessions and downturns of recent times have thrown up some substantial winners, especially in areas like retail (clothing retailer Next, for example, created a brand during the slump of the early 1990s by taking advantage of cheap advertising rates). By far most organizations – and most jobs – survive a downturn.

For these companies there are even some benefits in a downturn: moving from a tight labour market, suddenly they faced less competition for skilled labour, so it became easier to retain staff, while at the same time macro-economic conditions meant there was less upward pressure on wage costs. Indeed, the sudden availability of specialist staff could even mean an opportunity to grow – this was particularly the experience of small- to medium-sized consultancy firms, who were able to snap up experienced talent released from the larger players who would otherwise have been out of their grasp in terms of package or job attractiveness. This leaves them poised to take advantage of new opportunities, just as some of their competitors are disadvantaged by leaving areas or downgrading areas of business.

There are substantial knowledge implications in all of this that have ramifications beyond the end of any downturn: it becomes important to manage knowledge with the awareness that the trade cycle is real, and that substantial knowledge assets residing in people – ranging from specialist knowledge to vast networks of contacts and intelligence – can become vulnerable at any time.

The first big impact is on trust – knowledge capture initiatives, where people are being invited to share their knowledge in some way, become substantially more difficult to implement in a downturn, and nearly impossible during wholesale downsizing. Knowledge harvesting projects (based on debrief interviews) depend hugely on cooperation. So do things like document publishing on intranets, discussion databases etc. 'What's in it for me?' becomes an even more burning question than in normal circumstances. It's only natural that people protect their knowledge when they don't feel safe. And if people feel aggrieved at their treatment, they are unlikely to divulge much that is of use.

There can also be a substantial impact on learning. In a tight cashflow situation, often the first cut is to training budgets and things like conference attendance. While understandable, this is a questionable practice, such actions endanger the very future of the organization (and also tend to engender a lack of trust which has the knock-on effects described above). If most people in most organizations are knowledge workers, cutting off the flow of knowledge is like cutting off the blood supply. In addition, removing altogether any means of personal development demoralizes people (especially the better ones) and can stifle the very innovation that might be needed to survive. (There is a caveat, however: training and development is an 'easy target' for cost-cutting, and if not sustained too long may be ultimately better than other options like job cuts.)

The third impact is an obvious one: the risk of loss to organizational memory. To simply dispose of people who have previously been productive members of an organization carries a great risk. Almost every downsize has been followed by stories of workers either hired back at additional salary, or at high day rates as consultants, because their skills should not have been dispensed with – or worse, hired by competitors. If you must lose people, it is vital to be extremely careful both about whom you let go, and how many. The knowledge you lose when these individuals leave is likely to be lost forever.

Some companies have adopted creative approaches to this: for example, several of the management consultancies in the 2001–2 downturn offered employees a 'sabbatical' on 20% of salary – a retainer, with ongoing access to company resources and a commitment to rehire them when things picked up. For those who failed to get another job (and despite the activities of the small consultancies, there weren't vacancies for all) this was a lifeline and provided a win–win for both company and employee at a difficult time.

However, *after* a downsize, restructuring (or even a merger), KM tools and techniques come into their own.

In the first instance, KM projects can be used to springboard new goals, processes, or organizational structures. Using knowledge as the thread that ties people, skills and organizations together is a useful way forward. When processes in particular are redesigned or reshaped, this is a golden opportunity to consider whether knowledge management or learning steps can be built in (for example, when doing projects, preparing bids, or processing customer transactions).

An approach to knowledge should in any case be at the heart of organizational strategy. Mobilizing what people and teams in companies know, learning from what they do and applying it to new situations, leveraging what has already been learned, are all essential capabilities for competing in the modern age.

KM strategy is about pulling things together – a knowledge approach to people and skills, business processes (formal and informal), technology infrastructure and content management – in an effort to properly exploit an organization's knowledge assets and resources (which are mostly in people), and build the key knowledge capabilities it needs to compete. This sort of root-and-branch evaluation is highly appropriate when considering courses of action to come out fighting at the end of a downturn.

Finally, learning: people need reassurance if they are to perform ... as soon as practically possible, organizations need to reinstate things like training and development programmes, attendance at conferences, and internal knowledge sharing and networking events. Such activities tell people they are valued and that the company sees them playing a part in its future. People will perform better if they feel safe – while the company won't die from being starved of new thinking.

7.3.4 Onwards to new horizons

We have focused in this book on the stories of large corporate firms and public sector bodies with many thousands of employees and large budgets. Yet the principles apply equally regardless of size. In fact, it becomes much easier to apply some of the principles and activities outlined in this book to smaller organizations – small to medium enterprises (SMEs), in agencies or small public sector bodies, or at the business unit level of larger organizations, not least because the benefits can be reaped much faster and more directly, while the knowledge sharing and communications difficulties that plague large companies can more easily be addressed in smaller ones.

We set out at the start to provide some tools and a formalized but flexible approach to help those concerned with improving

organizational performance build new and innovative programmes to mobilize knowledge and information within their
companies. Our goal was to guide people through the background thinking and terminology, present the various issues,
tools and approaches, and set out an approach for mapping
these to specific organizational needs, based on learning from
the past seven years or so of working in this discipline. We
hope we have successes in this, that the tools and techniques
presented will prove useful, and that your journey will be as
full of interest and excitement as ours has been.

The empires of the future are the empires of the mind. (Sir Winston
Churchill 1874–1965)

Appendix 1 Issue identification

The following template can be used to assist in capturing knowledge issues during an audit.

Ref.	Issue	Why important?	Impact of not resolving	Urgency/Priority	Owner	Follow-up action

Examples of possible 'Issue':

(Based on knowledge-based business benefits – Breu, Grimshaw and Myers 2000)

- New products/services
- Research and development
- New business opportunities
- Developing new markets
- Innovative capability
- Reducing geographical barriers
- Organizational integration
- Organizational flexibility
- Sharing ideas
- Organizational learning
- Speed of decision-making
- Customer retention
- Customer service
- Meeting customer needs
- Product/services quality
- Supply chain efficiency
- Integration of logistics
- Supplier relationships
- Sustaining existing markets
- Time-to-market
- Process innovation
- Capability for change
- Operational efficiency
- Project management
- Product/services management
- Staff morale
- Quality of decision-making

Examples of 'Why important':

- Scope: number of people
- Scope: number of groups
- Impact on objectives (personal and organizational), e.g. financial, customer, processes, learning, growing
- Motivation
- Time, cost, quality

Examples of 'Impact of not resolving':

- Something negative will start to happen
- Something negative will increase
- Something negative will not change
- Something positive will reduce
- Something positive will stop happening

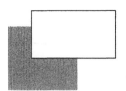

Appendix 2 Knowledge role audit

The following template can be used to assist in capturing knowledge role information during an audit.

Role Name & Brief Outline
e.g. Customer facing, Internal operations, Internal support

Purpose/Key Objectives
e.g. Highlight any knowledge-related areas

Scope
e.g. Exists in different locations, clusters exist, always work with other specific roles, estimated numbers

Knowledge/Information Inputs	Suppliers

Knowledge/Information Outputs	Customers

Significant Processes

Rating: In top 5?

e.g. Do they make a real difference to customers? Do they help your organization be better than competitors? Do they make it a better place to work?

Role Champion:	Contact:

Appendix 3 Knowledge process audit

The following template can be used to assist in capturing knowledge process information during an audit.

Process Name & Brief Outline

e.g. Customer facing, Suppliers facing, Internal operations, Internal support, Across internal organizational boundaries

Purpose/Key Objectives/Measures

e.g. Highlight any knowledge-specific areas

Scope

e.g. Performed in different locations, what are the boundaries that this process exists within, any specific IT systems used

Knowledge/Information Inputs	Suppliers

Knowledge/Information Outputs	Customers

Roles performed by

Rating: In top 5?
e.g. Do they make a real difference to customers? Do they help your organization be better than competitors? Do they make it a better place to work?

Process Owner:	Contact:

Appendix 4 Resistance to change

Resistance to change

In all but exceptional circumstances some levels of resistance to change will surface – something with potential to seriously slow up the programme, or even cause its failure. A useful analysis of resistance was undertaken by Milan Kubr (1996), and the following is developed from his work – intended here to provide some insight into the dynamics of change in organizations for those leading the KM programme.

Lack of conviction that change is needed

If people are not properly informed and the purpose of change not explained to them, they are likely to view the present situation as satisfactory and an effort to change as useless and upsetting.

Routine is something most people enjoy – and most people would need a good reason to go through the pain of change. There needs to be a compelling feeling that either staying in the current situation is too painful, or that the new situation will bring enough benefit that it is worth the journey. Communication is essential in the programme, for the knowledge management project is all about changing people's behaviour – without the right messages, fully understood, then it will be extremely difficult to build sufficient conviction to see change through until the project is successful.

Dislike of imposed change

In general, people do not like to be treated as passive objects. They resent changes that are imposed on them and about which they cannot express any views.

There is an element of 'loss of control here', but also potentially resistance to the style and approach of the change. If change is performed in an authoritarian manner, then it is likely to be experienced as imposed. The mitigating factor here is leadership and involvement: good leadership seeks to excite people about the change, and involves them to some extent in its design and implementation.

Dislike of surprises

People do not want to be kept in the dark about any change that is being prepared; organizational changes tend to be resented if they come as a surprise.

Communication is essential and if the right information is not available, then misinformation starts to spread. In the authors' experience, there is a fine line to tread in such projects: telling people too much too quickly can raise expectations, potentially leading to boredom or cynicism about the change. On the other hand, keeping too much information back risks falling victim to rumour and supposition.

In a large organization the authors were involved with there were a number of open online 'chat' sessions with members of the executive board, using the company intranet, with transcripts of the sessions published afterwards (along with answers to questions that were too complex to answer straight away) – very useful step in building dialogue and trust.

Fear of the unknown

Basically, people do not like to live in uncertainty and may prefer an imperfect present to an unknown and uncertain future.

Honesty is essential in change projects, although there are times when sensitive information cannot be disclosed. It is much easier and safer to be honest when discussing or giving face-to-face briefings: when written down this sort of information can have the habit of resurfacing out of context and in the wrong hands. With knowledge management there must be a level of confidence in the organization to encourage people to share and get involved. If people are uncertain about the future they are more likely to act as individuals cut off from others.

Reluctance to deal with unpopular issues

Managers and other people often try to avoid unpleasant reality and unpopular actions, even if they realise that they will not be able to avoid these forever.

There is an element of fear of 'loss of face' about this – but this is really about courage and about the passion, commitment and self-confidence of those driving the change that the benefits anticipated will be met, and will be substantial enough to warrant the change in the first place. Those individuals who are on the receiving end of change must have the opportunity to submit hard and difficult questions to those in charge. The example above concerning the chat online with members of the executive board was an ideal opportunity for some new and interesting questions to be submitted. It also helped everyone feel as if they were not the only person giving the issue serious thought, but that they were part of a community, and that management were open to dealing with unpopular or contentious questions.

Fear of inadequacy and failure

Many people worry about their ability to adjust to change, and maintain and improve their performance in a new work situation. Some of them may feel insecure, and doubt their ability to make a special effort to learn new skills and attain new performance levels.

One opportunity that a mobilizing knowledge approach can offer is the development of task support communities, potentially involving additional training and support for day-to-day jobs. When coupled with business process improvement, the objective is to enrich people's jobs, and to provide additional technology and process support. Again communication is essential in helping people understand what the changes will mean.

In the authors' experience the best way of tackling these feelings is sometimes a programme of common education and training in generic skills such as customer care, the management of change, or team working. When combined with discussion, these sessions can be light hearted, and help open up the individuals to share their concerns.

Disturbed practices, habits and relations

Following organizational change, well established and fully mastered practices and work habits may become obsolete, and familiar relationships may be altered or totally destroyed. This can lead to considerable frustration and unhappiness.

Loss of control and insecurity are the main fears here – and yet with knowledge management change, there is little reason why this should be a significant problem. By encouraging increased communication and knowledge sharing, then an increased feeling of community should begin to develop to help reaffirm existing relationships and to build new ones. Knowledge management is not about ripping out old routines that add value, but a more pragmatic approach. Where old routines do not add value any more then these must of course be considered for change. Involving people in the change, listening to concerns, and having a strong leader can help in this area.

Lack of respect and trust in the person promoting change

People are suspicious about change proposed by a manager whom they do not trust and respect, or by an external person whose competence and motives are not known and understood.

This is such a common problem in organizations, and that is why leadership is so important. Having a trusted leadership figure as the focus for the change is an essential component to ensure the change is a success.

The Change Equation

A short but nevertheless useful way of expressing resistance to change is the change equation. Change can be properly successful only if:

$$B > P + E$$

In words, this can be expressed as: the **Benefit** expected or experienced must be greater than the **Pain** people are experiencing before the change, plus the **Effort** involved in making the change.

To deconstruct this a little: the main variable here is the benefit. The programme must be designed to deliver benefit on a large number of fronts, and these must be communicated properly and understood by those about to undergo the change. The key change tool is therefore the benefits map, backed up by case studies and evangelism from those leading the project.

Little can be done about the pain – but making people more aware of the day-to-day difficulties and frustrations they are facing can be used to build awareness of the need to change (for example, the burning platform analogy: we can't stay here or we are doomed).

Finally, the effort people are asked to make may be substantial, but it should be possible to chunk this up into acceptable steps: good project and programme management is about ensuring successful delivery through achievable and appropriate phasing of project deliverables.

References

Ajzen, I. and Fishbein, M. (1980) *Understanding Attitudes and Predicting Social Behaviour* Prentice Hall: New York.

Arc Group (2002) *Knowledge Management* 5(6).

Breu, K., Grimshaw, D. and Myers, A. (2000) *Releasing the Value of Knowledge: A Survey of UK Industry 2000*. Cranfield University, School of Management.

British Quality Foundation (1998) *Guide to the Business Excellence Model – Defining World Class*. British Quality Foundation: 32–34 Great Peter Street, London.

Champy, J. (1995) *Reengineering Management – The Mandate for New Leadership*. HarperCollins: London.

Davenport, T.H. and Prusak, L. (2000) *Working Knowledge. How Organisations Manage What They Know*. Harvard Business School Press: Boston MA.

de Geus, A. (1999) *The Living Company*. Nicholas Brealey Publishing Ltd.

Department of Health (2001) *Knowledge Management Strategy Report* (Crown Copyright material is reproduced with the permission of the controller of HMSO).

Dictionary.com online 2002 available: http://www.dictionary.com (10 February 2002).

Drucker, P.F. (1969) *The Age of Discontinuity: Guidelines to Our Changing Society* London: Heinemann

EFQM online 2002 available: http://www.efqm.org (10 February 2002).

Garvin, D. (1998) *Building a Learning Organisation*. Harvard Business Review on Knowledge Management: Boston MA 47–80.

Goffee, R. and Jones, G. (2001) Followership: It's Personal Too. *Harvard Business Review*, Vol. 79, No. 11, December 2001. Harvard Business School Publishing.

Grant, R.M. (1998) *Contemporary Strategy Analysis: Concepts, Techniques, Applications* (3rd ed.). Blackwell Publishers Ltd, Oxford.

Hammer, M. and Champy, J. (1993) *Reengineering the Corporation – A Manifesto for Business Revolution*. Nicholas Brealey Publishing Limited: London.

Hammer, M. and Stanton, S.A. (1995) *The Reengineering Revolution: A Handbook*. Harper Business, New York.

Hammer, M. (1996) *Beyond Reengineering – How the Process-Centred Organization is Changing our Work and our Lives*. HarperCollins: New York.

Johnson, G. and Scholes, K. (1999) *Exploring Corporate Strategy* (5th ed.). Prentice Hall Europe.

Kaplan, R.S. and Norton, D.P. (1996) *Translating Strategy into Action – The Balanced Scorecard*. Harvard Business School Press.

Kotter, J.P. (1996) *Leading Change*. Harvard Business School Press.

Kotter, J.P. (2001) What Leaders Really Do. *Harvard Business Review*, Vol. 79, No. 11, December 2001. Harvard Business School Publishing.

Kotter, J.P. (1997) *Marketing Management Analysis, Planning, Implementation, and Control* (9th ed.). Prentice Hall, Englewood Cliffs, NJ.

Kubr, M. (1996) *Management Consulting – a Guide to the Profession*, 3rd edn. International Labour Office: Geneva.

Leonard-Barton, D. (1995) *Wellsprings of Knowledge. Building and Sustaining the Sources of Innovation*. Harvard Business School Press.

Marx, Karl (1999) *Capital*. Oxford University Press.

Murray, P. (1999) *Emerging Patterns in Knowledge Management in European Business*. Unicorn: London, pp. 27–35.

Murray, P. and Myers, A. (1997) The Facts About Knowledge. *Information Strategy*, Sept., pp. 31–33.

Nonaka, I. and Takeuchi, H. (1995) *The Knowledge Creating Company. How Japanese Companies Create the Dynamics of Innovation*. OUP: New York.

OU (1999) *Managing Knowledge Course B823*. The Open University Business School: Milton Keynes.

Peters, T. and Waterman, R.H. (1982) *In Search of Excellence*. Harper-Collins, London.

Polanyi, M. (1967) *The Tacit Dimension*. Routledge & Kegan Paul: London.

Porter, M.E. (1985) *Competitive Advantage: Creating and Sustaining Superior Performance*. Collier Macmillan, London.

Porter, M.E. (1980) *Competitive Strategy* (new ed.).

PRINCE2 (online) (2002) available: http://www.ogc.gov.uk/prince/ (10 February 2002).

Probst, G., Raub, S. and Romhardt, K. (2000) *Managing Knowledge – Building Blocks for Success*. John Wiley & Sons Ltd: Chichester.

Ruggles, R.L. (ed.) (1997) *Knowledge Management Tools*. Butterworth Heinemann: Boston, MA.

Senge, P.M. (1993) *The Fifth Discipline: The Art and Practice of the Learning Organisation*. Random House Business Books.

Skandia, (online) (1999) available: http://www.skandia.com (21 February 2002).

Skyrme, D. and Amidon, D. (1997) Creating the Knowledge-based Business. *Business Intelligence*.

Smith, A. (1982) *The Wealth of Nations*. Penguin Books, London.

Sveiby, K.E. (1997) *The New Organizational Wealth*. Berrott-Koehler Publishers Inc.

Taylor, F.W. (1967) *Principles of Scientific Management*. W.W. Norton, London.

Thorp, J. and DMR Consulting (1999) *The Information Paradox: Realizing the Benefits of Information Technology*. McGraw-Hill Education, Canada.

Index

3G mobile technologies, 177, 222
3M, 39, 189

Access, 147, 154
Access to technology, 145
After action reports and reviews, 108, 122
Aggregation, 169
Alta Vista, 168
American Civil War, 6
Amidon, D, 13
Annual report, 46
Apple Macintosh, 166
Application access, 169
Appraisal systems, 119
Apprenticeship route, 106
Armed forces, 11
Armoury methods, 6
Artisans, 5
Assets, 8
Asynchronous collaborative tools, 183
Audio conferencing, 150, 184
Audit process, 14
Audit tool, 112
Authentication, 155
Automated indexing, 158
Automatic categorization, 158, 159

Balanced scorecard, 7, 70, 71, 74,178
   customer perspective, 72
   financial perspective, 72
   internal-business-process perspective, 73
   learning and growth perspective, 73
Barclays Bank, 213
Behaviours, golden rule, 3, 42, 85, 103, 197, 210, 220,
Beliefs, 104, 106
Benchmarking, 206
Benefit categories, 78, 178
   business process, 84
   competence, 82
   knowledge and information availability, 78
Benefits, 35, 37, 38, 41, 42, 77
   golden rules, 3, 38, 42, 196, 204, 219
Benefits management, 219
Best practice, 84
Blockers, 94, 208
Bluetooth, 155, 222
Boolean search, 171
Bottom up, 197
BP, 214
BPR, 1, 2, 27, 140
Breu, K, 28
British Airways, 118
Building a KM delivery team, 102
Building a vision, 59
Burning platform analogy, 207
Business benefits see Benefits
Business case, 48, 65, 68, 70, 90, 201, 206, 216

Business case template, 90
Business intelligence, 154, 177
Business intelligence software, 177
Business priority, quick win, 67
Business process, 80, 85, 127
Business process functionality, 169
Business Process Re-engineering, 1,
   2, 27, 140
Business strategy, 15
Business unit, role of, 198

Cabinet office, 193
Capabilities, 59
Capacity, 86
Case studies, 190, 191, 218
Categorization, automatic, 158
Champy, James, 141, 142
Change, 206, 218, 220
   capacity to, 87
   equation, 240
   imposed, 238
   leaders and leadership, 96, 206,
      209
   resistance to, 237
Changing environment, 46
Chaos theory, 222
'Chasm of faith', 69, 76
   bridging the chasm, 75
Chief knowledge officer, 98
Cisco, 177, 224
Classification systems, 149
Collaboration, 116, 119, 146, 150,
   164, 178
Collaborative tools, 154, 183
Collaborative working, 183
Combination, 125
Communities, 97, 116, 169
Communities of practice, 97, 123,
   124, 175, 181
Competencies, 82, 114
Complexity theory, 222
Content:
   aggregation, 154, 170
   indexing, 149
   management systems, 149, 154,
      173, 174
   sources, integration, 169
   management-related records,
      163
Context, 122
Context search, 172
Continuous improvement, 133, 204

Corporate, 88
   drivers, 203
   portal, 169
   strategy, 43, 44, 216
   taxonomies, 157, 158
Costs, 90
Craftsmen, 5, 6
Cranfield University, 47
CRM, 222
Cross-functional teams, 118
Cultural:
   frames of reference, 111
   web, 112, 209
   web audit, 112, 113
Culture, 110
   and knowledge climate, 55
   change programmes, 222
   of an organization, 50
Custom 110
Customer and stakeholder, 87
Customer knowledge, 30
Customer relationship management,
   30, 106, 121
Customers, suppliers and markets, 80

Data processing revolution, 14
Data protection laws, 162
Data warehousing, 154, 177
Data, information and knowledge,
   12
Databases of expertise, 121
Davenport, Thomas, 13, 151
de Geus, Arie, 10, 61, 62, 189, 211,
   212
Delayering, 9
Delivery of technology, 144
Delivery team:
   building a team, 102
Deming, W. Edward, 1
Department of Health, 60, 192, 197,
   200
Directories, 155, 156
Directories of expertise, 154, 182
Directory services, 154, 155, 182
Discovery, 148, 154, 170
Discussion forums, 185, 186
Document management, 122, 147,
   154, 162, 163, 164, 181
Document sharing, 122, 154, 160, 162,
   181
Documents repository, 203
Downsizing, 9, 228

Downturns, 225
Drucker, Peter, 6, 7
Dynamics of knowledge, 214

e-business, 222
EFQM, 205, 219
Electronic records management, 154, 164
Email, 149, 154, 155, 117, 147, 178
    attachments, 180
    categories and headers, 180
    document sharing, 181
    filtering, 180
    mailbox size, 179
    overload, 179
    use, 154
Enterprises, small to medium, 229
Environment, 110
Epistemology, 4, 20
e-procurement, 222
European Foundation for Quality
    Management, 205, 219
Exit interviews, 107
Expert knowledge, 31
Expert systems, 1
Expertise, 154
Expertise database, 149
Explicit knowledge, 19, 20, 120
External environment, 57
Externalization, 121

Fear:
    of inadequacy and failure, 239
    of the unknown, 238
File storage, 147, 154, 160
FileNet, 163
Financial measures, 71
First direct, 134
Five forces model, 214
Five Golden rules see Golden rules
Five-stage strategic framework, 35, 215
Flextronics, 224
Ford, Henry, 6, 7, 117
Formal methodologies, 202
Freedom of information, 162, 193
Fujitsu, 56, 121, 123, 182, 194
Functional groups, 53

Gatekeeper, 124
Golden rules, 84, 215, 223
    behaviours, 3, 42, 103, 197, 210, 220

benefits, 3, 38, 42,196, 204, 219
leadership, 4, 42, 101, 210, 220
learning, 4, 42,189, 206, 214, 220
process, 4, 42, 129, 143
Google, 168
GPRS, 155, 177, 222
Grant, Robert M., 8
Grimshaw, D, 28
Groupware, 150

Hammer and Stanton's five roles, 102
Hammer, Michael, 141, 142
Hand-held devices, 148
Health, Department of, 60, 192, 197, 200
Hewlett-Packard, 224
Hot desking, 118

ICL see Fujitsu, 118, 123, 182, 194
Implementation programme, 198
Improvement, continuous, 204
Indexing, automated, 158
Individual support, 81
Induction of staff, 107
Information, 41
    and technology, 144
Information Age, the, 14
Information classification, 154, 156
Information, content and skills
    audit, 54
Information literacy, 114
Information management, 148, 154, 170
    audit, 147
Information overload, 16
Information professional, 99
Information sharing, 162
Infrastructure, 147,153, 154, 155
Infrastructure exploitation, 146
Infrastructure initiative, 29
Innovation, 28, 33, 189, 204
    capacity to innovate, 86
Integration, 169
Intellectual property, 19
Internalization, 125
Interviews, exit, 107
Intranet, 16, 123, 148, 151, 154, 163, 165, 175
Intranet-based tools, 162
IT infrastructure, 152

Japanese view of knowledge,
    definition, 18
Johnson, Gerry, 8, 111, 142
'Joined-up government', 60

'Kaizen', 117
Kaplan, R. S., 70, 72
Keyword search, 171
KLIMT, 193, 197
Know how, 21
Know that, 23
Know when, 23
Know where, 24
Know who, 22
Know why, 22
Knowledge:
    context knowledge, 22
    customer and/or supplier
        knowledge, 30
    explicit knowledge, 19, 20, 120
    mobilizing knowledge, 24, 42
    process knowledge, 30
    product and service knowledge,
        30
    project knowledge, 30
    tacit knowledge, 19, 20,120
    technical or expert knowledge, 31
    vision for, 43
Knowledge acquisition, 131
Knowledge and information types,
    137, 138
Knowledge architecture, 93
Knowledge assessment, 132
Knowledge assets, 19
Knowledge audit, 20, 49, 191
Knowledge base, 1
Knowledge-based business benefits,
    48
Knowledge broker, 9, 100, 208
Knowledge capture initiatives, 226
Knowledge creation, 127
Knowledge development, 132
Knowledge dynamics, 214
Knowledge economy, 15, 166
Knowledge goals, 131
Knowledge harvesting, 107, 226
Knowledge identification, 131
Knowledge, Learning and
        Information Management
        Toolkit, 193, 197
Knowledge literacy, 115
Knowledge management, 140

building a delivery team, 102
leadership roles, 97
Knowledge management strategy,
    34, 43, 44, 45, 60, 65, 191, 196
    analysis and conclusions, 65
    management summary, 65
    method outline, 65
    moving forward, 62
    pilot, 67
    prerequisite, 67
    programme of action, 66
Knowledge management
    technologies, 152
Knowledge map, 151
Knowledge mobilization, golden
    rules, 42
Knowledge network, 192
Knowledge process audit, 235
Knowledge processes, 52, 130, 132
Knowledge programme director, 98
Knowledge resources:
    management, 85
    quality, 85
Knowledge retention, 132
Knowledge role audit, 233
Knowledge roles, 51
Knowledge sharing/distribution,
    132
Knowledge technology audit, 147
Knowledge utilization, 132
Knowledge work, 125
Knowledge workers, 11, 95, 183
    soldiers, 11
Knowledge workplace, 50, 128

Lank, Elizabeth, 25
Laptops, 148
Layoffs, 225
Leadership, 32, 40, 43, 93, 95,197
    golden rule, 4, 42, 101, 197, 210,
        220
Leadership and change, 96
Leadership roles, 97
Learning, 227, 89, 214
    golden rule, 4, 42,189, 206, 214,
        220,
Learning organization, 2, 206, 211,
    212
Leonard Barton, Dorothy, 16, 142,
    211
Lessons learned, 10
Levers of change, 94, 217

Lifecycle content, 149
Lifecycle management, 173
Lotus Notes, 149, 192

Mailbox size, 179
Management information systems, 154, 177
Management theory, 222
Managing identity information, 156
Managing risk, 204
Manufacturing, 224
Marx, Karl, 7
Mass population, 6
Mass production, 6
M-commerce, 222
Medieval period, 5
Meeting spaces, 118
Merchant classes, 5
Merger and acquisition, 8
Meridio, 163
Metadata, 14, 154, 165, 166, 181
Metadirectory services, 154, 155
Methodologies, formal, 202
Microsoft Data Warehousing Framework, 177
Microsoft Exchange, 160
Microsoft Office, 192
Microsoft Outlook, 160
Microsoft SharePoint Portal server, 161
Microsoft Windows, 192
Microsoft Windows CE, 176
Microsoft X Box, 224
Millennium bug, 146, 152
Ministry of Defence, 183
Mobile phones, 176
Mobile telephony, 153
Mobilizing knowledge, 24
Mobilizing knowledge community, 124
Mobilizing knowledge programme, 183
Modernizing Government agenda, 193
Monasteries, 5
Motivation, 103, 104, 106
Myers, A, 28

National Health Service 192
  'no blame' environment, 108

.Net, 222
Neuro-linguistic programming, 103
News feed, 175
Newsgroups, 185
Newspaper systems, 209
Nine knowledge types, 137
'No blame' environment, 108
Nonaka, Ikujiro, 8. 17, 119, 142
Norton, D. P., 70, 72

Online chat, 185
Open Text Livelink, 161
Orbital's Organik, 186
Organization, response of, 216
Organizational:
  capabilities, 8, 10
  development, 222
  information, 81
  learning see Learning
  memory, 228
  strategy, 214
  structure, 213
Ownership, 196
Ownership of information, 147

Peer2Peer, 185
People, 40, 79, 103
  and technology, 144
Performance management, 119
Personalization, 165, 169
Peters, Tom, 9
Philosophy, Eastern:
  Japanese view, 17
Philosophy, Western, 17
  justified true belief, 17
Phrase search, 172
Pilot groups, 195
Pilot projects, 93, 189, 191
Planning, scenario planning, 213
Point solution, 29
Portal alignment, 174
Portals, 148, 165, 166, 168, 175
  role of, 154, 165
Porter, Michael, 214, 223
Presentation, 169
Presentation layer, 176
Pressure to change, 45, 216
Prices, 88
PRINCE2, 202
Prior knowledge, 122

Process *see also* BPR, 40
  audit, 52
  golden rule, 4, 42, 129,143
  knowledge, 30
  redesign, 133
Product knowledge, 30
Professional bodies, 5
Profit, improved, 90
Programme design, 198
Programme ownership, 196
Project knowledge, 30
Project leadership, 97
Project management, 196
'Proof of concept', 93
Proprietary systems, 147
Prusak, Larry, 13, 151
Public folders, 181
Public Records Office, 161

Quality management, 1, 9, 117
Quality of knowledge resources, 85
Quantum physics, 222
'Quick win', 183

Radical business change, 133, 134,
    140
Real time, 184
Records, digital, 154
Records management, 163, 164
Reformation, the, 5
Remote access, 148
Repurposing, 173, 176
Resources, 59
Restructuring, 228
Risk management, 204
Risks, 89
Rolex, 223

Scenario planning, 213
Scholes, Kevan, 8, 111, 142
Search, 154, 165, 169, 170, 173
  Boolean, 171
  context, 172
  keyword, 171
  phrase, 172
Search tools, 149, 181
Senge, Peter, 211
Serendipity, 185, 186
Service industries, 224
Service knowledge, 30

Shared network drive, 160
Shareholder value increase, 90
Sharing, 116, 119
Six investigators, 20, 21
  know how, 21
  know that, 23
  know when, 23
  know where, 24
  know who, 22
  know why, 22
Skandia Navigator method, 71
Skills, 103, 114
Skills and training, 79
Skills auditing, 115
Skills shortage, 6
Skoda, 225
Skyme, David, 13
Slump, economic, 226
Small to medium enterprises
    (SMEs), 229
Smart cards, 213
SMART criteria, 199
Smith, Adam, 7, 222
Socialization, 121
Spiral of innovation, 119, 120
Staff induction, 107
Stakeholders, 87
STEP analysis, 58
Storytelling, 23, 33, 109
Strategy see Knowledge
    management strategy
Supplier knowledge, 30
Suppliers, access to information, 148
Sveiby, Karl, 56
Swiss watch industry, 223
Synchronous collaborative tools, 183

Tacit knowledge, 19, 20, 120
Takeuchi, Hirotaka, 17, 119, 142
Taxonomy, 149, 154, 156, 157, 165,
    168
Taylor, Frederick W., 116, 222
Team working, 118
Technical knowledge, 31
Technology, 41, 144
  access to, 145
  and collaboration, 146
  delivery, 144
  discovery, 146
  information, 144
  people, 144
  time, 144

Technology audit, 53
Technology literacy, 114
Tesco, 130
Time and technology, 144
Time-shifted, 185
Top down, 197
Trade unions, 5
Training budgets, 228
Transaction costs, 7
Translation, 173
Trust, 122, 123, 240

US Army:
    after action reviews, 108

Value chains, 223
Value networks, 223
Values, 104
Video conferencing, 150, 184
Vision for knowledge, 43
Volkswagen, 225

Wealth, 26
'What's in it for me?', 94, 227
Whiteboards, 150, 185
Wireless Access Protocol, 176
Wireless network infrastructures,
    153
Workflow, 176
Workflow management, 173, 176
Workgroups:
    effectiveness, 85
    efficiency, 86
    support, 82
Workplace audit, 49
World Bank, 25
World Wide Web, 15

X Box, 224
XML, 222

Y2K, 146, 152
Yahoo, 157

Printed and bound by CPI Group (UK) Ltd, Croydon, CR0 4YY

17/10/2024

01775697-0006